The

MASLOW

BUSINESS

READER

Abraham H. Maslow
Edited by Deborah C. Stephens

JOHN WILEY & SONS, INC.
New York • Chichester • Weinheim • Brisbane • Singapore • Toronto

Published by John Wiley & Sons, Inc.
Published simultaneously in Canada.

This publication is designed to provide accurate and authoritative information in regard to the subject matter covered. It is sold with the understanding that the publisher is not engaged in rendering legal, accounting, or other professional services. If legal advice or other expert assistance is required, the services of a competent professional person should be sought.

Library of Congress Cataloging-in-Publication Data:
Maslow, Abraham H. (Abraham Harold)
    The Maslow business reader / Abraham H. Maslow ; with Deborah C. Stephens, editor.
        p.   cm.
    Includes bibliographical references and index.
    ISBN 0-471-36008-2 (cloth : alk. paper)
    1. Psychology, Industrial.   2. Self-actualization (Psychology)   3. Maslow, Abraham H.
(Abraham Harold)—Contributions in management.   4. Maslow, Abraham H. (Abraham
Harold)—Diaries.   I. Stephens, Deborah C. (Deborah Collins)   II. Title.
HF5548.8.M3753   2000
158.—dc17

                                                                99-055086

Printed in the United States of America.

10   9   8   7   6   5   4   3   2   1

To Lily, Aaron, and Mike
for always supporting me.

To Morton H. Meyerson
who demonstrates the importance of
the human experience in all that he does.

Contents

Preface

Six years ago, I was re-introduced to the works of Douglas Mc-Gregor. The out-of-print book, *The Professional Manager,* contained more wisdom and compelling thoughts than the majority of business books I had read over the years. Yet, written during an era when large mainframe computers were considered innovative and employees stayed with one company for life, McGregor's ideas and theories about managerial leadership seemed to be decades ahead of his time. Little did I know that my interest in the work of McGregor would lead me to an intense two-year study of the works of Abraham Maslow.

Anyone who has taken Psychology 101, studied organizational development, or raised a child has heard of the brilliant psychologist, Abraham Maslow. Maslow changed the science of psychology and left an indelible imprint on business and society. Yet, it was Douglas McGregor who introduced the icon to the world of business and organizational issues. While McGregor was at M.I.T. and Maslow was making a worldwide reputation for himself and his theories at Brandeis University, both men developed theories that are now imperative to the success of business in a global economy. Both men were prolific authors, and their best work is resurfacing today—for a new generation of leaders to read. Perhaps today's leaders are the audience the two men were writing for in the first place.

WHY MASLOW MATTERS

In the fall of 1997, I received a phone call that would become a defining moment. Ann Maslow Kaplan, the eldest daughter of Abraham Maslow, had learned of my interest in Douglas McGregor's work. Since Maslow and McGregor were colleagues and friends while alive, she wanted to know if I would be interested in reading through a set of journals her father had kept. The journals contained his thoughts and ruminations about management, self-actualizing work, creativity, leadership, and other pertinent business topics. Published in 1960 under the unusual name *Eupsychian Management,* few people, other than academics, had read the journals. I eagerly agreed.

Written in the late 1950s and early 1960s, Maslow wrote about entrepreneurship as if he were describing what transpires daily in Silicon Valley. He described a world where creativity, innovation, and reinvention were paramount to success. Ironically, he wrote many passages of this journal in Menlo Park, California, and kept an office on Sand Hill Road—a legendary place today, where ideas meet money and often create new industries overnight. A place where I have spent most of my adult life living and working.

Today, Silicon Valley (and the surrounding Bay Area) leads the world in seven key industry clusters: computers and electronics, telecommunications, multimedia, bioscience, banking and finance, environmental technology, and tourism. Some describe the area as ground zero for where new ideas emerge to enhance technological advances. A place where innovation and raw brainpower form global markets. Where start-up firms begin in a garage and result in the American Dream. Where people, from secretary to CEO, believe that their work can change the world. A place where failure is looked upon as a badge of courage and a stumble is just a quicker way to the finish line. And yet the reason Maslow matters today, nearly three decades after his death, is precisely because of places like Silicon Valley. His wisdom and thoughts and research can guide us through the transformations ahead. As we embrace innovation and human capital as prime factors in competitive advantage, Maslow matters more today than when he lived.

Maslow matters because he understood human nature and motivation and self-actualizing performance better than anyone alive today does. His messages are clear:

- Human beings are capable of extraordinary accomplishment.
- Creativity and innovation are a natural element in our make up.
- Long-term relationships with customers are the wisest strategy for long-term growth.

- Teamwork, although imperative to business outcomes, is an overlooked source of community and esteem for people.

- Enlightened management not only improves products and earnings per share; it improves people and thus improves the world.

- These thoughts that Maslow wrote about so many year ago, speak to us today in a clear and authoritative voice.

INNOVATION DRIVEN ECONOMIES

My work on the book, *Maslow on Management,* offered me the chance to meet many American business leaders. After its publication, my network expanded exponentially and I was deluged with correspondence from business leaders in hundreds of industries from around the world. There has been a common theme in many of these conversations. It is best illustrated by a question asked to me by a student in the Stanford Professional Development Program for which I was a faculty member. He wanted to know how Silicon Valley companies were able to create such vast technological breakthroughs.

While more brilliant minds than I have been asked the same question. My answer today is quite different than it would have been several years ago. I have learned from Maslow's work that the "people practices" of Silicon Valley companies play as vital a role in technological and wealth creation as do other factors. Yet, it has been my experience that few organizations are ready to commit full-heartedly to the re-invention they will need to undertake to tap the innovation and creativity of their employees. We often still turn to the quick fixes or feel more secure in investing millions in hardware and software than changing the cultures of our companies: Cultures where creativity and innovation become strategic initiatives.

Maslow's work gives us many ideas for creating self-actualizing companies where people can make extraordinary contributions. While I would encourage any leader to immerse themselves in Maslow's work, this book can be a starting point. In compiling this book, I have selected works that I believe are of utmost importance to leaders today. I have also added essays and letters from Maslow's personal papers that contain information that will be valuable to those attempting to make changes in their organizations.

I would like to thank the many students and executives who have helped me become a better leader and educator. In addition, I would like to thank Jeanne Glasser of John Wiley & Sons and Ann Maslow Kaplan for their support. To Jackie Speier, Linda Allan, Anne Robinson, Nancy Olsen, and Jan Yanehiro, I thank you for your friendship and encouragement. To Mort Meyerson for so generously passing along wisdom and advice about life and business that I cherish. To Warren Bennis for the encouragement he extended to me throughout the past two years. To Dr. Tom Kosnik of Stanford University, I thank you for being a wonderful mentor and cherished friend. To my family Mike, Aaron, and Lily, for always being a mirror reflective of what is truly important in life.

DEBORAH C. STEPHENS

San Carlos, California

Acknowledgments

I would like to thank Deborah Stephens for her wonderfully sensitive job of editing this book.

Ann R. Kaplan

PART ONE

SELF-ACTUALIZING WORK

A musician must make music, and an artist must paint, a poet must write, if he is to ultimately be at peace with himself. What a man can be, he must be. This need we may call self-actualization. . . . It refers to man's desire for self-fulfillment, namely to the tendency for him to become actually in what he is potentially; to become everything that one is capable of becoming.

A.H. Maslow, *Maslow on Management*

INTRODUCTION

Maslow's defining work was the development of the hierarchy of needs. Maslow believed that human beings aspire to become self-actualizing. He viewed human potential as a vastly underestimated and an unexplained territory. The now-famous pyramid has come to illustrate his concept:

1

Most discussions of people's needs in the world of work usually begin with a basic understanding of the work generally associated with Abraham Maslow. Its central thesis is that human needs are organized in a hierarchy, with needs for survival, food, and shelter, for example, as its base. At progressively higher levels in Maslow's hierarchy are needs for security and social interaction, with the highest level being the need to learn, grow, and reach one's potential. As lower level needs become reasonably satisfied, successively higher needs become more influential in motivating human behavior. When lower level needs remain unsatisfied, factors such as learning, creativity, innovation, or self-esteem remain stagnant, never rising to the surface.

In applying Maslow's hierarchy of needs to the world of work, reasonable satisfaction is achieved when, in the perception of the individuals involved, environmental factors like pay and job security are adequately addressed and equitably administered. People who feel that they are adequately and fairly paid do not spend most of their days thinking about their salary unless other environmental factors lead them to do so. When discipline is handled consistently, most people are able to manage the risk of failure without allowing that risk to unnecessarily distract them.

This is not to say that when lower level needs are satisfied, they are no longer an issue. On the contrary, Maslow noted that people seem to have an insatiable ability to become dissatisfied with what he referred to as "environmental factors." Even when survival is not in question and people are reasonably well paid, they usually want to be paid better. Also, it's a rare individual who is completely secure in his or her work environment (though today, more than ever, that insecurity may be well-founded). As for social needs, they wax and wane on the strength of our personal relationships and our participation with others in the organization.

In organizations, factors such as performance appraisal, incentives, and internal competition prevent employees from concentrating their efforts on learning, growth, and innovation. Understanding the hierarchy and its implications for building self-actualizing workplaces may be beneficial to those concerned with building high performance teams and organizations. The following essays and excerpts from Abraham Maslow's work allow the reader to understand these concepts as well as to apply them to the workplace.

The Hierarchy
of Needs

*Maslow's hierarchy of needs is still frequently cited by all
types of professionals in any number of industries. In this
short article, written in 1943, Abraham Maslow describes
and explains the hierarchy in a very clear and concise way.*

There are at least five sets of goals which we may call basic needs. These are briefly physiological, safety, love, esteem, and self-actualization. In addition, we are motivated by the desire to achieve or maintain the various conditions upon which these basic satisfactions rest and by certain more intellectual desires.

These basic goals are related to each other, being arranged in a hierarchy of prepotency. This means that the most prepotent goal will monopolize consciousness and will tend of itself to organize the recruitment of the various capacities of the organism. The less prepotent needs are minimized, even forgotten or denied. But when a need is fairly well satisfied, the next prepotent ("higher") need emerges, in turn to dominate the conscious life and to serve as the center of organization of behavior, since gratified needs are not active motivators.

Thus, man is a perpetually wanting animal. Ordinarily the satisfaction of these wants is not altogether mutually exclusive, but only tends to be. The average member of our society is most often partially satisfied and partially unsatisfied in all of his wants. The hierarchy principle is usually empirically observed in terms of increasing percentages of nonsatisfaction as we go up the hierarchy. Reversals of

Source: A.H. Maslow, "A Theory of Human Motivation," *Psychological Review,* vol. 50, 1943, pp. 394-395. © 1943 by the American Psychological Association. Reprinted with permission.

the average order of the hierarchy are sometimes observed. Also it has been observed that an individual may permanently lose the higher wants in the hierarchy under social conditions. There are not only ordinarily multiple motivations for usual behavior, but in addition many determinants other than motives.

Any thwarting or possibility of thwarting of these basic human goals, or danger to the defenses which protect them, or to the conditions upon which they rest, is considered to be a psychological threat. With a few exceptions, all psychopathology may be partially traced to such threats. A basically thwarted man may actually be defined as a "sick" man, if we wish.

What practical consequences did these results have?

Management regarded these experiments as an attempt to compile a sound body of knowledge upon which to base executive policy and action. And although it was recognized that such research is a long-term proposition, management was ready to make use of any findings which seemed to have been sufficiently tested.

What impressed management most were the stores of latent energy and productive cooperation which could be obtained from people working under the right conditions. Among the factors making for these conditions the attitudes of the employees stood out as being predominant.

The conclusions led to further studies. The Interviewing Program, 1928–30, covering 21,000 employees, provided data of immediate value in improving working conditions, supervisory training, and other employee relations activities conducted by management. Of even more historical significance, it developed insights into methods of listening to and understanding an employee's view of his own personal situation. In short, this part of the program perfected the interviewing technique itself.

Later, the Bank Wiring Observation Room (1931–32) was set up to observe the worker in his work environment. It developed a method of studying group behavior that supplemented interviewing with actual on-the-job data on behavior patterns in the working group. Out of this phase came the concept of the informal organization and its influence on productivity, as well as other new information demonstrating the impact of social factors in the industrial setting.

The Attitude of
Self-Actualizing People to
Duty, Work, Mission

This is the simplest way of saying that proper management of the work lives of human beings, of the way in which they earn their living, can improve them and improve the world and in this sense be a utopian or revolutionary technique.

A.H. Maslow, *Maslow on Management*

We can learn from self-actualizing people what the ideal attitude toward work might be under the most favorable circumstances. These highly evolved individuals assimilate their work into the identity into the self, that is, work actually becomes part of the self part of the individual's definition of himself. Work can be psychotherapeutic, psychogogic (making well people grow toward self-actualization). This of course is a circular relationship to some extent, that is, given fairly o.k. people to begin with, in a fairly good organization, then work tends to improve the people. This tends to improve the industry, which in turn tends to improve the people involved, and so it goes. This is the simplest way of saying that proper management of the work lives of human beings, of the way in which they earn their living, can improve them and improve the world and in this sense be a utopian or revolutionary technique.

I gave up long ago the possibility of improving the world or the whole human species via individual psychotherapy. This is impracticable. As a matter of fact it is impossible quantitatively. (Especially in view of the fact that so many people are not suitable for individual psychotherapy.) Then I turned for my utopian purposes to education as a way of reaching the whole human species. I then thought of the lessons from individual psychotherapy as essentially research data, the most important usefulness of which was application to the eupsychian improvement of educational institutions so that they could make people better en masse. Only recently has it dawned on me that as important as education perhaps even more important is the work life of the individual since everybody works. If the lessons of psychology, of individual psychotherapy, of social psychology, and so forth, can be applied to man's economic life, then my hope is that this too can be given a enlightened direction, thereby tending to influence in principle all human beings.

It is quite clear that this is possible. My first contact with the management literature and with enlightened management policy indicates that management has already in its most advanced forms taken an enlightened, as well as a synergic, direction. Many people seem to have discovered, simply in terms of improved production, improved quality control, improved labor relations, improved management of creative personnel, that the Third Force kind of psychology works.

For instance, the intuitive conclusions that Peter Drucker has arrived at about human nature parallel very closely the conclusions of the Third Force psychologists. He has come to his conclusions simply by observation of industrial and management situations, and apparently he knows nothing of scientific psychology or of clinical psychology or of professional social psychology. [The fact that Drucker comes to approximately the same understanding of human nature that Carl Rogers has achieved, or Erich Fromm, is a most remarkable validation of the hope that the industrial situation may serve as the new laboratory for the study of psychodynamics, of high human development, of ideal ecology for the human being.] This is very different from my own mistake, which I fell into automatically, of regarding industrial psychology as the unthinking application of scientific psychological knowledge. But it's nothing of the sort. It is a *source* of knowledge, replacing the laboratory, often far more useful than the laboratory.

Of course the opposite is also true or at least can be more true than Drucker realizes. There are rich gold mines of research data that the industrial psychologist and the management theorist can use and can apply to the economic situation. My guess is that Drucker and his colleagues took a quick look at what passes for scientific psychology and gave it up at once. It is obviously true that the rats and the pigeons and the conditioned reflexes and the nonsense syllables are of no earthly use in any complex human situation, but in throwing out the nonsense in psychology they also threw out the gold nuggets of which there are also plenty.

Insofar as my own effort is concerned, it has in any case always been an ethical one, an attempt to wed science with humanistic and ethical goals, with efforts to improve individual people and the society as a whole. For me industrial psychology opens up a whole new horizon; for me it means a new source of data, very rich data. Also it represents for me a whole set of validations of hypotheses and theories that I have based on purely clinical data. Furthermore it represents to me a new kind of life-laboratory, with going-on researches where I can confidently expect to learn much about the standard problems of classical psychology, for example, learning, motivation, emotion, thinking, acting, and so forth.

(This is part of my answer to Dick Farson's question, "Why are you so hopped up about all of this stuff? What are you looking for? What do you hope to get out of it? What do you hope to put into it?" What this amounts to is that I see another path for enlightened thinking.)

One advantage that the industrial situation has over individual psychotherapy as a path of personal growth is that it offers the homonomous[1] as well as the autonomous gratifications. Psychotherapy tends to focus too exclusively on the development of the individual, the self, the identity, and so forth. I have thought of creative education and now also of creative management as not only doing this for the individual but also developing him via the community, the team, the group, the organization—which is just as legitimate a path of personal growth as the autonomous paths. Of course, this is especially important for those who are not available for symbolic psychotherapy, psychoanalysis, insight therapy, and so forth. This holds true especially for the feeble-minded and for those reduced to the concrete, who are now mostly beyond the reach of Freudian-style therapy. The good community, the good organization, the good team can help these people where the individual therapist often is helpless.

[1] A. Angyal, *Neurosis and Treatment* (John Wiley & Sons, Inc., 1965).

Letter to John D. Rockefeller III

Mr. John D. Rockefeller III
Room 5600
30 Rockefeller Plaza
New York, New York 10020

Dear Mr. Rockefeller:

I found your Manila talk on "The Quality of Life" interesting, and even fascinating, for reasons beyond the overt face value of the common sense and good judgment of the paper itself. In addition to this, I was extremely absorbed by the convergence between the results of your personal thinking and probing and final judgments on one hand, and the very similar conclusions that come from the findings of the psychotherapists, the theoretical psychologists, the management scientists, and so on. They too have found that part of the human essence is what you have called human dignity, belonging, attaining full potential, caring, and beauty. I have gone so far as to coin a word for these basic needs and aspirations of human nature. I call them *instinctoid,* to indicate by belief that the evidence makes them defining qualities of human nature itself, aspects of its essence, aspects of specieshood.

I am sure also that you will find of the greatest interest my finding that self-actualizing people, that is, people who have been reasonably gratified in their needs for safety, belongingness, affection, dignity, and freedom to develop their own personal potentialities, that such people then become motivated no longer by their *basic needs* but, rather, by what I have called *metamotives*—but which turn out to be essentially the intrinsic values, the eternal verities, the values of Being. These include, as you have pointed out, beauty. But also there is considerable evidence to show that you can add to fill out the picture of these *metaneeds* truth, excellence, order (in the mathematical sense), unity, perfection, and so on.

For me this has been a very heartening thing, to realize that at least for some human beings—I don't know what percentage yet—as the basic aspects that make up the quality of life become fulfilled, they can move on to higher and higher aspirations. That is to say that if there was fulfillment of the aspects of the quality of life that you have listed, you could confidently expect that at least some human beings would move on to become more fully human, closer to the ideally good person. This is not to say that they would be saints, because I also have found that aspirations never cease (or to say it in a negative way, that grumbling, complaining, and wanting more and more never cease). One can say this in an encouraging way—that man's aspirations are endless and higher and higher—or one can say it in a negative way. In any case, we have evidence to indicate that the static notion of the good person, or of the good society, or even of the good heaven, must all give way to the person or the society reaching ever higher and higher and higher, to levels that we cannot even conceive of today.

Let me add my personal gratitude that you used your influence to focus simultaneously on that which is immediately urgent and sine qua non, in this case population control, but also found it possible to talk about aspirations that go beyond our most immediate and urgent problems. As I mentioned in our conversation, I find it extremely helpful, even in the middle of today's turmoil, in the middle of the hurricane so to speak, to have in my hand a compass that tells me the direction toward which I must steer even through the storm and beyond it. I know that it is easy to fall into the utopian spirit and think only of far-off ideals, and I agree with you that this is a great danger. Yet it is equally dangerous, I feel, to focus oneself entirely and exclusively on the immediate, on the fire that is raging now, without also thinking about tomorrow, next year, the next generation, and even the next century. Having this kind of compass helps me, at least, to know what to do at this moment, today, in the middle of an immediately demanding problem.

Of the various basic needs that have been discovered, you have covered them all but one, which I would certainly recommend that you add. This is the need for safety, security, stability, continuity, trust in the environment. I would use the words law and order here if they have not developed particular political accretions of meaning. But those would be fair words to use as aspects of the basic needs for safety, security, and so on. This is an especial problem in the underdeveloped countries (for instance, in Mexico, which I studied for a time): the law itself cannot be trusted, policemen and public officials must be bribed and they are not public servants but care for their own selfish interests first. Or it could be said in another way: where there is violence on the campuses and in the streets; where fear reigns after dark; where the government, the army, the police all seem helpless to ensure the ability to walk without anxiety, without fear, let us say, through Central Park. This is a profound and basic and instinctoid need of all human beings as a species. It is

(continued)

(Continued)

perfectly true that this can be subsumed under the material needs, or even of belongingness, but I have found it helpful to separate it out and to speak of it as a separable need that commands attention and fulfillment.

Another general scientific finding that I think would be helpful to you in your thinking about the quality of life is the finding that these basic needs are organized into what I have called a "hierarchy of prepotency." That is, although these are all universal human needs that demand gratification on pain of developing illness, some of them are more urgent, more prepotent, more demanding then others. The hierarchy of prepotency is an order of urgency or demandingness. The findings are so far that most urgent are the material needs; then come the safety-security needs; then comes belongingness; then come loving and caring, friendship, and affection; then come respect and self-respect and dignity; and then, finally, comes fulfilling one's own individual potentials, what I have called self-actualization. As you point out, self-actualization or dignity and so on are quite expendable when the person is hungry.

Certain basic needs are more urgent than others. This same hierarchy, or something very much like it, has been found to exist, for instance, not only in the order of priority of unconscious needs in the neurotic person but also in the history of what labor unions have struck for, the order of urgency of the problems of the underdeveloped nations, the order of kinds of satisfactions and kinds of pay that upwardly mobile and economically successful individuals in the United States seek for, the order of importance of the human needs that supervisors and managers had better satisfy in our factories, and so on. That is to say, it looks like a universal individual and social principle.

I do hope that these remarks may be helpful. Perhaps they will help you to see why I so much enjoyed your paper.

Cordially,

A.H. Maslow

Source: Letter from John D. Rockefeller III to A.H. Maslow, reprinted with the permission of Ann R. Kaplan and the *Archives of the History of American Psychology.*

Additional Notes on Self-Actualization, Work, Duty, Mission

To do some idiotic job very well is certainly not real achievement. I like my phrasing, "what is not worth doing is not worth doing well."

A.H. Maslow, *Maslow on Management*

After talking recently with various students and professors who "wanted to work with me" on self-actualization, I discovered that I was very suspicious of most of them and rather discouraging, tending to expect little from them. This is a consequence of long experience with multitudes of starry-eyed dilettantes—big talkers, great planners, tremendously enthusiastic—who come to nothing as soon as a little hard work is required. So I have been speaking to these individuals in a pretty blunt and tough and nonencouraging way. I have spoken about dilettantes, for instance (as contrasted with workers and doers), and indicated my contempt for them. I have mentioned how often I have tested people with these fancy aspirations simply by giving them a rather dull but important and worthwhile job to do. Nineteen out of twenty fail the test. I have learned not only to give this test but to brush them aside completely if they don't pass it. I have preached to them about joining the "League of Responsible Citizens" and down with the free-loaders, hangers-on, mere talkers, the permanent passive students who study forever with no results. The test for any person is—that is you want to find out whether he's an apple tree or not—Does He Bear Apples? Does He Bear Fruit? That's the way you tell the difference between fruitfulness and sterility, between talkers and doers, between the people who change the world and the people who are helpless in it.

Another point that has been coming up is the talk about personal salvation. For instance, at the Santa Rosa existential meetings there was much of this kind of talk, and I remember exploding in a kind of irritation and indicating my disrespect for such salvation seekers. This was on the grounds that they were selfish and did nothing for others and for the world. Besides, they were psychologically stupid and psychologically incorrect because seeking for personal salvation is *anyway* the wrong road to personal salvation. The only real path, one that I talked about in my public lecture there, was the path set forth in the Japanese movie "Ikiru," that is, salvation via hard work and total commitment to doing well the job that fate or personal destiny calls you to do, or any important job that "calls for" doing.

I remember citing various "heroes," people who had attained not only personal salvation but the complete respect and love of everybody who knew them; all of them were good workers and responsible people, and furthermore all of them were as happy as was possible for them to be in their circumstances. This business of self-actualization via a commitment to an important job and to worthwhile work could also be said, then, to be the path to human happiness (by contrast with the direct attack or the direct search for happiness—happiness is an epiphenomenon, a by-product, something not to be sought directly but an indirect reward for virtue). The other way—of seeking for personal salvation—just doesn't work for anybody I have *ever* seen—that is the introspection, the full-time-in-a-cave all by one's self some place. This may work for people in India and Japan—I won't deny that—but I have never seen it work for anybody in all my experience in the United States. The only happy people I know are the ones who are working well at something they consider important. Also, I have pointed out in my lecture and in my previous writings that this was universal truth for all my self-actualizing subjects. They were metamotivated by metaneeds (B-values) expressed in their devotion to, dedication to, and identification with some great and important job. This was true for every single case.

Or I can put this very bluntly: Salvation Is a By-Product of Self-Actualizing Work and Self-Actualizing Duty. (The trouble with most of these youngsters who have been after me is that it seems they have in the back of their heads some notion of self-actualization as a kind of lightning stroke which will hit them on the head suddenly without their doing anything about it. They all seem to want to wait passively for it to happen without any effort on their part. Furthermore, I think that practically all of them have tended unconsciously to define self-actualization in terms of the getting rid of all inhibitions and controls in favor of complete spontaneity and impulsivity. My impatience has been largely because of this, I guess, that they had no stubbornness, no persistence, no frustration tolerance, and so forth—apparently just these qualities they consider as the opposite of self-actualization. Maybe this is what I should talk about more specifically.)

One thing about this whole business is that self-actualization work transcends the self without trying to, and achieves the kind of loss of self-awareness and of self-consciousness that the easterners, the Japanese and Chinese and so on, keep on trying to attain. S-A work is simultaneously a seeking and fulfilling of the self *and* also an achieving of the selflessness which is the ultimate expression of *real* self. It resolves the dichotomy between selfish and unselfish. Also between inner and outer—because the cause for which one works in S-A work is introjected and becomes part of the self so that the world and the self are no longer different. The inner and the outer world fuse and become one and the same. The same is true for the subject-object dichotomy.

A talk that we had with an artist at Big Sur Hot Springs—a real artist, a real worker, a real achiever—was very illuminating on this point. He kept on pressing Bertha (my wife) to get to work on her sculpture, and he kept on waving aside all her defenses and her explanations and excuses, all of which were flossy and high-toned. "The only way to be an artist is to work, work, and work." He stressed discipline, labor, sweat. One phrase that he repeated again and again was "Make a pile of chips." "Do something with your wood or your stone or your clay and then if it's lousy throw it away. This is better than doing nothing." He said that he would not take on any apprentice in his ceramics work who wasn't willing to work for years at the craft itself, at the details, the materials. His good-by to Bertha was, "Make a pile of chips." He urged her to get to work right after breakfast like a plumber who has to do a day's work and who has a foreman who will fire him if he doesn't turn out a good day's work. "Act as if you have to earn a living thereby." The guy was clearly an eccentric and talked a lot of wild words—and yet he *had* to be taken seriously because there were his products—the proofs that his words were not merely words.

(Bertha had a very good research idea when we talked about this conversation: The hypothesis is that the creative person loves his tools and his materials, and this can be tested.)

(A good question: Why do people *not* create or work? Rather than, Why *do* they create? Everyone has the motivation to create and to work, every child, every adult. This can be assumed. What has to be explained are the inhibitions, the blocks, and so forth. What stops these motivations which are there in everyone?)

(Side idea: About D-motivated creators, I have always attributed this to special talent alone, that is, to special genius of some sort which has nothing to do with the health of the personality. Now I think I must add just plain hard work, for one thing, and for another, just plain nerve, for example, like someone who arbitrarily defines himself as an artist in a nervy and arrogant way and therefore *is* an artist. Because he treats himself like an artist, everybody tends to also.)

If you take into yourself something important from the world, then you yourself become important thereby. You have made yourself important thereby, as important as that which you have introjected and assimilated to yourself. At once, it matters if you die, or if you are sick, or if you can't work, and so forth. Then you must take care of yourself, you must respect yourself, you have to get plenty of rest, not smoke or drink too much, and so forth. You can no longer commit suicide—that would be too selfish. It would be a loss for the world. You are needed, useful. This is the easiest way to feel needed. Mothers with babies do not commit suicide as easily as nonmothers. People in the concentration camps who had some important mission in life, some duty to live for or some other people to live for tended to stay alive. It was the other ones who gave up and sank into apathy and died without resistance.

This is an easy medicine for self-esteem: Become a part of something important. Be able to say, "We of the United Nations. . . ." or "We physicians. . . ." When you can say, "We psychologists have proven that. . . ." you thereby participate in the glory, the pleasure, and the pride of all psychologists any place.

This identification with important causes, or important jobs, this identifying with them and taking them into the self thereby enlarging the self and making it important, this is a way of overcoming also actual existential human shortcomings for example, shortcomings in I.Q., in talent, in skill, and so forth. For instance, science is a social institution, with division of labor and colleaguehood *and* exploitation of characterological differences—this is a technique for making uncreative people creative, for enabling unintelligent men to be intelligent, for enabling small men to be big, for permitting limited men to be eternal and cosmic. *Any* scientist must be treated with a certain respect, no matter how minor a contributor he may be—because he is a member of a huge enterprise and he demands respect by participation in this enterprise. He represents it, so to speak. He is an ambassador. (This makes a good example also: The ambassador from a great country is treated differently from the ambassador from some dopey or inefficient or ineffective or corrupt country—even though they are both individual human beings with individual human shortcomings.)

The same is true for a single soldier who is a member of a huge victorious army by contrast with a single soldier who is a member of a defeated army. So all the scientists and intellectuals and philosophers, and so forth, even though they are limited figures taken singly, taken collectively they are very important. They represent a victorious army, they are revolutionizing society; they are preparing the new world; they are constructing Eupsychia. So they become heroes by participation in heroic enterprises. They have found a way for small men to make themselves big. And since there exists in the world only small men (in various degrees) perhaps some form of participation in, or identification with, a worthwhile cause may be essential for any human being to feel a healthy and strong self-esteem. (That's why working in a "good" company [prestige, good product, and so forth] is good for the self-esteem.)

This is all related to my thinking on "Responsibility as a Response to the Objective Requirements of the Situation." "Requirements" equals that which "calls for" an appropriate response, that which has "demand-character," which rests so heavily on the self-perceived constitution or temperament or destiny of the perceiver. That is, it is that which *he* feels impelled to make right, to correct; it is the burden that fits *his* shoulders, the crooked picture on the wall that *he* of all people in the world has to straighten. To some extent this is like a recognition of one's self out there in the world. Under ideal conditions there *would* be isomorphism, a mutual selection between the person and his S-A work (his cause, responsibility, call, vocation, task, and so forth). That is, each task would "call for" just that one person in the world most uniquely suited to deal with it, like a key and a lock, and that one person would then feel the call most strongly and would reverberate to it, be tuned to its wavelength, and so be responsive to its call. There is an interaction, a mutual suitability, like a good marriage or like a good friendship, like being designed for each other.

What happens then to the one who denies this unique responsibility? who doesn't listen to his call-note? or who can't hear at all any more? Here we can certainly talk about intrinsic guilt, or intrinsic unsuitability, like a dog trying to walk on his hind legs, or a poet trying to be a good businessman, or a businessman trying to be a poet. It just doesn't fit; it doesn't suit; it doesn't belong. One must respond to one's fate or one's destiny or pay a heavy price. One must yield to it; one must surrender to it. One must permit one's self to be chosen.

This is all very Taoistic. It's good to stress this because responsibility and work are seen unconsciously under the terms of Douglas McGregor's Theory X, as duty, as picking up a burden reluctantly because forced to do so by some external morality, some "should" or "ought" which is seen as different from natural inclination, different from free choice through delight or through tasting good. Under ideal conditions—that is, of healthy selfishness, of deepest, most primitive animal spontaneity and free choice, of listening to one's own impulse voices—one embraces one's fate as eagerly and happily, as one picks one's wife. The yielding (surrender, trusting response receptivity) is here the same as in the embrace of the two people who belong together. The polarity between activity and passivity is here transcended and resolved just as it is in the love embrace or in the sexual act when this is ideal. So also is the will-trust dichotomy resolved. So also the difference between the Western and the Eastern. So also the dichotomy between free will and being determined. (One can embrace one's determinants—but even that statement is too dichotomous. Better said—one can recognize that what *appear* to be one's determinants out there in the world are really one's self which seems to be out there, which appear to be different from the self because of imperfect perception and imperfect fusion. It's a kind of self-love, or a kind of embracing one's own nature. Those things that belong together melt into each other and enjoy that melting, preferring it to being separated.)

(So, Letting-Go [rather than self-control] equals Spontaneity and is a *kind* of activity, which is not other than, which is not separated from, which is not different from passivity.)

So—to recognize one's responsibility or one's work out there is like a love relationship, a recognition of a belongingness, a *Zusammenhang;* it has many of the paradoxical or dichotomy-transcending qualities of sexual intercourse and love embracing, of two becoming one perfectly. This also reminds me of C. Daly King[1] and his notion of "paradic design" which equals a recognition of suitability and belongingness and normality and rightness through the recognition of the intention or fate implied by the design.

Applying this whole notion to the relationship between a person and his work destiny is difficult and subtle, but not much more so than applying this principle to the relationships between the two people who should get married as compared to two people who obviously should not get married. One personality can be seen to fit with another personality in this same paradic design.

If work is introjected into the self (I guess it always is, more or less, even when one tries to prevent it), then the relationship between self-esteem and work is closer than I had thought. Especially healthy and stable self-esteem (the feeling of worth, pride, influence, importance, and so forth) rests on good, worthy work to be introjected, thereby becoming part of the self. Maybe more of our contemporary malaise is due to introjection of nonprideful, robotized, broken-down-into-easy-bits kind of work than I had thought. The more I think about it, the more difficult I find it to *conceive* of feeling proud of myself, self-loving and self-respecting, if I were working, for example, in some chewing gum factory, or a phony advertising agency, or in some factory that turned out shoddy furniture. I've written so far of "real achievement" as a basis for solid self-esteem, but I guess this is too general and needs more spelling out. Real achievement means inevitably a worthy and virtuous task. To do some idiotic job very well is certainly *not* real achievement. I like my phrasing, "What is not worth doing is not worth doing well."

[1] C. D. King, "The Meaning of Normal," *Yale Journal of Biology and Medicine,* 1945, *17,* 493–501.

Self-Actualized Duty

*Every age but ours has had its model, its ideal. All of these
have been given up by our culture; the saint, the hero, the
gentleman, the knight, the mystic . . . Perhaps we shall soon
be able to use as our guide and model the fully growing and
self-fulfilling human being. The one whom all potentialities
are coming to full development, the one whose inner nature
expresses itself freely . . .*

A.H. Maslow, *Maslow on Management*

At the point where the S-A job is assimilated into the identity
or into the self by introjection, then such work can be therapeutic and self-therapeutic. This is because the work or the
task out there which has become part of the self can be worked on, attacked, struggled with, improved, corrected in a way that the person
cannot do directly with his own inner self. That is to say, his inner
problems can be projected out into the world as outer problems where
he can then work with them far more easily and with less anxiety,
less repression than he could by direct introspection. As a matter of fact
this may be one main unconscious reason for projecting an inner problem into the outer world, that is, just so that it can be worked on with
less anxiety. I think probably the best examples here and the most easily acceptable ones are, first, the artist (certainly everybody will agree
that he does exactly this with his inner problems, putting them on his
canvasses), and second, many intellectual workers who do about the
same thing when they select some problems to work with which are
really projections of their own inner problems, even though they don't
recognize them as such.

Creativity in
Self-Actualizing People

Maslow had mentioned the "creativeness" of self-actualizing people only briefly in his earlier writings on self-actualization. The present chapter, which is a revised version of a lecture delivered at Michigan State University, February 28, 1959, represents his first attempt to expand upon the issue. His subsequent observations on creativeness/creativity can be found in Chapters 4, 5, 6, and 7 of his posthumously published collection of papers entitled The Farther Reaches of Human Nature *(New York: Viking Press, 1971).*

I first had to change my ideas about creativity as soon as I began studying people who were positively healthy, highly evolved and matured, self-actualizing. I had first to give up my stereotyped notion that health, genius, talent and productivity were synonymous. A fair proportion of my subjects, though healthy and creative in a special sense that I am going to describe, were *not* productive in the ordinary sense, nor did they have great talent or genius, nor were they poets, composers, inventors, artists or creative intellectuals. It was also obvious that some of the greatest talents of mankind were certainly not psychologically healthy people, Wagner, for example, or Van Gogh or Byron. Some were and some weren't, it was clear. I very soon had to come to the conclusion that great talent was not only more or less independent of goodness or health of character but also that we know little about it. For instance, there is some evidence that great musical talent and mathematical talent are more inherited than acquired. It seemed clear then that health and special talent were separate variables, maybe only slightly correlated, maybe not. We may as well admit at the beginning that psychology knows very little about special talent of the genius type. I shall say nothing more about it, confining myself instead to that more widespread kind of creativeness which is the universal heritage of every human being that is born, and which seems to co-vary with psychological health.

Furthermore, I soon discovered that I had, like most other people, been thinking of creativeness in terms of products, and secondly, I had unconsciously confined creativeness to certain conventional areas only of human endeavor, unconsciously assuming that *any* painter, *any* poet, *any* composer was leading a creative life. Theorists, artists, scientists, inventors, writers could be creative. Nobody else could be. Unconsciously I had assumed that creativeness was the prerogative solely of certain professionals.

But these expectations were broken up by various of my subjects. For instance, one woman, uneducated, poor, a full-time housewife and mother, did none of these conventionally creative things and yet was a marvellous cook, mother, wife and homemaker. With little money, her home was somehow always beautiful. She was a perfect hostess. Her meals were banquets. Her taste in linens, silver, glass, crockery and furniture was impeccable. She was in all these areas original, novel, ingenious, unexpected, inventive. I just *had* to call her creative. I learned from her and others like her that a first-rate soup is more creative than a second-rate painting, and that, generally, cooking or parenthood or making a home could be creative while poetry need not be; it could be uncreative.

Another of my subjects devoted herself to what had best be called social service in the broadest sense, bandaging up wounds, helping the downtrodden, not only in a personal way, but in an organization which helps many more people than she could individually.

Another was a psychiatrist, a "pure clinician who never wrote anything or created any theories or researches but who delighted in his everyday job of helping people to create themselves. This man approached each patient as if he were the only one in the world, without jargon, expectations or presuppositions, with innocence and naivete and yet with great wisdom, in a Taoistic fashion. Each patient was a unique human being and therefore a completely new problem to be understood and solved in a completely novel way. His great success even with very difficult cases validated his "creative" (rather than stereotyped or orthodox) way of doing things. From another man I learned that constructing a business organization could be a creative activity. From a young athlete, I learned that a perfect tackle could be as esthetic a product as a sonnet and could be approached in the same creative spirit.

It dawned on me once that a competent cellist I had reflexly thought of as "creative" (because I associated her with creative music? with creative composers?) was actually playing well what someone else had written. She was a mouthpiece, as the average actor or "comedian" is a mouthpiece. A good cabinet-maker or gardener or dressmaker *could* be more truly creative. I had to make an individual judgment in each instance, since almost any role or job could be either creative or uncreative.

In other words, I learned to apply the word "creative" (and also the word "esthetic") not only to products but also to people in a characterological way, and to activities, processes, and attitudes. And furthermore, I had come to apply the word "creative" to many products other than the standard and conventionally accepted poems, theories, novels, experiments or paintings.

The consequence was that I found it necessary to distinguish "special talent creativeness" from "self-actualizing (SA) creativeness" which sprang much more directly from the personality, and which showed itself widely in the ordinary affairs of life, for instance, in a certain kind of humor. It looked like a tendency to do *anything* creatively: for example, housekeeping, teaching, and so forth. Frequently, it appeared that an essential aspect of SA creativeness was a special kind of perceptiveness that is exemplified by the child in the fable who saw that the king had no clothes on (this too contradicts the notion of creativity as products). Such people can see the fresh, the raw, the concrete, the idiographic, as well as the generic, the abstract, the rubricized, the categorized and the classified. Consequently, they live far more in the real world of nature than in the verbalized world of concepts, abstractions, expectations, beliefs and stereotypes that most people confuse with the real world. This is well expressed in Rogers' phrase "openness to experience."

All my subjects were relatively more spontaneous and expressive than average people. They were more "natural" and less controlled and inhibited in their behavior, which seemed to flow out more easily and freely and with less blocking and self-criticism. This ability to express ideas and impulses without strangulation and without fear of ridicule turned out to be an essential aspect of SA creativeness. Rogers has used the excellent phrase, "fully functioning person," to describe this aspect of health.

Another observation was that SA creativeness was in many respects like the creativeness of *all* happy and secure children. It was spontaneous, effortless, innocent, easy, a kind of freedom from stereotypes and cliches. And again it seemed to be made up largely of "innocent" freedom of perception, and "innocent," uninhibited spontaneity and expressiveness. Almost any child can perceive more freely, without a priori expectations about what ought to be there, what must be there, or what has always been there. And almost any child can compose a song or a poem or a dance or a painting or a play or a game on the spur of the moment, without planning or previous intent.

It was in this childlike sense that my subjects were creative. Or to avoid misunderstanding, since my subjects were after all not children (they were all people in their 50's or 60's), let us say that they had either retained or regained at least these two main aspects of child-likeness, namely, they were non-rubricizing or "open to experience" and they were easily spontaneous and expressive. If children are naive, then my subjects had attained a "second naivete," as Santayana called it. Their innocence of perception and expressiveness was combined with sophisticated minds.

In any case, this all sounds as if we are dealing with a fundamental characteristic, inherent in human nature, a potentiality given to all or most human beings at birth, which most often is lost or buried or inhibited as the person gets enculturated.

My subjects were different from the average person in another characteristic that makes creativity more likely. SA people are relatively unfrightened by the unknown, the mysterious, the puzzling, and often are positively attracted by it, that is, selectively pick it out to puzzle over, to meditate on and to be absorbed with. I quote from my description: "They do not neglect the unknown, or deny it, or run away from it, or try to make believe it is really known, nor do they organize, dichotomize, or rubricize it prematurely. They do not cling to the familiar, nor is their quest for the truth a catastrophic need for certainty, safety, definiteness, and order, such as we see in an exaggerated form in Goldstein's brain-injured or in the compulsive-obsessive neurotic.

They can be, when the total objective situation calls for it, comfortably, disorderly, sloppy, anarchic, chaotic, vague, doubtful, uncertain, indefinite, approximate, inexact, or inaccurate (all at certain moments in science, art, or life in general, quite desirable).

"Thus it comes about that doubt, tentativeness, uncertainty, with the consequent necessity for abeyance of decision, which is for most a torture, can be for some a pleasantly stimulating challenge, a high spot in life rather than a low."

One observation I made has puzzled me for many years but it begins to fall into place now. It was what I described as the resolution of dichotomies in self-actualizing people. Briefly stated, I found that I had to see differently many oppositions and polarities that all psychologists had taken for granted as straight line continua. For instance, to take the first dichotomy that I had trouble with, I couldn't decide whether my subjects were selfish or unselfish. (Observe how spontaneously we fall into an either-or, here. The more of one, the less of the other, is the implication of the style in which I put the question.) But I was forced by sheer pressure of fact to give up this Aristotelian style of logic. My subjects were very unselfish in one sense and very selfish in another sense. And the two fused together, not like incompatibles, but rather in a sensible, dynamic unity or synthesis very much like what Fromm has described in his classical paper on healthy selfishness. My subjects had put opposites together in such a way as to make me realize that regarding selfishness and unselfishness as contradictory and mutually exclusive is itself characteristic of a lower level of personality development. So also in my subjects were many other dichotomies resolved into unities, cognition vs. conation (heart vs. head, wish vs. fact) became cognition "structured with" conation as instinct and reason came to the same conclusions. Duty became pleasure, and pleasure merged with duty. The distinction between work and play became shadowy. How could selfish hedonism be opposed to altruism, when altruism became selfishly pleasurable? These most mature of all people were also strongly childlike. These same people, the strongest egos ever described and the most definitely individual, were also precisely the ones who could be most easily ego-less, self-transcending, and problem-centered.

But this is precisely what the great artist does. He is able to bring together clashing colors, forms that fight each other, dissonances of all kinds, into a unity. And this is also what the great theorist does when he puts puzzling and inconsistent facts together so that we can see that they really belong together. And so also for the great statesman, the great therapist, the great philosopher, the great parent, the great inventor. They are all integrators, able to bring separates and even opposites together into unity.

We speak here of the ability to integrate and of the play back and forth between integration within the person, and his ability to integrate whatever it is he is doing in the world. To the extent that creativeness is constructive, synthesizing, unifying, and integrative, to that extent does it depend in part on the inner integration of the person.

In trying to figure out why all this was so, it seemed to me that much of it could be traced back to the relative absence of fear in my subjects. They were certainly less enculturated; that is, they seemed to be less afraid of what other people would say or demand or laugh at. They had less need of other people and therefore, depending on them less, could be less afraid of them and less hostile against them. Perhaps most important, however, was their lack of fear of their own insides, of their own impulses, emotions, thoughts. They were more self-accepting than the average. This approval and acceptance of their deeper selves then made it more possible to perceive bravely the real nature of the world and also made their behavior more spontaneous (less controlled, less inhibited, less planned, less "willed" and designed). They were less afraid of their own thoughts even when they were "nutty" or silly or crazy. They were less afraid of being laughed at or of being disapproved of. They could let themselves be flooded by emotion. In contrast, average and neurotic people wall off fear, much that lies within themselves. They control, they inhibit, they repress, and they suppress. They disapprove of their deeper selves and expect that others do, too.

What I am saying in effect is that the creativity of my subjects seemed to be an epiphenomenon of their greater wholeness and integration, which is what self-acceptance implies. The civil war within the average person between the forces of the inner depths and the forces of defense and control seems to have been resolved in my subjects and they are less split. As a consequence, more of themselves is available for use, for enjoyment and for creative purposes. They waste less of their time and energy protecting themselves against themselves.

As we have seen in previous chapters, what we know of peak-experiences supports and enriches these conclusions. These too are integrated and integrating experiences which are to some extent, iso-morphic with integration in the perceived world. In these experiences also, we find increased openness to experience, and increased spon-taneity and expressiveness. Also, since one aspect of this integration within the person is the acceptance and greater availability of our deeper selves, these deep roots of creativeness become more available for use.

PRIMARY, SECONDARY, AND INTEGRATED CREATIVENESS

Classical Freudian theory is of little use for our purposes and is even par-tially contradicted by our data. It is (or was) essentially an id psychol-ogy, an investigation of the instinctive impulses and their vicissitudes, and the basic Freudian dialectic is seen to be ultimately between im-pulses and defenses against them. But far more crucial than repressed impulses for understanding the sources of creativity (as well as play, love, enthusiasm, humor, imagination, and fantasy) are the so-called primary processes which are essentially cognitive rather than conative. As soon as we turn our attention to this aspect of human depth-psychology, we find much agreement between the psychoanalytic ego-psychology—Kris, Miller, Ehrenzweig, the Jungian psychology, and the American self-and-growth psychology.

The normal adjustment of the average, common sense, well-adjusted man implies a continued successful rejection of much of the depths of human nature, both conative and cognitive. To adjust well to the world of reality means a splitting of the person. It means that the person turns his back on much in himself because it is dangerous. But it is now clear that by so doing, he loses a great deal too, for these depths are also the source of all his joys, his ability to play, to love, to laugh, and, most important for us, to be creative. By protecting himself against the hell within himself, he also cuts himself off from the heaven within. In the extreme instance, we have the obsessional person, flat, tight, rigid, frozen, controlled, cautious, who can't laugh or play or love, or be silly or trusting or childish. His imagination, his intuitions, his soft-ness, his emotionality tend to be strangulated or distorted.

The goals of psychoanalysis as a therapy are ultimately integrative. The effort is to heal this basic split by insight, so that what has been repressed becomes conscious or preconscious. But here again we can make modifications as a consequence of studying the depth sources of creativeness. Our relation to our primary processes is not in all respects the same as our relation to unacceptable wishes. The most important difference that I can see is that our primary processes are not as dangerous as the forbidden impulses. To a large extent they are not repressed or censored but rather are "forgotten," or else turned away from, suppressed (rather than repressed), as we have to adjust to a harsh reality which demands a purposeful and pragmatic striving rather than revery, poetry, play. Or, to say it in another way, in a rich society there must be far less resistance to primary thought processes. I expect that education processes, which are known to do rather little for relieving repression of "instinct," can do much to accept and integrate the primary processes into conscious and preconscious life. Education in art, poetry, dancing, can in principle do much in this direction. And so also can education in dynamic psychology; for instance, Deutsch and Murphy's "Clinical Interview," which speaks in primary process language, can be seen as a kind of poetry. Marion Milner's extraordinary book, *On Not Being Able to Paint,* perfectly makes my point.

The kind of creativeness I have been trying to sketch out is best exemplified by the improvisation, as in jazz or in childlike paintings, rather than by the work of art designated as "great."

In the first place, the great work needs great talent which, as we have seen, turned out to be irrelevant for our concern. In the second place, the great work needs not only the flash, the inspiration, the peak-experience; it also needs hard work, long training, unrelenting criticism, perfectionistic standards. In other words, succeeding upon the spontaneous is the deliberate; succeeding upon total acceptance comes criticism; succeeding upon intuition comes rigorous thought; succeeding upon daring comes caution; succeeding upon fantasy and imagination comes reality testing. Now come the questions, "Is it true?" "Will it be understood by the other?" "Is its structure sound?" "Does it stand the test of logic?" "How will it do in the world?" "Can I prove it?" Now come the comparisons, the judgments, the evaluations, the cold, calculating morning-after thoughts, the selections and the rejections.

If I may say it so, the secondary processes now take over from the primary, the Apollonian from the Dionysian, the "masculine" from the "feminine." The voluntary regression into our depths is now terminated, the necessary passivity and receptivity of inspiration or of peak-experience must now give way to activity, control, and hard work. A peak-experience happens *to* a person, but the person *makes* the great product.

Strictly speaking, I have investigated this first phase only, that which comes easily and without effort as a spontaneous expression of an integrated person, or of a transient unifying within the person. It can come only if a person's depths are available to him, only if he is not afraid of his primary thought processes.

I shall call "primary creativity" that which proceeds from and uses the primary process much more than the secondary processes. The creativity which is based mostly on the secondary thought processes I shall call "secondary creativity." This latter type includes a large proportion of production-in-the-world, the bridges, the houses, the new automobiles, even many scientific experiments and much literary work. All of these are essentially the consolidation and development of other people's ideas. It parallels the difference between the commando and the military policeman behind the lines, between the pioneer and the settler. That creativity which uses *both* types of process easily and well, in good fusion or in good succession, I shall call "integrated creativity." It is from this kind that comes the great work of art, or philosophy, or science.

CONCLUSION

The upshot of all of these developments can, I think, be summarized as an increased stress on the role of integration (or self-consistency, unity, wholeness) in the theory of creativeness. Resolving a dichotomy into a higher, more inclusive, unity amounts to healing a split in the person and making him more unified. Since the splits I have been talking about are within the person, they amount to a kind of civil war, a setting of one part of the person against another part. In any case so far as SA creativeness is concerned, it seems to come more immediately from fusion of primary and secondary processes rather than from working through repressive control of forbidden impulses and wishes. It is, of course, probable that defenses arising out of fears of these forbidden impulses also push down primary processes in a kind of total, undiscriminating, panicky war on *all* the depths. But it seems that such lack of discrimination is not in principle necessary.

To summarize, SA creativeness stresses first the personality rather than its achievements, considering these achievements to be epiphenomena emitted by the personality and therefore secondary to it. It stresses characterological qualities like boldness, courage, freedom, spontaneity, perspicuity, integration, self-acceptance, all of which make possible the kind of generalized SA creativeness, which expresses itself in the creative life, or the creative attitude, or the creative person. I have also stressed the expressive or Being quality of SA creativeness rather than its problem-solving or product-making quality. SA creativeness is "emitted," or radiated, and hits all of life, regardless of problems, just as a cheerful person "emits" cheerfulness without purpose or design or even consciousness. It is emitted like sunshine; it spreads all over the place; it makes some things grow (which are growable) and is wasted on rocks and other ungrowable things.

Finally, I am quite aware that I have been trying to break up widely accepted concepts of creativity without being able to offer in exchange a nice, clearly defined, clean-cut substitute concept. SA creativeness is hard to define because sometimes it seems to be synonymous with health itself, as Moustakas has suggested. And since self-actualization or health must ultimately be defined as the coming to pass of the fullest humanness, or as the "Being" of the person, it is as if SA creativity were almost synonymous with, or a *sine qua non* aspect of, or a defining characteristic of, essential humanness.

Some Basic Propositions of a Growth and Self-Actualization Psychology

Maslow notes in the Preface to the first edition of Toward a Psychology of Being *that the propositions presented in this chapter "are a summary of the whole of this book and of my previous one." Most of the content of the chapter was drafted in 1958.*

When the philosophy of man (his nature, his goals, his potentialities, his fulfillment) changes, then everything changes, not only the philosophy of politics, of economics, of ethics and values, of interpersonal relations and of history itself, but also the philosophy of education, of psychotherapy and of personal growth, the theory of how to help men become what they can and deeply need to become.

We are now in the middle of such a change in the conception of man's capacities, potentialities and goals. A new vision is emerging of the possibilities of man and of his destiny, and its implications are many, not only for our conceptions of education, but also for science, politics, literature, economics, religion, and even our conceptions of the non-human world.

I think it is now possible to begin to delineate this view of human nature as a total, single, comprehensive system of psychology even though much of it has arisen as a reaction *against* the limitations (as

Source: A.H. Maslow, *Toward a Psychology of Being, 3rd ed.* (New York: John Wiley & Sons, 1968, 1999). Copyright © 1968, 1999 by John Wiley & Sons, used with permission.

philosophies of human nature) of the two most comprehensive psychologies now available—behaviorism (or associationism) and classical, Freudian psychoanalysis. Finding a single label for it is still a difficult task, perhaps a premature one. In the past I have called it the "holistic-dynamic" psychology to express my conviction about its major roots. Some have called it "organismic" following Goldstein. Sutich and others are calling it the Self-psychology or Humanistic psychology. We shall see. My own guess is that, in a few decades, if it remains suitably eclectic and comprehensive, it will be called simply "psychology."

I think I can be of most service by speaking primarily for myself and out of my own work rather than as an "official" delegate of this large group of thinkers, even though I am sure that the areas of agreement among them are very large. A selection of works of this "third force" is listed in the bibliographies. Because of the limited space I have, I will present here only some of the major propositions of this point of view. I should warn you that at many points I am way out ahead of the data. Some of these propositions are more based on private conviction than on publicly demonstrated facts. However, they are all in principle confirmable or disconfirmable.

1. We have, each one of us, an essential inner nature which is instinctoid, intrinsic, given, "natural," that is, with an appreciable hereditary determinant, and which tends strongly to persist.

It makes sense to speak here of the hereditary, constitutional and very early acquired roots of the *individual* self, even though this biological determination of self is only partial, and far too complex to describe simply. In any case, this is "raw material" rather than finished product, to be reacted to by the person, by his significant others, by his environment, and so forth.

I include in this essential inner nature instinctoid basic needs, capacities, talents, anatomical equipment, physiological or temperamental balances, prenatal and natal injuries, and traumata to the neonate. This inner core shows itself as natural inclinations, propensities or inner bent. Whether defense and coping mechanisms, "style of life," and other characterological traits, all shaped in the first few years of life, should be included is still a matter for discussion. This raw material very quickly starts growing into a self as it meets the world outside and begins to have transaction with it.

2. These are potentialities, not final actualizations. Therefore they have a life history and must be seen developmentally. They are actualized, shaped or stifled mostly (but not altogether) by extra-psychic determinants (culture, family, environment, learning, and so forth). Very early in life these goalless urges and tendencies become attached to objects ("sentiments") by canalization but also by arbitrarily learned associations.

3. This inner core, even though it is biologically based and "instinctoid," is weak in certain senses rather than strong. It is easily overcome, suppressed or repressed. It may even be killed off permanently. Humans no longer have instincts in the animal sense, powerful, unmistakable inner voices which tell them unequivocally what to do, when, where, how and with whom. All that we have left are instinct-remnants. And furthermore, these are weak, subtle and delicate, very easily drowned out by learning, by cultural expectations, by fear, by disapproval, and so forth. They are *hard* to know, rather than easy. Authentic selfhood can be defined in part as being able to hear these impulse-voices within oneself, that is, to know what one really wants or doesn't want, what one is fit for and what one is *not* fit for, and so forth. It appears that there are wide individual differences in the strength of these impulse-voices.

4. Each person's inner nature has some characteristics which all other selves have (species-wide) and some which are unique to the person (idiosyncratic). The need for love characterizes every human being that is born (although it can disappear later under certain circumstances). Musical genius however is given to very few, and these differ markedly from each other in style, for example, Mozart and Debussy.

5. It is possible to study this inner nature scientifically and objectively (that is, with the right kind of "science") and to discover what it is like (*discover*—not invent or construct). It is also possible to do this subjectively, by inner search and by psychotherapy, and the two enterprises supplement and support each other. An expanded humanistic philosophy of science must include these experiential techniques.

6. Many aspects of this inner, deeper nature are either (a) actively repressed, as Freud has described, because they are feared or disapproved of or are ego-alien, or (b) "forgotten" (neglected, unused, overlooked, unverbalized or suppressed), as Schachtel has described. Much of the inner, deeper nature is therefore unconscious. This can be true not only

for impulses (drives, instincts, needs) as Freud has stressed, but also for capacities, emotions, judgments, attitudes, definitions, perceptions, and so forth. Active repression takes effort and uses up energy. There are many specific techniques of maintaining active unconsciousness, such as denial, projection, reaction-formation, and so forth. However, repression does not kill what is repressed. The repressed remains as one active determinant of thought and behavior.

Both active and passive repressions seem to begin early in life, mostly as a response to parental and cultural disapprovals.

However, there is some clinical evidence that repression may arise also from intra-psychic, extra-cultural sources in the young child, or at puberty, that is, out of fear of being overwhelmed by its own impulses, of becoming disintegrated, of "falling apart," exploding, and so forth. It is theoretically possible that the child may spontaneously form attitudes of fear and disapproval toward its own impulses and may then defend himself against them in various ways. Society need not be the only repressing force, if this is true. There may also be intra-psychic repressing and controlling forces. These we may call "intrinsic counter-cathexes."

It is best to distinguish unconscious drives and needs from unconscious ways of cognizing because the latter are often easier to bring to consciousness and therefore to modify. Primary process cognition (Freud) or archaic thinking (Jung) is more recoverable by, for example, creative art education, dance education, and other non-verbal educational techniques.

7. Even though "weak," this inner nature rarely disappears or dies, in the usual person, in the U.S. (such disappearance or dying is possible early in the life history, however). It persists underground, unconsciously, even though denied and repressed. Like the voice of the intellect (which is part of it), it speaks softly but it *will* be heard, even if in a distorted form. That is, it has a dynamic force of its own, pressing always for open, uninhibited expression. Effort must be used in its suppression or repression from which fatigue can result. This force is one main aspect of the "will to health," the urge to grow, the pressure to self-actualization, the quest for one's identity. It is this that makes psychotherapy, education and self-improvement possible in principle.

8. However, this inner core, or self, grows into adulthood only partly by (objective or subjective) discovery, uncovering and acceptance

of what is "there" beforehand. Partly it is also a creation of the person himself. Life is a continual series of choices for the individual in which a main determinant of choice is the person as he already is (including his goals for himself, his courage or fear, his feeling of responsibility, his ego-strength or "will power," and so forth.). We can no longer think of the person as "fully determined" where this phrase implies "determined only by forces external to the person." The person, insofar as he *is* a real person, in his own main determinant. Every person is, in part, "his own project" and makes himself.

9. If this essential core (inner nature) of the person is frustrated, denied or suppressed, sickness results, sometimes in obvious forms, sometimes in subtle and devious forms, sometimes immediately, sometimes later. These psychological illnesses include many more than those listed by the American Psychiatric Association. For instance, the character disorders and disturbances are now seen as far more important for the fate of the world than the classical neuroses or even the psychoses. From this new point of view, new kinds of illness are most dangerous, for example, "the diminished or stunted person," that is, the loss of any of the defining characteristics of humanness, or personhood, the failure to grow to one's potential, valuelessness, and so forth.

That is, general-illness of the personality is seen as any falling short of growth, or of self-actualization, or of full-humanness. And the main source of illness (although not the only one) is seen as frustrations (of the basic needs, of the B-values, of idiosyncratic potentials, of expression of the self, and of the tendency of the person to grow in his own style and at his own pace) especially in the early years of life. That is, frustration of the basic needs is not the only source of illness or of human diminution.

10. This inner nature, as much as we know of it so far, is definitely not primarily "evil," but is rather what we adults in our culture call "good," or else it is neutral. The most accurate way to express this is to say that it is "prior to good and evil." There is little question about this if we speak of the inner nature of the infant and child. The statement is much more complex if we speak of the "infant" as he still exists in the adult. And it gets still more complex if the individual is seen from the point of view of B-psychology rather than D-psychology.

This conclusion is supported by all the truth-revealing and uncovering techniques that have anything to do with human nature: psychotherapy, objective science, subjective science, education and art. For instance, in the long run, uncovering therapy lessens malice, fear, greed, and so forth, and increases love, courage, creativeness, kindness, altruism, and so forth, leading us to the conclusion that the latter are "deeper," more natural, and more intrinsically human than the former, that is, that what we call "bad" behavior is lessened or removed by uncovering, while what we call "good" behavior is strengthened and fostered by uncovering.

11. We must differentiate the Freudian type of superego from intrinsic conscience and intrinsic guilt. The former is in principle a taking into the self of the disapprovals and approvals of persons other than the person himself, fathers, mothers, teachers, and so forth. Guilt then is recognition of disapproval by others.

Intrinsic guilt is the consequence of betrayal of one's own inner nature or self, a turning off the path to self-actualization, and is essentially justified self-disapproval. It is therefore not as culturally relative as is Freudian guilt. It is "true" or "deserved" or "right and just" or "correct" because it is a discrepancy from something profoundly real within the person rather than from accidental, arbitrary or purely relative localisms. Seen in this way it is good, even *necessary,* for a person's development to have intrinsic guilt when he deserves to. It is not just a symptom to be avoided at any cost but is rather an inner guide for growth toward actualization of the real self, and of its potentialities.

12. "Evil" behavior has mostly referred to unwarranted hostility, cruelty, destructiveness, "mean" aggressiveness. This we do not know enough about. To the degree that this quality of hostility is instinctoid, mankind has one kind of future. To the degree that it is reactive (a response to bad treatment), mankind has a very different kind of future. My opinion is that the weight of the evidence so far indicates that indiscriminately *destructive* hostility is reactive, because uncovering therapy reduces it, and changes its quality into "healthy" self-affirmation, forcefulness, selective hostility, self-defense, righteous indignation, and so forth. In any case, the *ability* to be aggressive and angry is found in all self-actualizing people, who are able to let it flow forth freely when the external situation "calls for" it.

The situation in children is far more complex. At the very least, we know that the healthy child is also able to be justifiably angry, self-protecting and self-affirming, that is, reactive aggression. Presumably, then, a child should learn not only how to control his anger, but also how and when to express it.

Behavior that our culture calls evil can also come from ignorance and from childish misinterpretations and beliefs (whether in the child or in the repressed or "forgotten" child-in-the-adult). For instance, sibling rivalry is traceable to the child's wish for the exclusive love of his parents. Only as he matures is he in principle capable of learning that his mother's love for a sibling is compatible with her continued love for him. Thus out of a childish version of love, not in itself reprehensible, can come unloving behavior.

In any case, much that our or any other culture calls evil need not be considered evil in fact, from the more universal, species-wide point of view outlined in this book. If humanness is accepted and loved, then many local, ethnocentric problems simply disappear. To take only one example, seeing sex as intrinsically evil is sheer nonsense from a humanistic point of view.

The commonly seen hatred or resentment of or jealousy of goodness, truth, beauty, health or intelligence ("counter-values") is largely (though not altogether) determined by threat of loss of self-esteem, as the liar is threatened by the honest man, the homely girl by the beautiful girl, or the coward by the hero. Every superior person confronts us with our own shortcomings.

Still deeper than this, however, is the ultimate existential question of the fairness and justice of fate. The person with a disease may be jealous of the healthy man who is no more deserving than he.

Evil behaviors seem to most psychologists to be reactive as in these examples, rather than instinctive. This implies that though "bad" behavior is very deeply rooted in human nature and can never be abolished altogether, it may yet be expected to lessen as the personality matures and as the society improves.

13. Many people still think of "the unconscious," of regression, and of primary process cognition as necessarily unhealthy, or dangerous or bad. Psychotherapeutic experience is slowly teaching us otherwise. Our depths can also be good, or beautiful or desirable. This is also becoming clear from the general findings from investigations of the sources of love, creativeness, play, humor, art, and so forth. Their roots are deep in the inner, deeper self, that is, in the unconscious. To recover them and to be able to enjoy and use them we must be able to "regress."

14. No psychological health is possible unless this essential core of the person is fundamentally accepted, loved and respected by others

and by himself (the converse is not necessarily true, that is, that if the core is respected, and so forth, then psychological health must result, since other prerequisite conditions must also be satisfied).

The psychological health of the chronologically immature is called healthy growth. The psychological health of the adult is called variously, self-fulfillment, emotional maturity, individuation, productiveness, self-actualization, authenticity, full-humanness, and so forth.

Healthy growth is conceptually subordinate, for it is usually defined now as "growth toward self-actualization," and so forth. Some psychologists speak simply in terms of one overarching goal or end, or tendency of human development, considering all immature growth phenomena to be only steps along the path to self-actualization (Goldstein, Rogers).

Self-actualization is defined in various ways but a solid core of agreement is perceptible. All definitions accept or imply, (a) acceptance and expression of the inner core or self, that is, actualization of these latent capacities, and potentialities, "full functioning," availability of the human and personal essence. (b) They all imply minimal presence of ill health, neurosis, psychosis, of loss or diminution of the basic human and personal capacities.

15. For all these reasons, it is at this time best to bring out and encourage, or at the very least, to recognize this inner nature, rather than to suppress or repress it. Pure spontaneity consists of free, uninhibited, uncontrolled, trusting, unpremeditated expression of the self, that is, of the psychic forces, with minimal interference by consciousness. Control, will, caution, self-criticism, measure, deliberateness are the brakes upon this expression made intrinsically necessary by the laws of the social and natural worlds outside the psychic world, and secondarily, made necessary by fear of the psyche itself (intrinsic counter-cathexis). Speaking in a very broad way, controls upon the psyche which come from *fear of the psyche* are largely neurotic or *psychotic,* or not intrinsically or theoretically necessary. (The healthy psyche is not terrible or horrible and therefore doesn't have to be feared, as it has been for thousands of years. Of course, the *unhealthy* psyche is another story.) This kind of control is usually lessened by psychological health, by deep psychotherapy, or by any *deeper* self-knowledge and self-acceptance. There are also, however, controls upon the psyche which do not come out of fear, but out of the necessities for keeping it integrated, organized and unified (intrinsic counter-cathexes). And there are also "controls," probably in another

sense, which are necessary as capacities are actualized, and as higher forms of expression are sought for, for example, acquisition of skills through hard work by the artist, the intellectual, the athlete. But these controls are eventually transcended and become aspects of spontaneity, as they become self. I propose that we call these desirable and necessary controls "Apollonizing controls" because they do not call into question the desirability of the gratification, but rather *enhance* pleasure by organizing, estheticizing, pacing, styling and savoring the gratification, for example, as in sex, eating, drinking, and so forth. The contrast is with repressive or suppressive controls.

The balance between spontaneity and control varies, then, as the health of the psyche and the health of the world vary. Pure spontaneity is not long possible because we live in a world which runs by its own, non-psychic laws. It *is* possible in dreams, fantasies, love, imagination, sex, the first stages of creativity, artistic work, intellectual play, free association, and so forth. Pure control is not permanently possible, for then the psyche dies. Education must be directed then *both* toward cultivation of controls and cultivation of spontaneity and expression. In our culture and at this point in history, it is necessary to redress the balance in favor of spontaneity, the ability to be expressive, passive, unwilled, trusting in processes other than will and control, unpremeditated, creative, and so forth. But it must be recognized that there have been and will be other cultures and other areas in which the balance was or will be in the other direction.

16. In the normal development of the healthy child, it is now believed that, much of the time, if he is given a really free choice, he will choose what is good for his growth. This he does because it tastes good, feels good, gives pleasure or *delight.* This implies that he "knows" better than anyone else what is good for him. A permissive regime means not that adults gratify his needs directly but make it possible for *him* to gratify his needs, and make his own choices, that is, let him *be.* It is necessary in order for children to grow well that adults have enough trust in them and in the natural processes of growth, that is, not interfere too much, not *make* them grow, or force them into predetermined designs, but rather *let* them grow and *help* them grow in a Taoistic rather than an authoritarian way.

(Though this statement sounds simple, it is in actuality misinterpreted extraordinarily. Taoistic let-be and respect for the child is actually quite difficult for most people, who tend to interpret it to mean total permissiveness, indulgence and over-protection, *giving* him things, arranging pleasure activities *for* him, protecting him against all dangers, forbidding risk-taking. Love without respect is quite different from love *with* respect for the child's own inner signals.)

17. Coordinate with this "acceptance" of the self, of fate, of one's call, is the conclusion that the main path to health and self-fulfillment for the masses is via basic need gratification rather than via frustration. This contrasts with the suppressive regime, the mistrust, the control, the policing that is necessarily implied by the belief in basic, instinctive evil in the human depths. Intrauterine life is completely gratifying and non-frustrating and it is now generally accepted that the first year or so of life had better also be primarily gratifying and non-frustrating. Asceticism, self-denial, deliberate rejection of the demands of the organism, at least in the West, tend to produce a diminished, stunted or crippled organism, and even in the East, bring self-actualization to only a very few, exceptionally strong individuals.

This statement is also often misunderstood. Basic need gratification is too often taken to mean objects, things, possessions, money, clothes, automobiles and the like. But these do not in themselves gratify the basic needs which, after the bodily needs are taken care of, are for (1) protection, safety, security, (2) belongingness, as in a family, a community, a clan, a gang, friendship, affection, love, (3) respect, esteem, approval, dignity, self-respect and (4) freedom for the fullest development of one's talents and capacities, actualization of the self. This seems simple enough and yet few people anywhere in the world seem able to assimilate its meaning. Because the lowest and most urgent needs are material, for example food, shelter, clothes, and so forth, they tend to generalize this to a chiefly materialistic psychology of motivation, forgetting that there are higher, non-material needs as well which are also "basic."

18. But we know also that the *complete absence* of frustration, pain or danger is dangerous. To be strong, a person must acquire frustration-tolerance, the ability to perceive physical reality as essentially indifferent to human wishes, the ability to love others and to enjoy their need-gratification as well as one's own (not to use other people only as means). The child with a good basis of safety, love and respect-need-gratification, is able to profit from nicely graded frustrations and become stronger thereby. If they are more than he can bear, if they

overwhelm him, we call them traumatic, and consider them danger-ous rather than profitable.

It is via the frustrating unyieldingness of physical reality and of animals and of other people that we learn about *their* nature, and thereby learn to differentiate wishes from facts (which things wishing makes come true, and which things proceed in complete disregard of our wishes), and are thereby enabled to live in the world and adapt to it as necessary.

We learn also about our own strengths and limits and extend them by overcoming difficulties, by straining ourselves to the utmost, by meeting challenge and hardship, even by failing. There can be great enjoyment in a great struggle and this can displace fear. Furthermore, this is the best path to healthy self-esteem, which is based not only upon approval from others, but also upon actual achievements and successes and upon the realistic self-confidence which ensues.

Overprotection implies that the child's needs are gratified *for* him by his parents, without effort of his own. This tends to infantilize him, to prevent development of his own strength, will and self-assertion. In one of its forms it may teach him to use other people rather than to re-spect them. In another form it implies a lack of trust and respect for the child's own powers and choices, that is, it is essentially condescending and insulting, and can help to make a child feel worthless.

19. To make growth and self-actualization possible, it is necessary to understand that capacities, organs and organ systems press to func-tion and express themselves and to be used and exercised, and that such use is satisfying, and disuse irritating. The muscular person likes to use his muscles, indeed, *has* to use them in order to "feel good" and to achieve the subjective feeling of harmonious, successful, uninhibited functioning (spontaneity) which is so important an aspect of good growth and psychological health. So also for intelligence, for the uterus, the eyes, the capacity to love. Capacities clamor to be used, and cease their clamor only when they *are* well used. That is, capacities are also needs. Not only is it fun to use our capacities, but it is also necessary for growth. The unused skill or capacity or organ can become a disease center or else atrophy or disappear, thus diminishing the person.

20. The psychologist proceeds on the assumption that for his pur-poses there are two kinds of worlds, two kinds of reality, the natural world and the psychic world, the world of unyielding facts and the

world of wishes, hopes, fears, emotions, the world which runs by non-psychic rules and the world which runs by psychic laws. This differentiation is not very clear except at its extremes, where there is no doubt that delusions, dreams and free associations are lawful and yet utterly different from the lawfulness of logic and from the lawfulness of the world which would remain if the human species died out. This assumption does not deny that these worlds are related and may even fuse.

I may say that this assumption is acted upon by *many* or *most* psychologists, even though they are perfectly willing to admit that it is an insoluble philosophical problem. Any therapist *must* assume it or give up his functioning. This is typical of the way in which psychologists bypass philosophical difficulties and act "as if" certain assumptions were true even though unprovable, for example, the universal assumption of "responsibility," "will power," and so forth. One aspect of health is the ability to live in both of these worlds.

21. Immaturity can be contrasted with maturity from the motivational point of view, as the process of gratifying the deficiency-needs in their proper order. Maturity, or self-actualization, from this point of view, means to transcend the deficiency-needs. This state can be described then as metamotivated, or unmotivated (if deficiencies are seen as the only motivations). It can also be described as self-actualizing, Being, expressing, rather than coping. This state of Being, rather than of striving, is suspected to be synonymous with selfhood, with being "authentic," with being a person, with being fully human. The process of growth is the process of *becoming* a person. *Being* a person is different.

22. Immaturity can also be differentiated from maturity in terms of the cognitive capacities (and also in terms of the emotional capacities). Immature and mature cognition have been best described by Werner and Piaget.[1] We can now add another differentiation, that between D-cognition and B-cognition (D = Deficiency, B = Being). D-cognition can be defined as the cognitions which are organized from

---

[1] Maslow does not list any of the writings of Jean Piaget in his bibliography. He was probably referring to the descriptions Piaget gave in *The Language and Thought of the Child* (New York: Harcourt Brace, 1926; also New York: Humanities Press, 1959) and *The Child's Conception of the World* (New York: Harcourt Brace, 1929).

the point of view of basic needs or deficiency-needs and their gratification and frustration. That is, D-cognition could be called selfish cognition, in which the world is organized into gratifiers and frustrators of our own needs, with other characteristics being ignored or slurred. The cognition of the object, in its own right and its own Being, without reference to its need-gratifying or need-frustrating qualities, that is, without primary reference to its value for the observer of its effects upon him, can be called B-cognition (or self-transcending, or unselfish, or objective cognition). The parallel with maturity is by no means perfect (children can also cognize in a selfless way), but in general, it is mostly true that with increasing selfhood or firmness of personal identity (or acceptance of one's own inner nature) B-cognition become easier and more frequent. (This is true even though D-cognition means for *all* human beings, including the mature ones, the main tool for living-in-the-world.)

To the extent that perception is desire-less and fear-less, to that extent is it more veridical, in the sense of perceiving the true, or essential or intrinsic whole nature of the object (without splitting it up by abstraction). Thus the goal of objective and true description of any reality is fostered by psychological health. Neurosis, psychosis, stunting of growth—all are, from this point of view, cognitive diseases as well, contaminating perception, learning, remembering, attending and thinking.

23. A by-product of this aspect of cognition is a better understanding of the higher and lower levels of love. D-love can be differentiated from B-love on approximately the same basis as D-cognition and B-cognition, or D-motivation and B-motivation. No ideally good relation to another human being, especially a child, is possible without B-love. Especially is it necessary for teaching, along with the Taoistic, trusting attitude that it implies. This is also true for our relations with the natural world, that is, we can treat it in its own right, or we can treat it as if it were there only for our purposes.

It should be noticed that there are considerable differences between the intrapsychic and the interpersonal. So far we have dealt mostly with the Self rather than with the relations between people and within groups, small and large. What I have discussed as the general human need for belongingness includes the need for community, for interdependence, for family, for fellowship and for brotherhood. From

Synanon,[2] from Esalen-type[3] education, from Alcoholics Anonymous, from the T-groups and the basic encounter groups and from many similar self-help-via-brotherhood groups, we learn again and again that we are social animals in a very fundamental way. Ultimately, of course, the strong person needs to be able to transcend the group when necessary. And yet it must be realized that this strength has been developed in him by his community.

24. Though, in principle, self-actualization is easy, in practice it rarely happens (by my criteria, certainly in less than one percent of the adult population). For this, there are many, many reasons at various levels of discourse, including all the determinants of psychopathology that we now know. We have already mentioned one main cultural reason, that is, the conviction that man's intrinsic nature is evil or dangerous, and one biological determinant for the difficulty of achieving a mature self, namely that humans no longer have strong instincts which tell them unequivocally what to do, when, where and how.

There is a subtle but extremely important difference between regarding psychopathology as blocking or evasion or fear of growth toward self-actualization, and thinking of it in a medical fashion, as akin to invasion from without by tumors, poisons or bacteria, which have no relationship to the personality being invaded. Human diminution (the loss of human potentialities and capacities) is a more useful concept than "illness" for our theoretical purposes.

25. Growth has not only rewards and pleasures but also many intrinsic pains and always will have. Each step forward is a step into the

---

[2] *Synanon* was a mind-control cult of the 1960s and 1970s, masquerading as a branch of the human-potential movement. Maslow was quite excited by what Synanon *appeared* to be in the early and mid-1960s, and even testified in court on its behalf. After spending a weekend at Synanon in January 1966, however, he came to realize that the appearance of "human potential" in this case concealed a rather ugly reality. In particular, he came to see that the founder of the "club," Charles Dederich, "*is* Synanon, & everyone else takes orders. He's the most powerful human being I have ever met personally—dominating, absolutely overwhelming, driving. A force of nature like an earthquake. . . . Absolutely blunt, candid, uncompromising." (R. Lowry [ed.], The Journals of A. H. Maslow [2 vol.]. Monterey, CA: Brooks/Cole, 1979, vol. 1, p. 585.) The story of Synanon culminated in 1980 when Dederich, along with two members of the cult, pleaded no contest to murder-conspiracy charges in Los Angeles Superior Court. The weapon of choice in this episode was a four and a half foot-long rattlesnake placed in the mailbox of the intended victim, allegedly at Dederich's behest.

[3] *The Esalen Institute* of Big Sur, California, was founded in 1962 "as an educational center devoted to the exploration of unrealized human capacities."

unfamiliar and is possibly dangerous. It also means giving up something familiar and good and satisfying. It frequently means a parting and a separation, even a kind of death prior to rebirth, with consequent nostalgia, fear, loneliness and mourning. It also often means giving up a simpler and easier and less effortful life, in exchange for a more demanding, more responsible, more difficult life. Growth forward *is in spite* of these losses and therefore requires courage, will, choice, and strength in the individual, as well as protection, permission and encouragement from the environment, especially for the child.

26. It is therefore useful to think of growth or lack of it as the resultant of a dialectic between growth-fostering forces and growth-discouraging forces (regression, fear, pains of growth, ignorance, and so forth). Growth has both advantages and disadvantages. Non-growing has not only disadvantages, but also advantages. The future pulls, but so also does the past. There is not only courage but also fear. The total ideal way of growing healthily is, in principle, to enhance all the advantages of forward growth and all the disadvantages of not-growing, and to diminish all the disadvantages of growth forward and all the advantages of not-growing.

Homeostatic tendencies, "need-reduction" tendencies, and Freudian defense mechanisms are not growth-tendencies but are often defensive, pain-reducing postures of the organism. But they are quite necessary and not always pathological. They are generally preponent over growth-tendencies.

27. All this implies a naturalistic system of values, a by-product of the empirical description of the deepest tendencies of the human species and of specific individuals. The study of the human being by science or by self-search can discover where he is heading, what is his purpose in life, what is good for him and what is bad for him, what will make him feel virtuous and what will make him feel guilty, why choosing the good is often difficult for him, what the attractions of evil are. (Observe that the word "ought" need not be used. Also such knowledge of man is relative to man only and does not purport to be "absolute.")

28. A neurosis is not part of the inner core but rather a defense against or an evasion of it, as well as a distorted expression of it (under the aegis of fear). It is ordinarily a compromise between the effort to seek basic need gratifications in a covert or disguised or self-defeating way, and the fear of these needs, gratifications and motivated behaviors.

To express neurotic needs, emotions, attitudes, definitions, actions, and so forth, means *not* to express the inner core or real self fully. If the sadist or exploiter or pervert says, "Why shouldn't *I* express myself?" (for example, by killing), or, "Why shouldn't *I* actualize myself?" the answer to them is that such expression is a denial of, and not an expression of, instinctoid tendencies (or inner core).

Each neuroticized need, or emotion or action is a *loss of capacity* to the person, something that he cannot do or *dare* not do except in a sneaky and unsatisfying way. In addition, he has usually lost his subjective well-being, his will, and his feeling of self-control, his capacity for pleasure, his self-esteem, and so forth. He is diminished as a human being.

29. The state of being without a system of values is psychopathogenic, we are learning. The human being needs a framework of values, a philosophy of life, a religion or religion-surrogate to live by and understand by, in about the same sense that he needs sunlight, calcium or love. This I have called the "cognitive need to understand." The value-illnesses which result from valuelessness are called variously anhedonia, anomie, apathy, amorality, hopelessness, cynicism, and so forth., and can become somatic illness as well. Historically, we are in a value interregnum in which all externally given value systems have proven to be failures (political, economic, religious, and so forth.), for example, nothing is worth dying for. What man needs but doesn't have, he seeks for unceasingly, and he becomes dangerously ready to jump at *any* hope, good or bad. The cure for this disease is obvious. We need a validated, usable system of human values that we can believe in and devote ourselves to (be willing to die for), because they are true rather than because we are exhorted to "believe and have faith." Such an empirically based Weltanschauung seems now to be a real possibility, at least in theoretical outline.

Much disturbance in children and adolescents can be understood as a consequence of the uncertainty of adults about their values. As a consequence, many youngsters in the United States live not by adult values but by adolescent values, which of course are immature, ignorant and heavily determined by confused adolescent needs. An excellent projection of these adolescent values is the cowboy, "Western" movie, or the delinquent gang.

30. At the level of self-actualizing, many dichotomies become resolved, opposites are seen to be unities and the whole dichotomous

way of thinking is recognized to be immature. For self-actualizing people, there is a strong tendency for selfishness and unselfishness to fuse into a higher, superordinate unity. Work tends to be the same as play; vocation and avocation become the same thing. When duty is pleasant and pleasure is fulfillment of duty, then they lose their separateness and oppositeness. The highest maturity is discovered to include a childlike quality, and we discover healthy children to have some of the qualities of mature self-actualization. The inner-outer split, between self and all else, gets fuzzy and much less sharp, and they are seen to be permeable to each other at the highest levels of personality development. Dichotomizing seems now to be characteristic of a lower level of personality development and of psychological functioning; it is both a cause and an effect of psychopathology.

31. One especially important finding in self-actualizing people is that they tend to integrate the Freudian dichotomies and trichotomies, that is, the conscious, preconscious and the unconscious (as well as id, ego, superego). The Freudian "instincts" and the defenses are less sharply set off against each other. The impulses are more expressed and less controlled; the controls are less rigid, inflexible, anxiety-determined. The superego is less harsh and punishing and less set off against the ego. The primary and secondary cognitive processes are more equally available and more equally valued (instead of the primary processes being stigmatized as pathological). Indeed, in the "peak-experience" the walls between them tend to fall together.

This is in sharp contrast with the early Freudian position in which these various forces were sharply dichotomized as (a) mutually exclusive, (b) with antagonistic interests, that is, as antagonistic forces rather than as complementary or collaborating ones, and (c) one "better" than the other.

Again we imply here (sometimes) a healthy unconscious, and desirable regression. Furthermore, we imply also an integration of rationality and irrationality with the consequence that irrationality may, in its place, also be considered healthy, desirable or even necessary.

32. Healthy people are more integrated in another way. In them the conative, the cognitive, the affective and the motor are less separated from each other, and are more synergic, that is, working collaboratively without conflict to the same ends. The conclusions of rational, careful thinking are apt to come to the same conclusions as those of the blind appetites. What such a person wants and enjoys is apt to be just what is

good for him. His spontaneous reactions are as capable, efficient and right as if they had been thought out in advance. His sensory and motor reactions are more closely correlated. His sensory modalities are more connected with each other (physiognomical perception). Furthermore, we have learned the difficulties and dangers of those age-old rationalistic systems in which the capacities were thought to be arranged dichotomously-hierarchically, with rationality at the top, rather than in an integration.

33. This development toward the concept of a healthy unconscious, and of a healthy irrationality, sharpens our awareness of the limitations of purely abstract thinking, of verbal thinking and of analytic thinking. If our hope is to describe the world fully, a place is necessary for perverbal, ineffable, metaphorical, primary process, concrete-experience, intuitive and esthetic types of cognition, for there are certain aspects of reality which can be cognized in no other way. Even in science this is true, now that we know (1) that creativity has its roots in the nonrational, (2) that language is and must always be inadequate to describe total reality, (3) that any abstract concept leaves out much of reality, and (4) that what we call "knowledge" (which is usually highly abstract and verbal and sharply defined) often serves to blind us to those portions of reality not covered by the abstraction. That is, it makes us more able to see some things, but *less* able to see other things. Abstract knowledge has its dangers as well as its uses.

Science and education, being too exclusively abstract, verbal and bookish, don't have enough place for raw, concrete, esthetic experience, especially of the subjective happenings inside oneself. For instance, organismic psychologists would certainly agree on the desirability of more creative education in perceiving and creating art, in dancing, in (Greek style) athletics and in phenomenological observation.

The ultimate of abstract, analytical thinking, is the greatest simplification possible, that is, the formula, the diagram, the map, the blueprint, the schema, the cartoon, and certain types of abstract paintings. Our mastery of the world is enhanced thereby, but its richness may be lost as a forfeit, *unless* we learn to value B-cognitions, perception-with-love-and-care, free-floating attention, all of which enrich the experience instead of impoverishing it. There is no reason why "science" should not be expanded to include both kinds of knowing.

34. This ability of healthier people to dip into the unconscious and preconscious, to use and value their primary processes instead of

fearing them, to accept their impulses instead of always controlling them, to be able to regress voluntarily without fear, turns out to be one of the main conditions of creativity. We can then understand why psychological health is so closely tied up with certain universal forms of creativeness (aside from special-talent), as to lead some writers to make them almost synonymous.

This same tie between health and integration of rational and irrational forces (conscious and unconscious, primary and secondary processes) also permits us to understand why psychologically healthy people are more able to enjoy, to love, to laugh, to have fun, to be humorous, to be silly, to be whimsical and fantastic, to be pleasantly "crazy," and in general to permit and value and enjoy emotional experiences in general and peak experiences in particular and to have them more often. And it leads us to the strong suspicion that learning *ad hoc* to be able to do all these things may help the child move toward health.

35. Esthetic perceiving and creating and esthetic peak-experiences are seen to be a central aspect of human life and of psychology and education rather than a peripheral one. This is true for several reasons. (1) All the peak-experiences are (among other characteristics) integrative of the splits within the person, between persons, within the world, and between the person and the world. Since one aspect of health is integration, the peak-experiences are moves toward health and are themselves, momentary healths. (2) These experiences are life-validating, that is, they make life worth while. These are certainly an important part of the answer to the question, "Why don't we all commit suicide?" (3) They are worth while in themselves, and so forth.

36. Self-actualization does not mean a transcendence of all human problems. Conflict, anxiety, frustration, sadness, hurt, and guilt can all be found in healthy human beings. In general, the movement, with increasing maturity, is from neurotic pseudo-problems to the real, unavoidable, existential problems, inherent in the nature of man (even at his best) living in a particular kind of world. Even though he is not neurotic he may be troubled by real, desirable and necessary guilt rather than neurotic guilt (which isn't desirable or necessary), by an intrinsic conscience (rather than the Freudian superego). Even though he has transcended the problems of Becoming, there remain the problems of Being. To be untroubled when one *should* be troubled can be a sign of sickness. Sometimes, smug people have to be scared "*into* their wits."

37. Self-actualization is not altogether general. It takes place via femaleness *or* maleness, which are prepotent to general-humanness. That is, one must first be a healthy, femalesness-fulfilled woman or maleness-fulfilled man before general-human self-actualization becomes possible.

There is also a little evidence that different constitutional types actualize themselves in somewhat different ways (because they have different inner selves to actualize).

38. Another crucial aspect of healthy growth of selfhood and full-humanness is dropping away the techniques used by the child, in his weakness and smallness for adapting himself to the strong, large, all-powerful, omniscient, godlike adults. He must replace these with the techniques of being strong and independent and of being a parent himself. This involves especially giving up the child's desperate wish for the exclusive, total love of his parents while learning to love others. He must learn to gratify his own needs and wishes, rather than the needs of his parents, and he must learn to gratify them himself, rather than depending upon the parents to do this for him. He must give up being good out of fear and in order to keep their love, and must be good because *he* wishes to be. He must discover his own conscience and give up his internalized parents as a sole ethical guide. He must become responsible rather than dependent, and hopefully must become able to *enjoy* this responsibility. All these techniques by which weakness adapts itself to strength are necessary for the child but immature and stunting in the adult. He must replace fear with courage.

39. From this point of view, a society or a culture can be either growth-fostering or growth-inhibiting. The sources of growth and of humanness are essentially within the human person and are not created or invented by society, which can only help or hinder the development of humanness, just as a gardener can help or hinder the growth of a rosebush, but cannot determine that it shall be an oak tree. This is true even though we know that a culture is a *sine qua non* for the actualization of humanness itself, for example, language, abstract thought, ability to love; but these exist as potentialities in human germ plasm prior to culture.

This makes theoretically possible a comparative sociology, transcending and including cultural relativity. The "better" culture gratifies all basic human needs and permits self-actualization. The "poorer" cultures do not. The same is true for education. To the extent that it fosters growth toward self-actualization, it is "good" education.

As soon as we speak of "good" or "bad" cultures, and take them as means rather than as ends, the concept of "adjustment" comes into question. We must ask, "What kind of culture or subculture is the 'well adjusted' person well adjusted *to?*" Adjustment is, very definitely, *not* necessarily synonymous with psychological health.

40. The achievement of self-actualization (in the sense of autonomy) paradoxically makes *more* possible the transcendence of self, and of self-consciousness and of selfishness. It makes it *easier* for the person to be homonous, that is, to merge himself as a part in a larger whole than himself (6). The condition of the fullest homonomy is full autonomy, and to some extent, vice versa, one can attain to autonomy only via successful homonomous experiences (child dependence, B-love, care for others, and so forth). It is necessary to speak of levels of homonomy (more and more mature), and to differentiate a "low homonomy" (of fear, weakness, and regression) from a "high homonomy" (of courage and full, self-confident autonomy), a "low Nirvana" from a "high Nirvana," union downward from union upward.

41. An important existential problem is posed by the fact that self-actualizing persons (and *all* people in their peak-experiences) occasionally live out-of-time and out-of-the-world (atemporal and aspatial) even though mostly they *must* live in the outer world. Living in the inner psychic world (which is ruled by psychic laws and not by the laws of outer-reality), that is, the world of experience, of emotion, of wishes and fears and hopes, of love, of poetry, art, and fantasy, is different from living in and adapting to the non-psychic reality which runs by laws he never made and which are not essential to his nature even though he has to live by them. (He *could,* after all, live in other kinds of worlds, as any science fiction fan knows.) The person who is not afraid of this inner, psychic world, can enjoy it to such an extent that it may be called Heaven by contrast with the more effortful, fatiguing, externally responsible world of "reality," of striving and coping, of right and wrong, of truth and falsehood. This is true even though the healthier person can also adapt more easily and enjoyably to the "real" world, and has better "reality testing," that is, doesn't confuse it with his inner psychic world.

It seems clear now that confusing these inner and outer realities, or having either closed off from experience, is highly pathological. The healthy person is able to integrate them both into his life and therefore has to give up neither, being able to go back and forth voluntarily. The difference is the same as the one between the person who can *visit* the slums and the one who is forced to live there always. (*Either* world is a slum if one can't leave it.) Then, paradoxically, that which was sick and pathological and the "lowest" becomes part of the healthiest and "highest" aspect of human nature. Slipping into "craziness" is frightening only for those who are not fully confident of their sanity. Education must help the person to live in both worlds.

42. The foregoing propositions generate a different understanding of the role of action in psychology. Goal-directed, motivated, coping, striving, purposeful action is an aspect or by-product of the necessary transactions between a psyche and a non-psychic world.

(a) The D-need gratifications come from the world outside the person, not from within. Therefore adaptation to this world is made necessary, for example, reality-testing, knowing the nature of the world, learning to differentiate this world from the inner world, learning the nature of people and of society, learning to delay gratification, learning to conceal what would be dangerous, learning which portions of the world are gratifying and which dangerous, or useless for need-gratification, learning the approved and permitted cultural paths to gratification and techniques of gratification.

(b) The world is in itself interesting, beautiful and fascinating. Exploring it, manipulating it, playing with it, contemplating it, enjoying it are all motivated kinds of action (cognitive, motor, and esthetic needs).

But there is also action which has little or nothing to do with the world, at any rate at first. Sheer expression of the nature or state or powers (Funktionslust) of the organism is an expression of Being rather than of striving. And the contemplation and enjoyment of the inner life not only is a kind of "action" in itself but is also antithetical to action in the world, that is, it produces stillness and cessation of muscular activity. The ability to wait is a special case of being able to suspend action.

43. From Freud we learned that the past exists *now* in the person. Now we must learn, from growth theory and self-actualization theory that the future also *now* exists in the person in the form of ideals,

hopes, duties, tasks, plans, goals, unrealized potentials, mission, fate, destiny, and so forth. One for whom no future exists is reduced to the concrete, to hopelessness, to emptiness. For him, time must be end- lessly "filled." Striving, the usual organizer of most activity, when lost, leaves the person unorganized and unintegrated.

Of course, being in a state of Being needs no future, because it is already *there*. Then Becoming ceases for the moment and its promis- sory notes are cashed in in the form of the ultimate rewards, that is, the peak-experiences, in which time disappears and hopes are fulfilled.

Notes on Self-Esteem
in the Workplace

. . . Where you try to move over from a strictly authoritarian managerial style to a more participative style, the first consequence of lifting the rigid restrictions of authority may well be some chaos, some release of hostility, some destructiveness, and the like. . . .

A.H. Maslow, *Maslow on Management*

If we expand and enrich our understanding of the self-esteem level of motivation, then I think we can clarify and crystallize much which is only half-conscious or groping in the management literature. Everybody seems to be aware at some level of consciousness of the

Human beings avoid	To be a nothing (Rather than a something)	A ludicrous figure regulated by others (like an object, to be treated like a physical object rather than like a person; to be rubricized, like an example rather than as unique)
Being manipulated	Unappreciated	Given orders
Dominated	Not respected	Forced
Pushed around	Not feared	Screwed (used, exploited)
Determined by others	Not taken seriously	Controlled
To be misunderstood	Laughed at	Helpless
		Compliant
		Deferent
		An interchangeable man

Source: A.H. Maslow, *Maslow on Management* (New York: John Wiley & Sons, 1998).

fact that authoritarian management outrages the dignity of the worker. He then fights back in order to restore his dignity and self-esteem, actively with hostility and vandalism and the like, or passively as a slave does, with all sorts of underhanded, sly and secretly vicious countermeasures. These reactions are puzzling to the dominator, but on the whole they are easily enough understood, and they make very real psychological sense, if they are understood as attempts to maintain one's dignity under conditions of domination or of disrespect.

Now, one approach to this is to pick out all the words from the literature, generally from the remarks of the dominated people about the way in which they view their own situations negatively. That is, it is like asking what is it they dislike, what are they avoiding, what makes them feel a loss of self-esteem.

What they are seeking for positively is:

To be a prime mover.

Self-determination.

To have control over one's own fate.

To determine one's movements.

To be able to plan and carry out and to succeed.

To expect success.

To like responsibility or at any rate to assume it willingly, especially for one's self.

To be active rather than passive.

To be a person rather than a thing.

To experience one's self as the maker of one's own decisions.

Autonomy.

Initiative.

Self-starting.

To have others acknowledge one's capabilities fairly.

The difference between the need for esteem (from others) and the need for self-esteem should be made very clear in the final write-up. Make the differentiation sharply, clearly, and unmistakably. Reputation or prestige or applause are very nice, and are for children and adolescents even absolutely necessary before real self-esteem can be built up. Or to say it the other way about, one of the necessary foundations for self-esteem is respect and applause from other people, especially in the younger years. Ultimately, real self-esteem rests upon all the things mentioned above, on a feeling of dignity, of controlling one's own life, and of being one's own boss. (Let's call this "dignity.") And then work out more carefully the interrelationship between dignity and self-esteem and the whole topic of real achievement, real skill, real mastery (by contrast with applause that may be undeserved). One has to *deserve* applause, prestige, medals, and fame, or at very deep unconscious levels, they can actually be hurtful and produce guilt; all sorts of psychopathogenic processes may start from undeserved applause.

Also, I think it will be extremely instructive to many people to expand considerably on the ways in which outraged dignity protects itself. Look up again John Dollard's *Caste and Class in a Southern Town*,[1] and other writings in which it is shown how the Afro-American, stepped upon and submerged, not being able to fight back physically, forced to swallow his rage, can yet strike back in all sorts of passive ways which can be very effective.

For instance, expand on the notion of pseudostupidity (and then pick out parallels in the industrial situation). The same for lethargy and laziness. The same for impulse freedom (which can be not only a form of self-assertion, but also a means of striking back at the oppressor). Do the same for the ways in which slaves, exploited people, oppressed minorities, and so on will fight back by fooling the oppressor secretly and then laughing at him; this too is a kind of retaliation psychodynamics which rests in the need for self-esteem. The same for passivity.

I think I can use in this context some of the examples that I've used in my *Need to Know and the Fear of Knowing*. I think we could teach managers and supervisors, not to mention professors of business management and industrial consultants and so on, that so many of these responses in workers, responses which they despise, which produce anger, may have been made by the worker just *in order to* produce that anger; maybe that was the *purpose* of it; maybe it was a striking back. In any case, if these psychodynamics are more readily recognized, then they can be taken for the valuable indicators that they are, just as a thermometer is very useful as an indicator of fever and of hidden sickness someplace. When these passive, sneaky, underhanded,

[1] New Haven: Yale University Press, 1935.

behind-the-back retaliations come, they come out of anger, anger generally about being exploited or dominated or being treated in an
undignified way.

And now I would ask the question, "How can any human being
help but be insulted by being treated as an interchangeable part, as
simply a cog in a machine, as no more than an appurtenance to an assembly line (an appurtenance less good than a good machine)? There
is no other human, reasonable, intelligible way to respond to this kind
of profound cutting off of half of one's growth possibilities than by
getting angry or resentful or struggling to get out of the situation.

If I ask the managers or bosses or professors about what they would
do in a similar situation, that is, how they would feel if they were put
into some kind of position in which they weren't treated as persons,
in which their names weren't known, but in which they were given
a number of some sort and in which they were treated not as unique
but absolutely as interchangeable, their answer usually implies that they
wouldn't resent it; they would work hard and work themselves out of
that situation. That is, they would look for a promotion of some sort.
They would regard this kind of work as a means to an end.

But this is an evasion of my question because then I would ask
them, "Suppose you had to do this for the rest of your life? Suppose
there were no promotions possible? Supposing this were the end of
the road?" Then I think these upper-level people would see the situation in a different way. My own expectation is that this more forceful, more decisive type would probably be the *most* hostile, most
revolutionary, most vandalistic, much more so than the average worker
now who has gotten used to the whole idea of living that way for the
rest of his life and who will commit only partial vandalisms and be
only partially hostile. I suspect that all these "time-study" people and
the "scientific management" people and the upper-class people in general who expect that the lower-class people will accept calmly, quietly,
peacefully, and without protest the status of slavery and of anonymity
and of interchangeability which is being dished out to them, that these
very same bosses put into similar situations would start a revolution or
a civil war almost immediately.

Such realizations would quickly force a change in the philosophy
of managers. Partly this would be because they could identify with,
and have intuitions of, and deeply understand and experience the
feelings of, a human being put into an interchangeable mechanistic

situation. The manager who shudders at the thought of being in such a situation would have more sympathy for the reactions of the person whom fate has forced for the time being into this mechanistic situation. He would understand, for instance, what the situation was if he meditated upon the fact that feeble-minded girls find themselves quite comfortable in these mechanistic and repetitive industrial situations. Should he ask that all people react like feeble-minded people?

Then I think also that this kind of psychodynamic understanding of self-esteem and of dignity would make a great difference in the industrial situation because the feeling of dignity, of respect and of self-respect are *so easy to give!* It costs little or nothing, it's a matter of an attitude, a deep-lying sympathy and understanding which can express itself almost automatically in various ways that can be quite satisfying, since they save the dignity of the person in the unfortunate situation.

Being in an unfortunate situation, or working hard in a mechanistic situation is itself quite tolerable, as we know, if the goals are good and are shared, and if also being in this situation is not threatening to the self-esteem of the person. But the situation can very easily be made unthreatening to the self-esteem in all sorts of simple and easy ways which the case histories in the management literature show by the dozens. I think here of careful and detailed case histories like those in M. Dalton's *Men Who Manage.*[2] One could make a good demonstration of the role of self-esteem in the industrial life simply by going through Dalton's book with this particular fine-tooth comb, that is, to pick out every instance in the whole book that has to do with the searching for self-esteem, with responses to threats to self-esteem, with retaliations, with self-healing efforts to restore wounded self-esteem, and so forth.

The more I think of this, the more I think it would pay to put this in the widest psychological context. I think it would pay to make a theoretical generalization from the responses of all exploited or minority groups of various kinds to construct a general abstract theory of responses to domination. I think I could do this by pulling together what I've already written about the relationships between the strong and the weak, between masculinity and femininity (where they are seen as mutually exploitative or rivalrous), between dominance and subordination,

[2] New York: John Wiley & Sons, 1959.

between adults and children, between the exploiter and the exploitee, between the general population and our despised minorities of various sorts, between the whites and Afro-Americans, especially in pre-Civil War days, but also more recently.

Perhaps the history of the relations between men and women in the patriarchal cultures would be as illustrative as anything. The ways in which women have responded to being dominated, exploited, and used without dignity and without respect in the past, these ways of retaliation have generally been seen as character traits, and have added up to a definition of femininity in the particular culture and in the particular time. For instance, reading in the Turkish or Arabic literature where women were treated as nothings, just as pieces of property, and nobody ever dreamed of using the word dignity with regard to them, the ways in which Turkish or Arabic men in the last couple of centuries characterized femininity, the feminine soul, the feminine character, adds up to practically all those forms of secret retaliation that we can find in the Negro slaves in the southern plantations, or in "typical" Negro behavior in the South perhaps thirty or forty years ago, where there was no possibility for them to retaliate openly with hostility. The techniques by which a child who is afraid of his parents and who is dominated by them (perhaps we should better say terrorized), manages to get along again comes very close to being the same as the list of characteristics of femininity in a patriarchal situation, or the Negro character in a slavery situation.

I think the point would be made unmistakably and clearly by such a juxtaposition, and with the clear possibility of making a general abstract theory of the relations between domination and subordination, not only for all human beings but even across the species lines. That is, this response of workers to domination and consequent loss of dignity, can be seen as a profoundly normal biologically rooted self-protection, and therefore can be seen itself as a symptom of human dignity. This comes out at the other end of the horn finally from the way in which most people today will see these responses of the outraged worker who is being stepped upon and who is defending himself, precisely as evidence of how low human nature is, how little it can be trusted, how worthless people are, how little they amount to. It is precisely these reactions which *I* can see as respectworthy which make other people lose all their respect for the worker.

The fact that slaves will revolt if not openly then covertly makes *me* proud of the human species; but I can understand quite well that it would make a slave owner or an exploiter or a dominator get very angry and contemptuous. I have seen this happen often in the individual clinical situation: The exploiter comes to take for granted the exploitee almost as a kind of character. This is very subtle and very hard to say, but it's also quite real. The wolf expects that the lamb will continue to behave like a lamb. If suddenly the lamb turns around and bites the wolf, then I can understand that the wolf would get not only surprised but also get very indignant. Lambs aren't supposed to behave that way. Lambs must lie quietly and get eaten up. Just so I have seen human wolves get very angry when their victims finally turn around and strike back.

Or another example that I have observed and which is usable in this situation is the very frequent conversation that one is apt to hear among older people who are wealthy and who always have been wealthy. The standard topic of conversation is how good the servants used to be and how bad they are now. Throughout this kind of conversation I have never detected the slightest doubt that God made it this way, that is, that these people assumed that it was absolutely just that they should be ladies and gentlemen and that servants should be servants. They never doubted for a moment that loyalty to the master in the servant was a very desirable and just and fair thing. Their indignation when the servants have an opportunity to become unexploited, to give up being slavish, is the kind of indignation I have spoken of above that the queenly wife might show when suddenly the slave of a husband revolted.

"This is not right, this is not becoming," they might say. "This is very ugly and dirty and very depressing. People shouldn't be that way."

What all these people are describing is really the good and well-adjusted slave who likes being a slave and is very well adjusted and adapted to that situation, and whose hostility has either disappeared or has been repressed so profoundly that there is just no surface indication of it anymore at all. But in a democratic society this is exactly the kind of person who should make us depressed instead of glad; this is the kind of person who is an argument *against* the higher possibilities of human nature, of creativeness, of growth, of self-actualization. Just in the same way as a neurosis can be seen either as a sign of sin and evil and human weakness and degradation on the one hand, or can be seen with deeper understanding and insight, as a frightened person's indirect struggle toward health, growth, and self-actualization, just so is the whole of the foregoing applicable to the response of the worker in a bad industrial situation. He may show his anger at being dehumanized in all sorts of sneaky ways, but these are essentially testimonials to his fear rather than to his lack of growth possibilities. The hostility shows that he wants to grow out of that situation. Or to say this in another way, the response of outrage when dignity is attacked is itself a validation of the human being's need for dignity.

The research questions then are: "How can we avoid the organizational situations which cut human dignity and make it less possible? In those situations which are unavoidable in industry, as with assembly lines, how can we decontaminate these so as to retain the dignity of the worker and his self-esteem as much as possible in spite of the circumstances?"

The Human
Side of Enterprise

*The following transcript are Maslow's notes from a lecture he
presented to the Harvard School of Business in 1965. Douglas McGregor's book,* The Human Side of Enterprise, *had
just been published. McGregor used Maslow's theory of motivation as a framework for the book. As a result, Maslow,
overnight, became widely known in the world of business.*

What I want to speak about today, obviously like humming
birds skimming and nipping at things, is on the general
topic of motivation theory and society, politics, industry,
organization. Mostly now I must speak of the material from industrial
psychology and from organization theory because that's where the research lies. The rest of it is about motivation theory in politics, motivation theory in economics, is really not research area but more
philosophical and theoretical discussions. The book that I want you to
read, let me say it that way. It is an assignment and I'll ask you about
it 10 years from today. It's by Douglas McGregor, *The Human Side
of Enterprise,* and I would like you to be large enough to see it not in
its ad hoc, not in its immediate aspect. Immediately this is an application of motivation theory to industry, to management, labor, economics, to things like that. I would like you to see it in the way that
I do as a first step in the direction of a new kind of thinking for the
next century or so. The drawing of the conclusions about society,
about utopia, eupsychia, about education. Everything he says here is

Source: A.H. Maslow lecture (May 17, 1965), to the Harvard Business School, reprinted with the permission of Ann R. Kaplan and the *Archives of the History of American Psychology.*

applicable for instance to our situation right here at Brandeis University on the campus. The problems are about the same. The whole application of our new knowledge of human nature to the general problems of society and of human organization and of interpersonal relationships and so on. I'd like you to see it that way. I've picked it rather than other books on the one hand because it's got some rooting in research. McGregor was a psychologist and also McGregor was President of Antioch College who made it into the good college it is today. It has an excellent reputation, deservedly so and he tried applying these principles not only to industry but also to the college. He was the Chairman of the Department of Industrial Management over at MIT until he died unexpectedly four or five months ago. It was a very great loss. This was a premature death. I'm sure that he would have gone on to generalize to the social problems, that is the relationship between human nature and society. The title should not really be "The Human Side of Enterprise" because I know many of you are not interested in business or the factory or labor-economics, or how you set wages or things like that. I wish he would have called it "The Human Side of Society," "The Human Side of Social Organizations" of "Social Institutions," all social institutions. That includes marriage and the college and the nursery school and politics and anything you can imagine. O.K. if you have time for one book, that's what I'd like you to read and I am going to have a few selections from that.

This came in and it looks very good. I've just thumbed it through. It's *The Psychology of Industrial Behavior,* Second Edition, by Henry Clay Smith. I've already recommended to you the book by John Gardner called *Self Renewal* which is of the same order where he raises the question there that McGregor also raises on a somewhat broader canvas. He asks there, he says "we have learned something about the self-renewing individual. We have learned something about the growing individual, the possibility of a human being who grows towards something larger. Is it possible to extrapolate this knowledge to society? Is it possible to speak about a self-renewing society? Is it possible to speak about social institutions which do not have the evils which social institutions inevitably have had through the millenia and the centuries? Is it possible to speak about an organization which is self-cleansing? Which is open to the future? Which is open to new information? Which is in the John Dewey sense therefore instrumental, experimental, scientific, open, ready to change with new information as institutions of course have always been unready to change? Bureaucracies tend to freeze. However beautiful the original impulse may have been they tend to freeze and to become holding companies and to resist the future. Of course it is very tempting for us to extrapolate out to the social institutions, to marriage, to parenthood, bringing up children, to our college situation where we have this perpetual going on debate between authority, freedom and what it means, and how possible it is to go and how much freedom will let you go. Are there limits to that which would endanger the growth? and so on and so on. This is the standing discussion, standing debate."

Now another angle on it. This comes from, I seem to be highly charged here, if you're not grounded watch yourself. This comes from the *New Statesman* and it's Michael Stewart. This is a British Journal. This is an editorial and it represents part of our debate, part of our discussion too because to some extent it is a debate between the Labor Party and the Tory Party. It's the question of the production of wealth, the sharing of wealth and in England much more than in this country, that's an open political debate all the time. It's between a particular British version of Socialism and a British version of Conservatism. The title of, this is labeled "Party Platform." The title of it is "The Quality of Life." This is off in a somewhat different direction from what I've just had but I want to read you a few sentences. "Production and sharing of wealth are major election issues"—this is in England—"Torys depict increasing productions and with less emphasis share prosperity. Yet the increase limps behind the country's real capacity and the gap between the least and most fortunate grows wider. Most profoundly, Torys fail to grasp to truths."

This is a guy speaking apparently officially for the Laborites. First the desire for non-material things. That is, he says "the Tories fail to grasp the true truths." I don't want to get involved in the good and the bad here. My impression is that many of the Laborites fail to grasp these two things. First, as a truth which they fail to grasp, is a desire for non-material things; scope for energy for instance; justice; the quality of life which is ultimately as essential to human nature as the desire for food. Secondly, these values do not conflict with material desires. Failure to acknowledge them frustrates material progress. Now that's about as good a summing up of what we have been talking about as I could imagine in a single paragraph. He goes on to talk about steel and nationalization and so on and so on, and I stick to the end of it. Or first, if I may, a little underlining, an exogenous of what's obvious here, what should be obvious: If we talk here about the hierarchy of human needs and speak of, what he is saying is not only the lower needs of human, essentially human, but also the higher needs are and even he implies what we've been calling here the metaneeds, metamotivations precisely as human as the lower needs for food or for shelter.

Thirdly, he makes the point that these values, higher needs or higher values, do not conflict with material desires. It's the failure to acknowledge them that frustrates material progress, he's saying here. If we deliberately, consciously, if we could add to the Bill of Rights for instance, to the Constitution or have some new declaration of psychological independence or add to the Four Freedoms another three or four or five of them, add these higher needs as worthy and essential and unavoidable and even intrinsic, biologically intrinsic human goals, human values, human meanings to strive for, the needs for dignity for instance, for self-respect, for freedom to be an identity, for freedom to be whatever your biological fate pushes you toward being, not to mention these other metaneeds for truth, beauty and so on; that if we understood those as real needs and built them into our theories of economics, our theories of business, if somehow we could manage to put them in the profit and loss statements which now we can't. The whole of accounting is really for objects and things, things which can be translated into numbers, dollars and so on. If somehow we could translate into dollars or into numbers of some sort the higher needs and the metaneeds and indicate that they are valuable to us in some way which can be roughly equated I've found out with dollars. You could put rough dollar evaluations upon them. They could go into the profit and loss statements and into our wages, our values. Brandeis by the way has started to do that, very intelligently I think. When I get a monthly or yearly statement of my salary I now have listed the dollar value of fringe benefits which are very considerable, perhaps as much as 10 percent of my salary, for the professors. Those are only the ones that can be translated into dollars too, but if we could translate other things into dollars, values and there are many of them and I do for myself, I know I try to put some kind of valuation on them so that I don't get too easily tempted by literal dollars from some place else, I think this would make us more realistic even about the material progress and wouldn't get into this trap in which so many of us are, of thinking somehow that more and more of the objects, that is more and more satisfactions for the lower needs will bring us this happiness which is somehow evading us all the time; that, well you thought an automobile would make you happy if you got it and you got it and then it made you happy for three days and then somehow you got restless again. Most people will think, "well I need a second automobile then." If that doesn't work it's a third, a fifth and a tenth and so on and so on. If we understood that getting these satisfactions makes the need so to speak die and yield to higher satisfactions and if we consciously look for those higher satisfactions and higher values, it would work out better, and that is what he is talking about here, about the quality of life.

The last here: Each of us interprets for himself the phrase "quality of life." To one it means well planned towns and a beautiful countryside; to another high standards of taste and wise uses of leisure, wise use of leisure; to a third, citizenship of a country which will be remembered for its services to mankind. The lack of policy for the location of industry can wreck the first planned value, that is the well-planned towns and beautiful countryside and an educational system can wreck the second, as in England it's been threatening to do; high standards of taste and wise use of leisure and thirdly citizenship of a country which will be remembered for its services to mankind, defense policies based on the dangers, vanities of dependent-independent deterents they are fighting in Great Britain about whether they should have their own atom bombs or not can wreck the third. Nor can these rejections of non-material values be justified as hardheaded and realistic, and this is the usual answer from turning aside from the reality of higher needs and higher values. Their practical effects—well, let's skip that.

Mankind does not have to choose between vision and kindness on the one hand and material progress and hardheaded common sense on the other. The two are bound together. Given the situation and courage, mankind can do both. Toryism by rejecting the first provides the depressing combination of hard hearts and soft heads and remember that's not—I think the Laborites—my impression—I don't read it very carefully, don't follow it very carefully, is that the Laborites are not terribly better about these things than the Torys there, that is about what I call the stupid materialist or mere materialist. That's a better word—mere materialist—because materialism is very fine. The satisfaction of lower needs, having a house, having food, having clothes, having shoes and so on. This is a very very nice thing for a person to have especially in cold weather. The dichotomizing tendencies is what makes the trouble there. It's the mere materialism, that is of trying to be content with just the shoes and the clothes and the house and the automobile and the refrigerator and so on. This is the depression combination of hard heart and soft head.

Now I'd like to read from McGregor a few passages which make this general point. What we have here in the new management theory and I would say also in the new economic theory propounded by this man that I mentioned, this Walter Weiskopf, so far as I know he is the only economist in the country who is aware of higher needs. I'll break this down here. There's some part of me that's electrified.

If I can say it very simply, I have said it this way often enough before but it can stand saying again, industrial theory, wage theory in this country, to this day, is on the surface. It consciously, verbally is still run by the carrot and the stick notion of quotation. People are supposed to be buyable. You hire their labor and if you pay them well enough they are supposed to do anything that you would want them to do. Wages is supposed to take care of things and money furthermore is supposed to be the universal medium of exchange for any satisfactions of any kind. The more money you get, the happier you're supposed to be. The more you are able to buy, presumably the more gratification and satisfaction you can get. The same thing is true in a very rough way it seems to me, both for this common sense, low brow or, if I may say it, this stupid political theory and economic theory which again also proceeds on the assumption that if the material satisfactions, the merely material satisfactions, that is all they are, that money and all the things that it can buy are what people work for and what they struggle in politics for—the whole of the public polling system is based upon selfish and material interests. It's assumed that people will vote their pocketbooks and so on. This on the whole is true, statistically speaking, the question of. By other standards whether it's true or not is another story. Or, if I can take what I mean there, the Nielsen ratings in television. The Nielsen ratings practically rule television entirely with practically no other considerations that are involved. The Nielsen ratings probably are not fake as some people say, and the principles of sampling are well known. The Gallup poll, the public opinion poll of sampling theory is probably sufficient and even the few thousand people through the country can make a fairly accurate, plus or minus two or three percent approximation of whether the Beverly Hillbillies or something else is the right thing. Well the Nielsen ratings are, what let's assume are a pretty accurate reflection of what exists, what is the case, what people in fact do want. The question here is about the tension between, you could say it one way, the is and the ought. It's a kind of Professor of Philosophy way of saying it. Or, what we can say here is that which exists and simultaneously enough our actuality and our potentiality, our conscious and introspectable self on the one and our deepest intrinsic core self on the other. You can talk about your lower self and your higher self. You can talk about what you are on the one hand and what you would like to be on the other hand. You can talk about your immediate wishes and your ultimate wishes and then the Nielsen ratings would look a little different. And it's a question of whether even the people who would want to, that is who would reach out, let's say the smoker who reaches out for a cigarette or the overweight person who reaches out for whipped cream and expresses his Nielsen rating so to speak by actually choosing this sandwich which he shouldn't have or the fourth cocktail which he shouldn't have, or the cigarette which he shouldn't have and which he knows damn well he shouldn't have. That he chooses as a kind of general way of expressing a conflict which goes on inside himself and which represents simply then one side of the conflict winning out, overlooking the other side of the conflict. The same who chooses the cigarette is simultaneously castigating himself and saying he shouldn't have it. Or the youngster, the child, the child who blackmails his father, the youngster who implies that his father is being cruel and unkind and that he will not love his father and so on—you know these tricks. They are pretty recent. As a matter of fact they may be still going on, of trying to get someone to do something for you, or as a matter of fact in a recent study as in the relationships between young men and young women and the findings of the very complex structure of the dominance structure in the young woman which shows up rather well with a little peeling away of layers and sometimes it's quite conscious of the young woman who tries to dominate her man deliberately, consciously tries to make her man and then despises him because he doesn't fight back and then will say, "Well, you let me do it. You shouldn't have let me do it. If you're so

weak as to let me dominate you, you deserve anything you get."
This is the kind of is and ought conflict that's involved here.

Now McGregor was the one who put this in a very very tangible
very simple way so that it could be understood. He spoke about language which is very widespread now. He called it the Theory X and
Theory Y approach to the management of men. Now that remember
means any men and men there means including women and children
and individuals as well as large masses of people. The Theory X mode
of management implies, it rests upon assumptions, generalizations, and
hypotheses. That is to say, on a theory, a theory about people. And
here's what McGregor talked about, how he tries to pluck out these
theoretical assumptions about people and says, "a manager for instance," now "the manager" for example states that he delegates to his
subordinates. When asked he expresses assumptions such as "people
need to learn to take responsibility." That's a theory about human nature, or "those closer to the situation can make the best decisions."
However, he has arranged, that's what he says, has arranged to obtain
a constant flow of detailed information about the behavior of the subordinate and he uses this information to police their behavior and second guess all their decisions. He says "I am held responsible so I need
to know what's going on." He sees no inconsistency in his behavior nor
does he recognize some other assumptions which are implicit. "People
cannot be trusted. They can't really make as good decisions as I can
make." Many of you by the way are precisely in that situation in relation to your parents. You're just about ripe for that now. Parents who
will talk about freedom and who mean it. You should be responsible.
You should be grown up. You should run yourself. You should run
your own life and so on. Old enough to do such and such and then in
effect will get mad at you for coming in after a certain hour or will
have to check about where exactly you were, where you are going to
be or will insist on your calling up and giving bulletins from the road
every 30 minutes or something of the sort. Or, in effect, will say, "well
I will give you an allowance while you are going to college, run this
your own way" and then will get mad at you because you spend five
bucks on something that he would not have spent five bucks on. These
are the kinds of things which McGregor actually observed and tried to
analyze out. He wrote down the words and he wrote down also the actions, the implied principles behind the actions. It's extremely difficult and I don't mean to sound snobby about the situation. It's a very

difficult situation on both sides, where again the balance between freedom and authority, where in general it turns out best to yield the freedom gradually, slowly as it is proven to be well used. I think most parents do it that way. For the parents who don't do it that way it doesn't work out very well. Parents who say on your 18th birthday "now you are a man" by calendar determination. Yesterday you weren't a man, today you are and then you're supposed to be able to do all sorts of things and so on, the sudden giving of freedom.

Well these are matters of strategy and tactics and they're real questions. It's peculiar that it's in the area of industrial management that we have most of our research materials. For instance we do not have much research material on the way in which a new wife and husband adjust to each other. We have practically no research on that. If they start inching in on each other's freedom, which must be so, I mean in principle no two human beings can live together. You start from that assumption and then well you do have to live together and want to live together and how are you going to manage it with the least possible friction. This means generally giving up the freedom at various times, giving up and making compromises of all sorts and the like. The same is true for this transition from dependency to freedom let's say during the adolescent years. This has not been studied in detail either. You have a lot of clinical material from breakdowns, problems, troubles, but we don't have much material on the good, on the healthy, the successful mode of giving freedom.

Now that relates to what I am talking about here: The Theory X attitude toward the human being, toward all these human beings that I have been mentioning is that the human being cannot be trusted. This is what I've called, I think I've labeled it in one of my chapters "our maligned human nature." The assumption that people—yes, here's one from McGregor about the Theory X now: "The average worker has an inherent dislike of work and will avoid it if he can." That's nonsense. It's wrong, incorrect as a generalization. There are certain circumstances in which that's true and there are certain circumstances in which it's not true. Any theory which implies that it's always true is wrong and stupid and will breed bad results. By the way I should say any theory which implies that it's never true will make the same mistakes and come to the same grief. What Smith does here is label them the traditional manager's theory and on the other side is the psychologist's theory, talking about certain psychologists, not all, but anyway we'll leave it. In contrast he says, "the average worker does not have an inherent dislike of work. Work is as natural as play or rest. Depending upon controllable conditions, work can be a source of satisfaction and will be sought after or it can be a source of punishment and will be avoided. It obviously depends on the kind of work, your attitude toward it, your own level of maturation.

Now for Theory X. "The average worker must be forcefully directed with punishment to get him to do a fair day's work." I would add to that the other side of it, "the average worker" works either out of fear and punishment or rewards. The average worker will work only if he gets three credits, a certificate, a gold star, a label, a cap and gown, a particular kind of thing that he puts on his head, a label that he puts on the wall, letters, a degree and so on, to translate it to our situation. If there are no credits for a course nobody will take it. If there are no punishments for a course nobody will come. Or in many places, unless attendance is required nobody will show up and so on and so on.

This is, to boil it down, the reward and punishment theory which McGregor puts under this Theory X notion of human nature.

The contrasting theory, Theory Y is "the average worker likes to and will exercise self-direction and self-control in the service of goals which he chooses and to which he is committed under such and such conditions." Thirdly, Theory X—"the average worker or the average student or the average child or the average adolescent likes to be directed, wants to avoid responsibility and seeks above all other things safety and security." Theory Y in contrast "the average worker or student or son or daughter likes responsibility and will seek it out and accept it under certain stated conditions." Theory X—"few workers have either the imagination, the intelligence or the ingenuity to solve organizational problems, industrial problems." Theory Y—"many workers have the capacity, not all, many workers have the capacity, and workers or students have the capacity to solve organizational problems. Under controllable conditions they will use this capacity."

Now I don't think we will have the time and I can refer you this for yourself, Chapter 2 in the Smith book. The label is "Why Men Work" and you can say also "Why Men Study" and go to college. You can get there some of the researchs which have been done which show this to be true under particular conditions. I'll cite very briefly just a few of these to indicate that what McGregor is talking about, what I'm talking about is essentially an empirical statement, an extrapolation or generalization from researches in the literature for you to look up in great detail. They are too lengthy to speak about at any length. For instance, I think the one study that comes to mind, it's a very good one, very famous one and to show you also that if you are interested you can do this study. It's a feasible kind of research. It's not laboratory research in the test tube kind of sense. It's another kind of laboratory. This was by James Clark. I don't have his specific reference. If you want the reference ask me—James Clark doing a study in Canada in an aluminum factory and having a good setup there where it was possible, there were several lines. That is, you couldn't have one big line for the whole factory. You could have different smelting lines because you could smelt only so much in the particular batch. He managed to observe without arranging it that the two different smelting lines ran in a very different way. The spirit was very different. The consequences were very different. So he studied these two lines. This was a doctoral dissertation by the way at the Harvard Business School. It wound up with a kind of Theory X or Theory Y situation to make it very simple. In this case the foreman in charge of the smelting line was all-powerful and could run it his way. One of them ran it on the Theory X assumptions. He had to watch everything. He had to keep his eye on everything. He trusted nobody. He assumed that everybody was stupid. He would tell them what to do. The instructions were always explicit. He worked very very hard running back and forth, he was very very tired because he had to be tired to do all of these things. As a consequence, by the way, the men were always insulted and angered, felt that they weren't being respected and did what they had to do of course. They took orders. On the whole the results from this line were not as good as from the other line in simple materialistic terms. The amount of aluminum that they got wasn't as much as from the other line. The quality of the aluminum—that is a more sensitive criteria by the way—the quality of the product was not as good. You have to love your work in order to turn out a high quality product because that's what needs the extra care all the time. There was more absenteeism—not faked necessarily—but there were more colds, somehow people stayed away from work more, more lateness, there was more vandalism and there was more wasted, more destruction of, they needed more X plus 10 percent in any particular parts as compared with the second smelting line.

The second line, the foreman without instructions from anybody, not from Clark, simply because he was that kind of guy, this was a natural experiment you might say, behaved in a very different way. He assumed that the men could do their jobs, that they did not need the constant supervision, they did not need careful instruction about everything, they did not have to be checked on it all the time and so on. There was this Theory Y. You assumed that they used their intelligence, enjoyed doing this and the like. The results are very clear and statistically significant in that kind of situation. That kind of natural experiment the industrial literature is full of. There are all sorts of experiments of this sort. That just happened so to speak. For instance one from, Babelas is the name. This is a very famous one because it happened all by itself. This is in a toy factory which was of an assembly line nature, one of those Charlie Chaplin kind of things. You know where there was a moving belt and the toys came along—these were dolls I think—and each one, there were women workers on the line and each one would sort of dab each doll as it went by with something or put in an eye or make a red spot or something of the sort and within this situation of making red spots for 40 years as the belt went by. Now they had a manager who was a Theory Y manager. You know what I mean by that, you don't need details. The girls said of him for instance that he was respectful. They felt that he liked them and was fond of them. They felt that he would listen respectfully and sympathetically and so on. They could talk with him. It was a very important business—there was communication even about complaints which is an ultimate test. You don't complain to a Theory X manager. What they did was to suggest—they had their bull sessions—one in which this kind of work is manageable. By the way it's not as bad as it sounds. I've done this kind of assembly line work or routine work. It can be very pleasant if the work gang remains the same and if you can chat while you are doing it. Finally the dab is done, you don't do it. Your hands sort of automatically do it. Meanwhile you are busy talking with your friends. And it's like a club. I know I was a kitchen man for some years, worked in a kitchen, chef's assistant and stuff like that. I remember the jobs that we all liked best were the most routine jobs. It used to be the best job of all in the kitchen, shelling peas. You get, oh six bushels of peas and then settle down for a nice quiet sociable day. You'll have four or five pals who will sit around and shell peas and the fingers work away and your four buddies and you sit and chat for a whole day and you get paid for it. That's not so bad. So don't think that this was a horrible thing necessarily. It's horrible only if you are not permitted to talk. Then it does become horrible.

Now in this situation, chatting away they decided that they would ask the foreman since this was routine, could they manage the speed of the belts because there was times when they got tired, just before quitting for instance or in the middle of the afternoon and he thought about it and said, "well there's no harm in trying it." He said, "O.K., you can regulate it as you wish" and he put in controls so he could slow down the belt or speed up the belt and what happened was then that they hit something which could be called a curve. I remember one of them was just before quitting time at 5 o'clock. I think it was that time that they slowed down the belt. There were other times when they speeded it up. Now reported satisfaction from the girls was great. This was a wonderful thing for them. Things changed a little bit. They felt very satisfied. The morale was high and this remember can be measured in terms of breakage, wasteage, vandalism, the deliberate breaking of things, the deliberate killing of time in the toilet, deliberate taking of coffee breaks that lasted two or two and one-half hours and stuff like that, or stay home altogether on one excuse or another and morale as measured was high. Now the crazy thing about this, the very unMarxian thing . . . I remember one argument with Herbert Marcuse on this, Herbert just didn't like this at all. This was a plot. The trouble was that the production of toys increased. That's crazy. The women were allowed to slow down the belts as they pleased and yet the toys increased. So morale was good, they felt happier, they felt better about the job yet the boss of the factory also made a greater profit. This is supposed to be not possible. These are incompatible Marxian theories, that in principle these are incompatible to managers. The interests of the workers inversely correlated with the interests of the boss. It turns out under Theory X management this is true. Theory X management could be called sort of Marxian if you want. I mean not necessarily Marx himself. I mean the interpretations of Marx. I don't think Marx is that foolish. Under Theory Y management it is somehow nonMarxian, more synergic. It seems to turn out that what's good for the workers seems to be also good for the boss or the stockholder. More frequently than you might expect, it's not always so. But rather commonly it turns out that the workers allowed to choose their own conditions set up it to their own tastes, then do a better job even in terms of production. This story is interesting, the next part of it, the sequel.

This worked along—everybody was very happy with this arrangement. It worked along until a new production manager came in. This was a very interesting story because he was so horrified. This was an authoritarian, a Theory X manager. He was so horrified at thoughts of the workers controlling their own lines. That in spite of the anguished outcries of the girls and their threats too but also of the foreman, this man who had permitted all of this and who had now a whole list of profit and loss statements and said "look it worked. It's not indulgence. It's not softness alone." Or you could say it this way: that in being soft improves the product. You get more toys. It's fine. This is good for the stockholder. It's good for the factory. The production manager who was an engineer absolutely refused. He took the controls away from the belt, insisted that it go at a constant speed in spite of the demonstration that this produced less toys, less products. Of course at this point you can get very Freudian if you want to and well one consequence was that the whole crew quit which made the whole thing worse and so on. This is a characteristic story and it's a characteristic experiment. This kind of experiment as I say there are literally dozens of in this literature. There are no experiments like this so far as I know in the experimental literature on motivation which is the kind of literature on motivation you will get on the textbooks on motivation and which I have not pressed upon you—the Cofer and Appley book which I mentioned and which I think is the best of the textbooks and which is certainly 75 percent occupied with white rats and monkeys and so on rather than with human beings. Human being experiments are practically entirely laboratory experiments, controlled-designed experiments rather than you might say the naturalistic experiments. These experiments I just mentioned by the way are not mentioned in the Cofer–Appley book. I regard them of course as great experiments in motivation theory. And you must decide for yourself there.

The American Dynamic

Although written in 1969, the following essay adequately portrays today's times. Maslow discusses his concerns regarding the American dream being expressed primarily in materialistic terms. He points out how materialistic values are a matter of selling short human nature in general and the American character in particular. Perhaps more relevant today, where dot.com mania and IPO millionaire dreams dominate the business literature, Maslow's essay will make us re-think the American dream.

The way I would analyze the present, prevailing situation is to say that the American value system—the American dream—is typically expressed in *lower-need* terms (for example, in terms of income) and almost entirely in materialistic terms. That is, personal success is generally defined in terms of the amount of money one receives and, along with it, the number of symbolic, status objects that one has attained in life, such as a fancy automobile, a boat, a big house in an upscale neighborhood, lavish vacations, and fine clothes.

But to enjoy a good life, *all* of these status objects are expendable. Not one of them is actually necessary for true fulfillment. Psychologists know that what *is* necessary for human nature is that, as our material gratifications are satisfied, we move upward in our needs through belongingness (community, brotherhood/sisterhood, friendliness), to love and affection, to achievement and competence with ensuing dignity and self-respect, and then on up to freedom for self-actualization and for expressing and resolving our unique idiosyncrasies. And then upward, still higher, to our *metaneeds* (the *Being-values*).

Source: A.H. Maslow essay (November 12, 1969), reprinted with the permission of Ann R. Kaplan and the *Archives of the History of American Psychology.*

But where has this conception been at all meaningfully articulated? Which U.S. president or senator has even attempted to speak in such terms? For that matter, which contemporary professor or philosopher has attempted to speak in such terms? It is no wonder that so many young people today see the entire social system of the United States as geared to making them adopt a wholly materialistic definition of success in life.

And because their lower needs generally have been satisfied and they have been raised by good parents who were kind, loving, and respectful, these youth are ready for the Being-values, for self-actualization, for real discussions about love, affection, dignity, respect, and cooperation. Then, they look about our current society, and they do not hear any such talk. No governmental official is speaking in these crucial terms. There is no official track toward the attainment of these goals. As a matter of fact, they are not discussed as goals at all even by presidential committees on national goals—committees who would much rather talk about materialist matters such as the gross national product, economic growth, or the amount of goods turned out by industry.

In other words, the young adults today who are confronting American society are not being offered the *metavalues* as a formal goal. For them, the higher values are, therefore, not part of the formal U.S. value system. Consequently, these youth perceive the United States as a limited system of lower motivation, lower needs, lower aspirations, and lower goals that any self-respecting, mature human being would despise and reject. Anyway, the whole American dream thing today is phrased materialistically.

Moreover, there is no clear track in our society upward to the *B-values*. How many young adults have come to me and said, "I would like to lead a good life. What shall I do? Where shall I go?" Frequently, I do not quite know how to answer them. I think of nice young people whom I know—who acquire a taste of the higher life from a group experience or from an inspiring book. Logically enough, they want to have more of the same and to go further with their personal development. But what can I tell them? Where shall I send them? There simply is no clear track. There is no vocational ladder for this sort of achievement. There is no formal, worked out, socially accepted system for becoming a higher, self-actualizing, B-valuing person.

It is bad enough that this problem exists, but worse, there is not even a language yet to deal with it meaningfully. The only words that are available for these lofty aspirations (which are embedded very deeply in human nature when our lower needs have been gratified)—which express what Buddhism calls the *Bodhisattvic* (saintly) path—are words with derogatory connotations like "do-gooder," "boy scout," and "bleeding heart." There is simply no way that a young adult today can unabashedly say, "I would like to be a good human being, as good as I can be, and I would like to live a fruitful, useful, and virtuous life." There is no one to speak to such a young person nor even to offer a way to address such sentiments except in the *Being-language* that I use.

Let's be honest: I can hardly offer myself as an example of a typical psychology professor or academician. Certainly, I can advise such youths what to do and where to go, but I am way out on the edge of regular American society. Would any mainstream, vocational-guidance expert or high school counselor offer similar advice? Would even a mainstream psychoanalyst or a psychotherapist tell them anything of the sort?

The American dream must be phrased explicitly. We have much to learn from the anomie of the hippies and of the politically radical Students for a Democratic Society (SDS), and I think that it can all be put down in words and well communicated. For an individual to experience the higher life is certainly possible in the United States, in an affluent society. There's really nothing against such attainment except the ignorance that the higher path exists and these goals are possible to obtain. It is not necessary to develop, as the hippies do, a reaction formation against what they call the "plastic" or materialistic culture—which is all that they know—and then to reject it entirely and to drop out of it.

Foolishly, the hippies are seeking to achieve instantaneously all the noble goals of the *Tzaddik* (Hebrew for saint)—love, lack of domination, community, brotherhood/sisterhood, and the like—immediately and without effort, seemingly just by willing it to be so.

So a paradoxical situation currently exists. The hippie creed does offer the highest values. But these young people don't at all know how to attain these, and so, they end up destroying the very goals for which they wish. Indeed, they find themselves generating the opposite situation of what they are seeking, that is, leading lives of hypocrisy, reaction formation, slovenliness, laziness, mutual exploitation, taking advantage of other people, and just being general nuisances—even though their verbalized values actually are wonderful goals.

The same issue holds true for the politically radical youths who, in effect, want to destroy American society in order to attain these very same goals. However, there is a difference in character structure, I suppose. The SDS types are more active, aggressive, and violent, whereas the hippie types are more passive, receptive, and quiescent. But it should be pointed out that their ultimate goals are identical.

Furthermore, it should be pointed out that these goals are the same goals that all great religions have sought for—as well as the Boy Scouts, the Kiwanis, and virtually every other benevolent organization. All these groups want love, peace, prosperity, social harmony, affection, trust, and the like. I can say it another way: The contemporary anomie in American society—especially of the young—means that they are not feeling loyal to mainstream values but, rather, view them with disgust and horror.

But then I would ask, "What *are* the U.S. values?" I would maintain that these values have not been articulated well and that, consequently, these young adults do not really know what they are. They have historically been phrased only in lower and materialist terms. In other words, there is actually a hierarchy of phrasings of U.S. values, and it seems to be my responsibility to phrase them at their very highest.

After this phrasing is accomplished—and there is a clear depiction of the Jeffersonian dream (which is, after all, truly possible to attain in the United States)—then I must next point out that our society has to legitimize the various professional tracks, educational paths, and vocational ladders to sustain life at these highest levels. This step would require a major revolution in the whole notion of vocational guidance and of personal-educational counseling.

In writing up this conceptualization, I also must be sure to differentiate between the hippies and the SDS youth on one hand—who are the products of affluence and of lower basic-need gratification so that their "grumbles" are actually "higher grumbles"—and the blacks, minority groups, and poor who are at a lower level of grumbles altogether. In the latter case, we could speak about social injustice and feel that there are easily soluble problems to end job discrimination or substandard housing—at least in principle if not in daily political practice. But in the former case, the problems essentially are philosophical, psychological, religious, and theoretical, that is, in terms of the values that people should seek for in everyday life. The former group is seeking for the very highest human values because its lower ones are already satisfied. So, the goals of these two groups are entirely different.

In writing up my analysis, I certainly must make the whole hierarchy of human needs and metaneeds quite explicit. I must say something like this: It is possible in American society to lead a life in which people are not endangered and can feel free of anxiety and fear; in which they can feel intimacy, belongingness, and brotherhood/sisterhood; and in which it is possible and probable that love needs can be satisfied—and that if it is possible to find people to love and to enter into loving relationships, then it is also possible to seek for dignity, pride, and self-respect.

If it is possible to have a society in which these qualities are freely given to everybody as a right, then it is possible to seek for self-actualization and for personal fulfillment of one's personal, unique potentialities and idiosyncrasies. Finally, it is possible to lead a life at the level of beauty, excellence, goodness, truth, perfection, and oneness.

Then, all of these principles can be framed in terms of the following: This is the American dream, or, at least, it *can* be. It certainly should be. That is, it should become a reality, not just remain a dream. This vision ought to be offered to young adults as a real possibility, something that they can choose voluntarily to do and pursue and that, if they work hard enough, they confidently can expect to attain. All the hippie goals actually can be attained; it is just that they are pursuing them in the wrong way. So also for the violent SDS revolutionaries and the black militants: Their goals can be attained, but they are seeking them in the wrong way.

It is important, though, to delineate the differences between protesting the problems of American society in "good faith" versus protesting them in "bad faith." Not only with groups like SDS, the hippies, and black militants is there a major discrepancy between means and ends in their talk. Worse, they frequently seek to disguise their goals of chaos, destruction, and violence by talking about "good ends" or goals. In this sense, they are definitely talking in bad faith.

I think it will help too if even the materialist and money goals of American society are pointed out to be at least *possibly* a good path toward the higher values. That is, wealth and power in the hands of good people are means to good ends. It is just that they are not necessarily so. In the hands of weak, bad, or immature people, money and power can be used for bad purposes, either personally or socially. Thus, part of the total picture should be to work out the reaction formation of many youth today against power and money *at any time and in any hands.*

The fact is that with a lot of money you can buy your way to the Being-values. You can support them, foster them, strengthen them, and the like. There are people in American society—I call them *aggridants*—who do this all the time. I can prove that this phenomenon exists. Money is not necessarily a contaminating thing. Neither are good clothes, fine houses, beautiful gardens, or big cars. These are all means to ends, and in the hands of good people, they are useful and good things.

Another point that Yablonsky (1968) makes is worth quoting:

> The lower-class American delinquent, therefore, is really affirming the validity of the goals of American society by striving for them at any cost. Traditional crime and delinquency in this context is a tribute to the goals and values of American society. The hippie reaction, in contrast, is a condemnation of the total American system. Most youths who drop out into the hippie movement have access to and usually can have all of the cultural prizes of American society. Their condemnation and rejection is total. They reject the American family, religion, education, government, the economic and materialist prizes of American society. More than that, they reject the "game-playing" approach for that acquisition. (p. 318)

But notice how throughout this relevant passage Yablonsky makes no distinction among the different possible phrasings of American values, among the cultural prizes, or among the various goals of American society. Rather, he implies here that, for both the criminals and the hippies, all that the American system has to offer are materialist things. This is simply not true. I think I will go on with this issue later.

I have one last thought in this context. I must speak about the bad job of salesmanship that American culture is doing. That is, the advertising and salesmanship techniques of Madison Avenue and the culture's other sections could very easily be used far better than they have been. Partly, this is a matter of the usual selling-short of human nature in general and of the American character in particular. This situation must be changed.

Dangers of Self-Actualization

The hierarchy of needs and self-actualization were often misunderstood and misconstrued. Maslow wrote the following chapter to correct what he perceived to be the widespread misunderstanding of his theories.

The aim of this chapter is to correct the widespread misunderstanding of self-actualization as a static, unreal, "perfect" state in which all human problems are transcended, and in which people "live happily forever after" in a superhuman state of serenity or ecstasy. This is empirically not so, as I have previously pointed out.

To make this fact clearer, I could describe self-actualization as a development of personality which frees the person from the deficiency problems of youth, and from the neurotic (or infantile, or fantasy, or unnecessary, or "unreal") problems of life, so that he is able to face, endure and grapple with the "real" problems of life (the intrinsically and ultimately human problems, the unavoidable, the "existential" problems to which there is no perfect solution). That is, it is not an absence of problems but a moving from transitional or unreal problems to real problems. For shock purposes, I could even call the self-actualizing person a self-accepting and insightful neurotic, for this phrase may be defined in such a way as to be almost synonymous with "understanding and accepting the intrinsic human situation," that is, facing and accepting courageously, and even enjoying, being amused by the "shortcomings" of human nature instead of trying to deny them.

It is these real problems which confront even (or especially) the most highly matured human beings, that I would like to deal with in the

Source: A.H. Maslow, *Toward a Psychology of Being,* 3rd ed. (New York: John Wiley & Sons, 1968, 1999). Copyright © 1968, 1999 by John Wiley & Sons, used with permission.

future, for example, real guilt, real sadness, real loneliness, healthy self-ishness, courage, responsibility, responsibility for others, and so forth.

Of course there is a quantitative (as well as qualitative) improvement that comes with higher personality evolvement, quite apart from the intrinsic satisfaction of seeing the truth rather than fooling oneself. Most human guilt, statistically speaking, is neurotic rather than real guilt. Being freed of neurotic guilt means absolutely to have lesser amounts of guilt, even though the probability of real guilt remains.

Not only this, but highly evolved personalities also have more peak-experiences, and these seem to be more profound (even though this may be less true of the "obsessional" or Apollonian type of self-actualization). That is to say, though being more fully human means to have problems and pains still (even though of a "higher" sort), yet it remains true that these problems and pains are quantitatively less, and that the pleasures are quantitatively and qualitatively greater. In a word, an individual is subjectively better off for having reached a higher level of personal development.

Self-actualizing people have been found more capable than the average population of a particular kind of cognition which I have called Being-cognition. This has been described in Chapter 6 (*Toward a Psychology of Being*) as cognition of the essence, or "is-ness," or intrinsic structure and dynamics, and presently existing potentialities of something or someone or everything. B-cognition (B = being) is in contrast to D-cognition (D = deficiency-need-motivation) or human-centered and self-centered cognition. Just as self-actualization does not mean absence of problems, so does B-cognition as one aspect of it hold certain dangers.

DANGERS OF B-COGNITION

1. *The main danger of B-cognition is of making action impossible or at least indecisive.* B-cognition is without judgment, comparison, condemnation or evaluation. Also it is without decision, because decision is readiness to act, and B-cognition is passive contemplation, appreciation, and non-interfering, that is, "let-be." So long as one contemplates the cancer or the bacteria, awe-struck, admiring, wondering, passively drinking in the delight of rich understanding,

then one does nothing. Anger, fear, desire to improve the situation, to destroy or kill, condemnation, human-centered conclusions ("This is bad for me," or, "This is my enemy and will hurt me") are all in abeyance. Wrong or right, good or evil, the past and the future, all have nothing to do with B-cognition, and are at the same time inoperative. It is not in-the-world, in the existentialist sense. It is not even human in the ordinary sense either; it is godlike, compassionate, non-active, non-interfering, non-doing. It has nothing to do with friends or enemies in the human-centered sense. It is only when the cognition shifts over to D-cognition that action, decision, judgment, punishment, condemnation, planning for the future becomes possible.

The main danger, then, is that B-cognition is at the moment incompatible with action.[1] But since we, most of the time, live in-the-world, *action is necessary* (defensive or offensive action, or selfishly centered action in the terms of the beholder rather than of the beheld). A tiger has a right to live (as do flies, or mosquitoes, or bacteria) from the point of view of its own "being"; but also so does a human being. And *there* is the unavoidable conflict. The demands of self-actualization may necessitate killing the tiger, even though B-cognition of the tiger is against killing the tiger. That is, even existentially, intrinsic and necessary to the concept of self-actualization, is a certain selfishness and self-protectiveness, a certain promise of necessary violence, even of ferocity. And therefore, self-actualization demands not only B-cognition but also D-cognition as a necessary aspect of itself. This means then that conflict and practical decisiveness and choice are necessarily involved in the concept of self-actualization. This means that fighting, struggle, striving, uncertainty, guilt, regret must also be "necessary" epiphenomena of self-actualization. It means that self-actualization involves *both* contemplation and action *necessarily*.

Now it is possible in a society that there be a certain division of labor. Contemplators may be exempted from action, if someone else can do the acting. We don't have to butcher our own beefsteaks.

---

[1] Probable parallels are perhaps found in the famous Olds experiments. A white rat, stimulated in the "satisfaction center" of his brain, stops dead, seemingly to "savor" the experience. So also the tendency of human beings having beatific experiences under drugs is to be quiet and nonactive. To hang on to the fading memory of a dream, it is best not to move.

Goldstein has pointed this out in a widely generalized form. Just as his brain-impaired patients can live without abstraction and without catastrophic anxiety because other people protect them and do for them what they themselves cannot do, so does self-actualization in general, at least in so far as it is a specialized kind, become possible because other people permit it and help it. (My colleague, Walter Toman, in conversations has also stressed that well-rounded self-actualization becomes less and less possible in a specialized society.) Einstein, a highly specialized person in his last years, was made possible by his wife, by Princeton, by friends, and so forth. Einstein could give up versatility, and self-actualize because other people did for him. On a desert island, alone, he *might* have self-actualized in Goldstein's sense ("doing the best with his capacities that the world permits"), but at any rate it could not have been the specialized self-actualization that it was. And maybe it would have been impossible altogether, that is, he might have died or become anxious and inferior over his demonstrated incapacities, or he might have slipped back to living at the D-need level.

2. *Another danger of B-cognition and of contemplative understanding is that it may make us less responsible especially in helping other people.* The extreme case is the infant. To "let-be" means to hinder him or even to kill him. We also have responsibility for non-infants, adults, animals, the soil, the trees, the flowers. The surgeon who gets lost in peak-wonder at the beautiful tumor may kill his patient. If we admire the flood, we don't build the dam. And this is true not only for the other people who suffer from the results of non-action, but also for the contemplator himself, since he must surely feel guilty at the bad effects upon others of his contemplation and non-action. (He *must* feel guilty because he "loves" them in one way or another; he is love-identified with his "brothers," and this means care for *their* self-actualization, which their death or suffering would cut off.)

The best examples of this dilemma are found in the teacher's attitude toward his students, the parent's attitude toward his children, and the therapist's attitude toward his patients. Here it is easy to see the relationship to be a relationship-of-its-own-kind. But we must also face the necessities that come from the teacher's (parent's, therapist's) responsibility in fostering growth, that is, the problems of setting limits, of discipline, of punishment, of *not* gratifying, of deliberately being the frustrator, of being able to arouse and endure hostility, and so forth.

3. *Inhibition of action, and loss of responsibility leads to fatalism,* that is, "What will be will be. The world is as it is. It is determined. I can do nothing about it." This is a loss of voluntarism, of free will, a bad theory of determinism, and is certainly harmful to everybody's growth and self-actualization.

4. *Inactive contemplation will almost necessarily be misunderstood by others who suffer from it.* They will think it to be lack of love, of concern, of compassion. This will not only stop growth toward self-actualization in them, but may also send them backwards in the growth incline since it can "teach" them that the world is bad, and that people are bad. As a consequence, their love, respect and trust in people will retrogress. This means then worsening the world especially for children and adolescents and weak adults. They interpret "let–be" as neglect, or lack of love, or even contempt.

5. *Pure contemplation involves, as a special case of the above, not writing, not helping, not teaching.* The Buddhists distinguish the Pratyekabuddha, who wins enlightenment only for himself, independently of others, from the Bodhisattva who, having attained enlightenment, yet feels that his own salvation is imperfect so long as others are unenlightened. For the sake of his own self-actualization, we may say, he must turn away from the bliss of B-cognition in order to help others and teach them.

Was Buddha's enlightenment a purely personal, private possession? Or did it also necessarily belong to others, to the world? Writing and teaching, it is true, are often (not always) steps back from bliss or ecstasy. It means giving up heaven to help others get there. Is the Zen Buddhist or the Taoist correct, who says, "As soon as you talk about it, it no longer exists, and is no longer true" (that is, since the *only* way to experience it is to experience it, and anyway words could never describe it, since it is ineffable)?

Of course there is some right on both sides. (That is why it is an existential dilemma, eternal, unsolvable.) If I find an oasis which other people could share, shall I enjoy it myself or save their lives by leading them there? If I find a Yosemite which is beautiful partly because it is quiet and non-human and private, shall I keep it or make it into a National Park for millions of people who, because they are millions, will make it less than it was or even destroy it? Shall I share my private beach with them and make it thereby unprivate? How right is the Indian who respects life and hates active killing and thereby lets the cows get fat while the babies die? What degree of enjoyment of food may I allow myself in a poor country where the starving children look on? Ought I starve too? There is no nice, clean, theoretical, a priori answer. No matter what answer is given, there must be some regret at least. Self-actualization must be selfish; and it must be unselfish. And so there must be choice, conflict, and the possibility of regret.

Maybe the principle of division of labor (tied in with the principle of individual constitutional differences) could help toward a better answer (although never toward a perfect answer). As in various religious orders some feel the call to "selfish self-actualization," and some feel the call to "doing good self-actualization," maybe the society could ask, as a favor (thereby relieving guilt), that some people become "selfish self-actualizers," pure contemplators. The society could assume that it would be worth its while to support such people for the good example they would set others, the inspiration, and the demonstration of the possibility that pure, out-of-the-world contemplation can exist. We do this for a few of our great scientists, artists, writers and philosophers. We relieve them of teaching, writing and social responsibilities not only for "pure" reasons, but also in a gamble that this will pay off for us as well.

This dilemma also complicates the problem of "real guilt" (Fromm's "humanistic guilt") as I have called it, to differentiate it from neurotic guilt. Real guilt comes from not being true to yourself, to your own fate in life, to your own intrinsic nature; see also Mowrer and Lynd.

But here we raise the further question, "What kind of guilt comes from being true to yourself but not to others?" As we have seen, being true to yourself may at times intrinsically and necessarily be in conflict with being true to others. A choice is both possible and necessary. And the choice can only rarely be completely satisfactory. If, as Goldstein teaches, you must be true to others in order to be true to yourself, and as Adler states, social interest is an intrinsic, defining aspect of mental health, then the world must be sorry as the self-actualizing person sacrifices some portion of himself in order to save another person. If, on the other hand, you must *first* be true to yourself, then the world must be sorry over the unwritten manuscripts, the paintings thrown away, the lessons we could have learned, from our pure (and selfish) contemplators who have no thought for helping us.

6. *B-cognition can lead to undiscriminating acceptance, to blurring of everyday values, to loss of taste, to too great tolerance.* This is so because every person, seen from the viewpoint of his own Being

exclusively, is seen as perfect in his own kind. Evaluation, condemnation, judging, disapproval, criticism, comparison are all then inapplicable and beside the point. While unconditional acceptance is a *sine qua non* for the therapist, let us say, or for the lover, the teacher, the parent, the friend, it is clearly not alone sufficient for the judge, the policeman, or the administrator.

We already recognize a certain incompatibility in the two interpersonal attitudes implied here. Most psychotherapists will refuse to assume any disciplining or punishing function for their patients. And many executives, administrators, or generals will refuse to take on any therapeutic or personal responsibility for the people to whom they give orders and whom they have to discharge or punish.

The dilemma for almost all people is posed by the necessity for being both "therapist" and "policeman" at various times. And we may expect that the more fully-human person, taking both roles more seriously, will probably be more troubled by this dilemma than is the average person, who is often not even aware that there *is* any dilemma.

Perhaps for this reason, perhaps for others, self-actualizing people so far studied are generally able to combine the two functions well, by being most often compassionate and understanding and yet also more capable of righteous indignation than the average person. Some data are available to indicate that self-actualizing people and healthier college students give vent to their justified indignation and disapproval more whole-heartedly and with less uncertainty than do average people.

Unless the capacity for compassion-through-understanding is supplemented by the capacity for anger, disapproval, and indignation, the result may be a flattening of all affect, a blandness in reaction to people, an inability to be indignant, and a loss of discrimination of and taste for real capacity, skill, superiority, and excellence. This may turn out to be an occupational hazard for professional B-cognizers if we can take at face value the widespread impression that many psychotherapists seem rather too neutral and unreactive, too bland, too even, too un-fiery in their social relations.

7. *B-cognition of another person amounts to perceiving him as "perfect" in a certain sense which he can very easily misinterpret.* To be unconditionally accepted, to be loved utterly, to be approved of completely, can be, as we know, wonderfully strengthening and growth-promoting, highly therapeutic and psychogogic. And yet, we must now be aware, this attitude can also be misperceived as an intolerable

demand to live up to unreal and perfectionistic expectations. The more unworthy and imperfect he feels, and the more he misinterprets the words "perfect" and "acceptance," the more he will feel this attitude to be a burden.

Actually, of course, the word "perfect" has two meanings, one for the realm of Being, the other for the realm of Deficiency, of striving, and of becoming. In B-cognition, "perfection" means totally realistic perceiving *and* acceptance of all that the person is. In D-cognition, "perfection" implies necessarily mistaken perceiving and illusion. In the first sense, every living human being is perfect; in the second sense, no person is perfect, nor ever can be. That is to say, we may see him as B-perfect, while he may think that we perceive him as D-perfect and, of course, may be made uncomfortable, unworthy and guilty thereby, as if he were fooling us.

We may reasonably deduce that the more capable a person is of B-cognition, the more he is able to accept and enjoy being B-cognized. We may also expect that the possibility of such misunderstanding may often pose a delicate problem of tactics upon the B-cognizer, the one who can totally understand and accept another.

8. *Possible over-estheticism is the last tactical problem entailed by B-cognition that I have space to speak of here.* The esthetic reaction to life often conflicts intrinsically with the practical and with the moral reaction to life (the old conflict between style and content). Depicting ugly things beautifully is one possibility. Another is the inept, unesthetic presentation of the true or the good or even the beautiful. (We leave aside the true-good-beautiful presentation of the true-good-beautiful as presenting no problem.) Since this dilemma has been much debated throughout history, I confine myself here merely to pointing out that it also involves the problem of social responsibility of the more mature for the less mature who may confuse B-acceptance with D-approval. A moving and beautiful presentation of, for example, homosexuality[2] or crime or irresponsibility, arising out of deep understanding, may be misunderstood as inciting to emulation. For the B-cognizer who lives in a world of frightened and easily misled people, this is an additional burden of responsibility to bear.

---

[2] Maslow would have been the first to acknowledge that one's views are conditioned by the surrounding culture, and that blind spots are more readily detected in others than in oneself. The words in this paragraph were written in 1959.

EMPIRICAL FINDINGS

What has been the relation between B-cognition and D-cognition in my self-actualizing subjects? How have they related contemplation to action? Though these questions did not occur to me at the time in this form, I can report retrospectively the following impressions. First of all, these subjects were far more capable of B-cognition and pure contemplation and understanding than the average population, as stated at the outset. This seems to be a matter of degree, since everyone seems to be capable of occasional B-cognition, pure contemplation, peak-experience, and so forth. Secondly, they were also uniformly more capable of effective action and D-cognition. It must be admitted that this may be an epiphenomenon of selecting subjects in the United States; or even that it may be a by-product of the fact that the selector of the subjects was an American. In any case I must report that I ran across no Buddhist-monk-like people in my searches. Thirdly, my retrospective impression is that the most fully-human people, a good deal of the time, live what we could call an ordinary life—shopping, eating, being polite, going to the dentist, thinking of money, meditating profoundly over a choice between black shoes or brown shoes, going to silly movies, reading ephemeral literature. They may be expected ordinarily to be annoyed with bores, to be shocked by misdeeds, and so forth, even though this reaction may be less intense, or more tinged by compassion. Peak-experiences, B-cognitions, pure contemplation, whatever their relative frequency may be, seem, in terms of absolute numbers, to be exceptional experiences even for self-actualizing people. This seems true even though it is also true that more matured people live all or most of the time at a higher level in some other ways, for example, more clearly differentiating means from ends, profound from superficial; being generally more perspicuous, more spontaneous and expressive, more profoundly related to the ones they love, and so forth.

Therefore the problem posed here is more an ultimate than an immediate one, more a theoretical problem than a practical one. And yet these dilemmas are important for more than the theoretical effort to define the possibilities and the limits of human nature. Because they are also breeders of real guilt, of real conflict, of what we might also call "real existential psychopathology," we must continue to struggle with them as personal problems as well.

PART TWO

MANAGEMENT AND LEADERSHIP ISSUES

We might ask the accountant: In which company would you prefer to invest your savings, one which had a high amount of human assets in the organization or one which had a low amount of human assets in the organization, quite irrespective of the profit picture for the last twelve months? In which company would you invest, one that had consumer goodwill or one that had used up its consumer good will? One which had good morale among the workers or one which had bad?

A.H. Maslow, *Maslow on Management*

INTRODUCTION

In the midst of great technological innovation, where products and markets emerge and disappear at a speed that would make our ancestors motion sick, many leaders simply forget that at its core, business is a fundamental human endeavor. An endeavor where individuals meet, talk, and work. It is much easier to mechanize business rather than to uncover the true barriers that stand in the way of breakthrough performance and reinvention. Yet, those very barriers prevent many organizations from capturing the potential of people.

Our natural progression to mechanizing the human organization is one Maslow warned against nearly 30 years ago. He predicted that such efforts would eventually alienate the people who form the core of the organization. He also commented on leaders' almost inherent need to place people into boxes or categories to better manage. He referred to this process as "rubricizing" and stated that such tactics prevented us from fully understanding the human condition. He defined rubricizing "as a cheap form of cognizing quick and easy cataloguing whose function is to make unnecessary the effort required by more careful idiographic perceiving or thinking. . . . To place a person in a system, he said, took less energy than to know him in his own right."

In too many organizations, we still continue to rubricize and mechanize the people part of the business. This approach underestimates the capabilities of people and does not allow for their natural growth.

Who better to help us understand the human side of enterprise than Abraham Maslow, the psychologist who was referred to as the great humanist? In the collection of articles and papers in Part Two, he comments on topics that are as timely today as they were out of place in his lifetime. Concepts such as long-term relationships with customers, customer loyalty, sales tactics that result in long-term relationships, the role of the entrepreneur in society, and the importance of communication.

The Necessity for Enlightened Management Policies

The more evolved people get, the more psychologically healthy they get, the more will enlightened management policy be necessary in order to survive in competition and the more handicapped will be an enterprise with an authoritarian policy.

A.H. Maslow, *Maslow on Management*

People are growing and growing, either in their actual health of personality, or in their aspirations, especially in the United States, and especially women and other underprivileged groups. The more grown people are, the worse authoritarian management will work, the less well people will function in the authoritarian situation, and the more they will hate it. Partly this comes about from the fact that when people have a choice between a high and a low pleasure, they practically always choose the high pleasure if they have previously experienced both. What this means is that people who have experienced freedom can never really be content again with slavery, even though they made no protest about the slavery *before* they had the experience of freedom. This is true with all higher pleasures; those people who have known the feeling of dignity and self-respect for the first time can never again be content with slavishness, even though they made no protest about it before being treated with dignity.

Treating people well spoils them for being treated badly. That is, they become much less contented and willing to accept lower life conditions. This means in general that the better the society grows, the better the politics, the better the education, and so forth, the less suitable will the people be for Theory X management, or for authoritarian politics, or for gangster rule, or for prison-type colleges, and the more and more they will need and demand eupsychian management, growth-permitting education, and so forth. For this they will work well; for the authoritarian hierarchical management they will work badly and will be rebellious and hostile. This should show up in pragmatic ways, that is, in terms of production, quality, identification with the managers, and so forth.

Giving people good conditions spoils them for bad conditions.

Now what all this means so far as the competitive situation is concerned in the U.S. is that considering the level of personality development in this society that eupsychian or enlightened management is already beginning to become a competitive factor. That is, old-style management is steadily becoming obsolete, putting the enterprise in a less and less advantageous position in competition with other enterprises in the same industry that are under enlightened management and are therefore turning out better products, better service, and so forth, and so on. That is to say that old-style management should soon be obsolete, even in the accounting sense, in the business sense, in the sense of competition, just in the same way that any enterprise will become obsolete and take a bad position in respect to competition if it has obsolete machinery.

The same is true for obsolete people. The more evolved people get, the more evolved psychologically, the more psychologically healthy they get, the more this will be true—the more will enlightened management policy be necessary in order to survive in competition and the more handicapped will be an enterprise with an authoritarian policy. This means all sorts of other theoretical things: for instance, the better our schools get, the greater the economic advantage for enlightened management. The more enlightened the religious institutions get, that is to say, the more liberal they get, the greater will be the competitive advantage for an enterprise run in an enlightened way, and so forth, and so on.

This is why I am so optimistic about the future of eupsychian management policy, why I consider it to be the wave of the future. The chances are that general political, social, and economic conditions will not change in any basic way; that is to say, I think we are in a stalemate of a military-political kind. Therefore, I expect that the present rates of growth and directions of growth in religion and industry, politics, education, and so forth, will continue in the same way. If anything, the tendency toward favoring eupsychian management should increase, because the tendency is toward more internationalism rather than less, which, in turn, will force all sorts of other growth-fostering changes in our society and in other societies as well. The same thing is probably true for the development of automation, although this, too, will bring all sorts of huge transitional problems along with it. The same thing is true for the possibility that we may shift over to a peace economy, laying much less stress on defense and military expenditures. This tendency will, I think, also favor enlightened management or democratic management over authoritarian or old-style management.

It looks as if it might be desirable eventually to coordinate, under one ninth vice president (in addition to Drucker's eight), what we might call the eupsychian tendency, the fostering of growth, the increasing of the personality level of all the employees of an enterprise including the managers. It is perfectly true now that this could be included and probably is included in enlightened plans under department seven of "worker-attitude and performance" and also under Drucker's department six, "managerial performance and development." I don't know that this ninth department is necessary *today,* but it may one day become professionalized and demanding a different kind, a different constellation of training, than either Drucker's department-six manager or Drucker's department-seven manager. For instance, a wide philosophical, psychological, and psychotherapeutic and educational training would certainly be very heavily involved in this ninth department.

This ninth department may soon turn out to be especially important and may be precipitated into action because of the requirement of the cold war. The way things are now, it looks as if there has been a military stalemate and a stalemate in the usefulness of physical, chemical, and biological weapons. These are no longer useful at all in the cold war except to prevent an open outbreak of war. The way in which the cold war will be won or will tip one way or the other will be in terms of the human products turned out by the Russian society and the American society. Since the cold war now really consists of all sorts of political, social, educational, and personal maneuvering before the neutral nations—that is, the effort is to win over *their* good opinion—then clearly all sorts of nonmilitary things come into account. One is race prejudice, in which the Russians have such a tremendous advantage over the Americans now, especially before the African nations.

But this will probably all add up ultimately in terms of the kind of person, the kind of average citizen, that is turned out by the two cultures. This is getting steadily more and more important as international travel gets easier and easier. It's the tourists, the visiting businessmen, the visiting scientists, the cultural exchanges that are now making a big impression and will get to be more and more important. If the Americans can turn out a better type of human being than the Russians, then this will ultimately do the trick. Americans will simply be more loved, more respected, more trusted, and so forth, and so on. If this is so, then the establishment of growth-fostering tendencies in industry becomes a matter of high national policy and even of crash programs of the atom bomb sort. If we were to put into this the kind of money that we put into the atom bomb and are now putting into missiles and the space program, we might get a hell of a lot more for our money in the political sense. It may yet become national policy to have this ninth psychological vice president in every industry, partly as a public service, partly at the request of the government, the state department, and so forth.

(This is still another instance of increased interrelatedness, both in theory and in practice, plus the increased synergy and symbiosis of any industry and of the whole society. Furthermore, this kind of thing guarantees that this symbiosis will increase year by year rather than decrease, that the ties between government and industry will be greater rather than less. Any industry represents the whole society. Any industry has also the function of making good citizens or bad citizens in a democracy.)

The quality of product turned out also has international, cold war status as well as personal, local, and national status. That this is a practical everyday kind of consideration is already very clear, even though America doesn't realize this as much as other countries do. The stereotype in most of the world is that an American fountain pen is more likely to be a good, workable, efficient fountain pen than if it comes from another country. And we have the recent example of the self-conscious cooperation between the government of Japan and its industries in deliberately shifting over to higher-quality products. The stereotype of Japanese products before the war was that they were shoddy and cheap or low-quality imitations. But already, we are getting to think of Japanese products in about the same way that we used to think of a German product in the old days, that is, as being of very high quality and of excellent workmanship. Countries to some extent get judged by the quality of automobile or camera that they turn out. I am told that German quality has gone down. If this is so, then the status of West Germany in the eyes of the whole world will go down. It will be considered in an unconscious way to have less status, to have poorer quality as a nation. This, of course, since every West German tends to identify with his country and tends to introject it, means a loss of self-esteem in every single citizen, just as the increased Japanese quality and the general respect for their products means an increase in the self-esteem of every Japanese citizen. The same thing is true for the United States in a very general way.

Letter from Peter Drucker

PETER F. DRUCKER
138 NORTH MOUNTAIN AVENUE
MONTCLAIR, NEW JERSEY 07042

September 15, 1966

Dr. Abraham H. Maslow
Brandeis University
Waltham, Massachusetts

Dear Professor Maslow,

This letter is about seven years late. For the last seven years or so I have always been on the point of writing you to tell you how very much I have learned from you and how deeply grateful I am. But every time I sat down to write, I started a long discussion—and in no time at all I found myself arguing some minor point and forgetting the really important reason why I wanted to write—namely, to express my gratitude.

This happened to me particularly after I read your "Eupsychian Management." (A measure of my gratitude is my willingness to put up with this title—for an old professional writer who has had a lifetime love affair with the language, this is tolerance indeed. What's wrong with "Well-tempered," or simply "Well-balanced?") I found it a book of tremendous insight and stimulation which made me understand a great many thoughts of my own, made me ask questions, and made me learn. And this is what I read a book for. I am afraid I shall never be the proper academic and be primarily interested in "what is right," let alone in "who is right." I shall always put first the question, "what do I get out of it?" and "what can I use this for?" And all your books have been of the greatest value and importance to me in respect to what I learned from them, in respect to what I got out of them, and in respect to what they enabled me to understand and to do. Whether I necessarily agree or not with everything is quite irrelevant—and therefore, the long arguments I found myself engaged in every time in the past I sat down to write to you are irrelevant too.

But I know that the moment I start reading your new book, "A Psychology of Science" which I just found on my desk when I returned from a trip in the Pacific, will again start me arguing with you. And before this delays even further my writing a "bread and butter letter" of simple but real gratitude, I thought I'd sit down and tell you how much I owe you, how much I have been learning from you, how much I admire the turn of your mind and the texture of your personality, tough and yet fine-grained, and altogether how much your writings have meant to me.

Maybe one of these days I shall have the pleasure of meeting you in the flesh and of being able to convey to you in person my admiration and my gratitude.

Sincerely yours,

Peter Drucker

Source: Peter Drucker letter to A.H. Maslow, reprinted with the permission of Ann R. Kaplan and the *Archives of the History of American Psychology.*

The Good Enlightened
Salesman and Customer

*A good sales person is the eyes and ears of the company . . .
he is the ambassador of the enterprise . . . He is the company
at a distance . . . any enterprise ought to have a very steady
feedback about consumer demand, about needs of markets,
about satisfaction and dissatisfaction of product and the salesperson is exactly the person to collect this information and feedback. He is the V.P. in charge of innovation and development
of future products as well as just the guy who sells something.*

A.H. Maslow, *Maslow on Management*

If we start with our standard assumption of the enterprise persist-
ing over a long period of time and remaining healthy, both in the
homeostatic sense and in the growth sense, and if we include all
the things that we have deduced such an enterprise needs in order to
remain healthy, then this will also make a difference in the definition
of the salesman and of the customer. The way things stand now, the
current conceptions and definitions of salesman and customer are only
slight modifications in principle from that of the snake-oil salesman
and the sucker. The relationship is seen very clearly in the language
which is used, which implies that either the customer screws the salesman or the salesman screws the customer, and there is much talk about
who gets screwed, who gets raped, who gets exploited, or who gets
taken advantage of. Or, it is as if the customer is sometimes spoken of
as a sheep with plenty of blood which is there to be sucked by the
smarter mosquitoes or leeches or whatever, that is, he is simply a host

animal who is not respected but who is there only to be used or taken advantage of.

The current stereotype is that the salesman is a short-range-in-time kind of person. That is, the salesman wants a quick score or quick success; he wants to make this particular sale and doesn't think too much of what will happen next week; nor does he think too much of what will happen to the enterprise in general or to other sales offices in other sections of the country, and so forth. He is focused on the here and now; he is not only short range in time but in space as well. This is the kind of person considered to be the salesman type; the successful, good salesman; he is simply the one who can sell a product today, all other conditions being equal, and the worse the product or the worse the conditions, the better salesman he is considered to be if he manages to sell.

But, realistic management and the healthy enterprise, of course, need a different kind of person and a different kind of relationship between salesman and customer. First of all, the salesman must be longer range in time and longer range in space and wider thinking in terms of causes and effects and holistic relationships. Why is this? Well, in general it's because the relationships between the healthy enterprise and its customer are very different when these customers are supposed to be kept for a century or two. A good customer, under ideal conditions or in eupsychia would be the person who wants the best product, who is intelligent, realistic, rational, virtuous and moral, and so forth, and who will choose in a rational way the best product, the cheapest price, the highest quality, but who also will tend to judge the product and the enterprise and everything connected with it in terms of the morality and integrity of the salesman and the enterprise in general. That is, he will get angry if he is swindled or lied to, or if something is palmed off on him that is not quite what it was supposed to be.

For instance, I can use the example of the way in which I tried to make my life simpler when I was the manager of a small plant. I told the suppliers that I did not want to spend time inspecting carefully whatever they brought to my plant; I wanted to be able to trust them. I told them that I would give them an order but not inspect the material supplied. Then, if I were swindled, I would make up for the swindle, certainly, and get my money back, but, also, I would never have anything to do with them thereafter, and they would lose the possibility of a profitable relationship. With one of these men this is exactly what happened. In a very stupid way he sent over some completely inadequate products. I had to go to the trouble of sending them back and getting my money back, and I told him never to deliver anything to me again, that I would never accept his products no matter what price he put on them. Thereafter he did try to underbid other people, but I refused to take advantage of this, and in fact, never had anything more to do with him. What he did, in effect, was to lose a customer. He behaved as if his business were going to run for only two weeks and then close up shop. He didn't care for my good opinion. The salesman who does this kind of thing, will, in the long run, destroy the enterprise that he is representing (and since we're dealing with long-run enterprise, this becomes essential). That is to say, a "good eupsychian customer" is one who doesn't like being fooled, one who appreciates it if his interests are kept in mind by the enterprise and its representative.

On the other hand, taking the customer's interests seriously and actually trying to serve him or to help him prosper, even though this sometimes means willingly and knowingly getting him to buy a rival product rather than one's own, is in the same way helpful because it builds in him a feeling of trust, and guarantees that if this enterprise eventually turns out a better product, it can assume that the customer will buy it.

All of this implies a kind of a virtue which certainly cannot be expected of most human beings today; that is to say, an enterprise manager would *want* the customer to buy the best product, even if it were produced by the rival factory. That is, he would see that this represents a kind of justice and virtue, and even if it hurt him at the moment, it would in the long run help him and everybody else—at least at the higher need levels and the metamotivational levels. This, of course, demands a very great deal of objectivity and detachment. The fact is, however, that we do get it once in a while in our society; for instance, a priest who has lost his religious faith, even though it is entirely private and within his own head, will do the gentlemanly thing and resign from his post. This is also expected from people in a political situation, that is, in certain kinds of government, anyhow: if they do not agree with the government, they give up their jobs voluntarily and resign. If good conditions were to prevail for some length of time, we would expect that more and more of this kind of objectivity and gentlemanliness and honesty would spread more and more. Very rarely today, but still sometimes, do we see this in the lover relationship.

I suppose it would be too much to ask for many or most businessmen and salesmen to point out to the customer that there is a rival product which he should try out and which might be better for his purposes, and yet, I think it can be shown that in a healthy, long-term enterprise exactly this will pay off; that is, this kind of virtue will pay under these good conditions. It also follows that what Andy Kay was trying to change over to is desirable as a kind of ideal condition, for instance, not bothering to curry the favor of, to bribe, to buy lunches for, or to mimic personal friendship with, all sorts of unlikable people, just in the hope that this might induce them to buy the product. It is quite reasonable to ask, as Kay did, What kind of life is this? What kind of a life will I be leading if I am forced to be a hypocrite and pretend to be friends with people that I actually don't feel friendly with? What's the good of being in business then, and controlling my own fate, if I don't have the freedom not to have lunch with the people I dislike?

This policy carries over also in the system of not giving budget credit for this kind of bribery, which is essentially a befuddling of the customer, a confusing of the issue, trying to get him, by implication, to buy a second-rate product out of personal gratitude or loyalty and the like. Here too, it can be pointed out that if the customer is a rational person, precisely this sort of thing is going to make him doubly suspicious about the worth of the product. A good product does not need this kind of contamination or befuddling or bribery. And just in the same way that an honest man will be repelled by the offer of bribery, so an honest man will be repelled by the necessity for offering the bribe.

Under ideal economic conditions all that any enterprise can ask or *should* ask is that the best product should win. This is fair, free and open, and desirable competition. Therefore, it follows that these same people who feel that the best product should win should find distasteful any factors in the situation that would confuse this basic issue (in any systematic presentation of this point of view it would be very desirable here to pile up the examples of instances in which true service to the customer paid off not only for the customer but for the enterprise itself).

The salesman for the enlightened enterprise, then, has functions which are different from the old conventional ones. For one thing, he should know his product as well as is necessary, he should be a knowledgeable man about the state of the market, about his customers needs, about the whole business, the whole section of industry he is involved in. Facts, candor, honesty, truth, efficiency—these should be his mottos. (Remember to point out that this is said not only on moral grounds, or on merely moral grounds or a priori grounds of any kind, but on the grounds that this will pay for the enterprise, that under these conditions in the long run virtue of this sort will actually pay off in selfish terms as well. But it is best to make the final statement in terms of synergy, that is, of teaching the reader that at a high level of good conditions and of good humanness, selfishness and unselfishness, private interest and public interest are not polar-opposites, or are not mutually exclusive, but do come together into a new kind of unity.) Another way of saying this is that the salesman then must be a man of integrity, a man who can be trusted, a man whose word will be believed, a man whose word is his bond, a man of honor, a gentleman (in clear contrast with the standard conventional stereotype of the old-time salesman, who is the opposite of all these things).

Finally, another thing has to be strongly stressed which is missing from the stuff on salesmanship that I've read, namely, that the salesman has another function entirely besides just selling. He is the eyes and ears of the company, and furthermore, he is the representative or the ambassador of the company. He is the company at a distance. For one thing, in good marketing situations, any enterprise ought to have a very steady feedback about consumer demands, about the needs of the market, about the satisfaction or dissatisfaction the product it giving, and the field representative or the salesman is exactly the person to collect this information and feedback. This implies, furthermore, that the salesman or the diplomat or the field representative or the marketer, whatever we will finally choose to call him (the word "salesman" is really not very good anymore), takes on himself every single function of anybody in the whole enterprise back home, insofar as these functions are important in his particular situation and in the particular moment: for instance, he is, let's say, the vice president in charge of innovation and future products as well as being just the guy who sells something.

Another way of looking at the future type of marketer is to shear away from the concept the overtone of manipulation. The way things are now, the average salesman considers himself to be a manipulator, considers the psychologist, for instance, to be a manipulator and a controller, that is, someone who functions partly on the basis of *hiding* information and truth. But, in principle, the new enlightened salesmanship or marketing must, like all the other aspects of any good enterprise, rest on full disclosure of facts, on candor, honesty, and truthfulness. Well, this takes a particular kind of character to be able to do. The stereotyped present-day salesman is not this kind of character. Therefore, there must be a change in the selection policies; the salesman who is hired now to work in an enlightened enterprise toward the future must be trained in a different way and must be the kind of personality who is capable of picking up these new requirements.

Further Notes on Salesmen
and Customers . . .

We should be able to institutionalize all the democratic, communicative, respecting, loving, listening, customer satisfaction kinds of things in the future by using the advantages of technology. In other words, keeping all the benefits of smallness but also capitalizing on the benefits of bigness.

A.H. Maslow, *Maslow on Management*

Themselvethe enlightened-type salesman and the enlightened customer are both based on the assumption of a good and worthwhile product. If the product they turn out is not good, then this Y type of management will destroy the whole enterprise, as truth generally will destroy untruth and phoniness and fakery. Another way to say this is that Theory Y management works only for virtuous situations, where everybody trusts the product and can identify with it and be proud of it. Contrariwise, if the product is not good and must be concealed and faked and lied about, then only Theory X managers, customers, and salesmen are possible. Countrariwise, if Theory X is actually used, then this indicates possible mistrust of the product and a mistrust of the rationality of the customer (assuming that he doesn't have sense enough to pick the best product, and assuming he is stupid enough to be fooled and swindled by irrelevant data). Actually, this suggests that the measurement of the level of the customer rationality would give us an indication of what type of management to use that would be most successful. Low rationality would indicate that a successful business would have to use Theory X philosophy. High customer rationality would indicate that it would be better and more successful to use Theory Y management.

Managerial Stuff

The following material is an eye-opening account of Maslow's application of human motivation theory to the workplace.

I happened to stumble across—in this one plant, this was an electronics factory—I happened to stumble across by accident the new building that they were putting up which struck me with kind of a thunderclap because it fulfilled right here on earth you might say practically all the extrapolated ideal conditions, the utopian conditions that I had set up on paper for creativeness, that is for creativeness in architecture. In this particular case I became very very curious as to how it was possible, how did this happen, how did this building, how was it possible that this plant, the man in charge, the people in charge had built so extraordinarily perfect a building, which was so extraordinarily adapted to the needs of the people who would work in it and live in it, and how had it happened that they had thrown away the standard architectural plant, for which they had paid a good deal of money by the way, and this was the way I got into this situation and found that well, for me, for the Professor of Psychology interested in motivation theory, what I had been doing ever since I started writing on motivation was trying to figure out ways of putting it to the test, experimental laboratory ways of deciding whether this was true or false, or confirmable or disconfirmable and I have always failed. So had everybody else. The experimental literature on motivation is very sad. It just doesn't amount to anything at all hardly as you can tell from the little that I've passed on to you. The text books on motivation are mostly concerned with triviality and with animal trivialities

Source: A.H. Maslow, McGregor, Likert, et al. lecture (1955), reprinted with the permission of Ann R. Kaplan and the *Archives of the History of American Psychology.*

at that. Now here what happened to me was that I realized that it was in the like situation, here particularly in the work situation and in the situation, where we could call it organization situation, where there are 300 or 400 people who are all involved with each other, that in this situation it occurred to me that they had been putting to the test practically all the theories of motivation, all the conceptions of motivation which had been written by the theorists, the clinicians, that they were putting them to the test and that they had data; that it was possible to observe what was going on and I still remember the moment in which it dawned on me how silly it had been for me to expect to be able to test these most basic of all aspects of human nature within a room, in a basement, some place in a psychology lab with a few animals maybe or whatever, some apparatus, that obviously these crucial aspects of human nature could be tested only in a like situation and that's what they were doing. I think in that moment I gave up the laboratory, at least for motivation studies anyway, and turned with great zest and great eagerness to the literature which I hadn't even known existed, literature on so-called organization theory, administration theory, the work situation, labor union theory, industrial psychology, personnel theory and so on and so on, is a huge mass not only of speculation of theories but also a very good research, research which is certainly far more impressive to me anyhow and I think it would be to you too, because it deals with actual whole human beings totally involved, fully immersed in the situation—it's not an artificial situation by any means that we have here—talked about—these studies—that these are life and death matters sometimes, that finally I would say it's almost the only way in which you could test on a large scale your attributions to human nature. That is, your guesses, your speculations on human nature. What I found was that the theory of motivation which I had derived almost entirely from clinical data. That is from the effort to cure neurotic people, to make them well. That this theory was being put to the test in this wholly other situation, the organization, the work, the factory situation. Since then, I found also in the army, the air force, any large grouping of people. Now I've gotten ambitious about trying them out at the education level too, on which very little has been done.

Now as I said last time—well, in the first place, this is a nice bridge between individual psychology and whole of social psychology and I say that in the largest possible framework. I may say that—for instance, I can refer you, if you want my thoughts on these subjects, I wrote a whole darn journal full of them, they're on reserve in the Library.

There's a mimeographed book there called "Summer Notes on the Social Psychology of Industry and Management." These are my reactions to all of this new stuff and suggestions and experiments and theories and so on. Was it a good thing to have that building built in what I considered an extremely intelligent way? The people who work in it, I've been checking on it after it was built, the people who work in it are very content, very happy with it, very pleased with it. And their work life is happier. It turns out also that more profits are made in fact, because the people who are happy just simply do a better job. It happens that they turn out in this particular plant a highly intricate, delicate, subtle, carefully made, very fine volt meter which is accurate to the thousandth of a volt, so it has to be quality work. It has to be done with love, let's put it that way, . . . Well it's a lousy volt meter. Now the question is, how can you get people to make volt meters . . . , an interesting question. You know that these volt meters are made in only two countries I believe. Most of the countries on the face of the earth—the workmen don't love their work enough so that they can do fine work, so that England and the United States, as I understand it, are the only ones who are turning out these fine volt meters. It can't be done any place else because it requires that much devotion. You have to love your job and you have to love your work and you have to love your product. Well, how about that?

The British socialists found out that it's not enough to have legal ownership of the coal mines. I mean it doesn't do the trick if you say to the coal miners "this is your coal mine now go down there and work for eight hours." It seems that it doesn't make much difference in the attitude toward the work, toward the job, toward the coal, where the profits go eventually, whether they go into the state treasury or they go into somebody's pocket. It doesn't seem to make much difference to the person spending his life right there in the coal mine. And labor morale in the coal mines has been just as bad after socialization of the coal mines as before. I think this is slowly penetrating—the Yugoslavs and the Russians and maybe some of the borderline, the Satellite countries—that, to make it brief, what I would suggest to them or what I would say to you is to disentangle ourselves from this, what I consider a spurious problem is that the question of making good volt meters or good fountain pens, or good anything that requires exactness and precision and love, let's say it that way; devotion, dedication to the job, that this problem is the same for Fascists, Communists, Socialists, Capitalists and anybody. For any society that wants to turn out fine fountain pens they are confronted with the stuff of human nature, with attitudes towards jobs, with basic needs, with how do you keep the workers happy and how do you keep them not happy, and how do you keep them for instance from getting into, let's say, the vandalism, the enmity toward the job that I found in this plant: for instance, a man who showed up—he was an industrial engineer who came from Columbia, Columbia, South America and who told us the way in which the workers who were—as nearly as we could make out—absolutely exploited, absolutely treated without dignity, absolutely treated at the lower need level and with a complete frustration of all higher needs satisfactions, that the inevitable happens, vandalism just for fun. I mean if you hate your boss it is a pleasure to gum up the works. You must have had that experience with a job, with a boss that you disliked very much. I know I did. In the summer notes I cite one job that I had a long time ago where vandalism—I know how it feels. It feels wonderful. Really gum up the works for a real stinking son of a bitch who tried to exploit you, to step on your neck and so on. This was a summer hotel that years ago—pre-union days—in which I got a job presumably as a waiter and then showed up and was put to work as a bus boy at one-tenth the income. I didn't have the money to get back to town and it was too late to get another job anyway and apparently this guy had done this to everybody around the place. He was just trying to squeeze out every nickle that he possibly could and we just fumed and boiled and simmered and the gastric ulcers started growing and finally we figured out something very good. The whole hotel was full, all jammed full on July 4th and we laid out I remember these orange baskets that so and so had kept us up all night making and we put those orange baskets on the table and the whole staff walked out. Just walked out. All the bus boys, waiters, kitchen help just walked out and left him with 300 people sitting at the table. I still enjoy the memory. Well this kind of vandalism, this kind of hatred of reactive, well righteous indignation which comes, this Colombian man told us about, people just deliberately on the job building into various machines. One thing I remember he told me, they put sugar water. It took a lot of effort to put sugar water into some kind of pipes where they would harden and where it was practically impossible to get it out without taking the whole machine apart. And that was fun, good clean fun.

I don't want to lose my point now. In a way that's kind of a reputation of Herbert Marcuse after he left, when he couldn't hear the comeback, he hauled off to Europe or somewhere, but I'll catch him in September, of making this point: that this same problem of keeping workers happy especially in a very delicate organization, of making the work life real life, making it worth while, making it pleasant to come to work and to stay for a whole day rather than to make it a torture and a turmoil, seems to be a pre-requisite condition for a good productiveness in any kind of a society whatsoever—anyone that can compete—that's for China or Yugoslavia, Romania, Russia, or for that matter, Spain or Paraguay or any place you can imagine. If you want fountain pens and if you want human beings to produce them and if they have to have fine points and it has to be done delicately and well, then you just have to do it this way. You have to proceed on the assumption that there are higher needs and that these must be satisfied and not frustrated in the work situation and then it turns out that you get kind of a synergic situation in which what it is good for the plant and what is good for the product and what is good for the society turns out to be what is good for the self-actualization of the particular working man. And you can start at either end. Let's say that if you started a society on some kind of utopian basis in which you didn't care about fountain pens particularly but which the main goal of every institution was the self-actualization of everybody there, that you would eventually wind up with this same kind of industrial organization because this is best for self-actualization. Or, in another society, if you started just cold blooded, cold hearted, absolutely selfish, just wanting as many profits as you possibly could in making these volt meters let's say, that you'd wind up with the same procedure, the same kind of form and the same kind of instructions, the same sort of an organization of the workers in relationship to each other and so on, because you would discover that you had transcended the dichotomy or the distinction between individual needs, individual motivation and the good of the society in general.

Well, let me dig into this just a little bit. I'm going to give you the references for the details. You'll have to look them up for yourself. We just don't have the time for going into. These are pretty elaborate researches which take a good deal of time to describe. One that I want to give you immediately is the one by R. Likert. It's called "New Patterns in Management." That comes from the University of Michigan Social Psychology Group. They have been working for about 20 years now at this sort of thing and this book is just full of their researches, their investigations and it sums up, although Likert didn't put it that way, it sums up in essence the finding that human beings do have higher needs. If you treat them that way and you try to gratify these higher needs, they work well and this is good for the organization in general. That was true for instance of bomber crews during the war. It's also true of factories that make toys and so on and so on. And if you treat these people without, as if they did not have higher needs, as if they didn't need respect and dignity and social groupings with each other, companionship, friendliness in the situation, then you wind up getting poor production, poor quality as a product, greater turnover—people quitting their jobs more frequently—more sick leave. You know that for yourself, how often the sick leave, is a matter of your own judgment. If you wake up in the morning one day, you have sort of a headache and your belly doesn't feel so good and so on and you speculate. Should I go to class or should I not and you think it depends on the class that you're going to, to some extent certainly. If it's a class you look forward to you're more apt to take a couple of asprins for your headache and go to class. If it's some class that you don't look forward to, that you don't enjoy, don't like, you're more apt to stay in bed and that happens in these work situations as well. There's a very great difference: the sick leave is used as a criterion of, oh good, things are working well and so on.

Let me turn now—I want to read you a few passages from this book by McGregor which I mentioned. That's probably the best book to start with, to make your entrance into this field of Social Psychology. By the way, for those of you who are interested in social psychology my personal opinion is that social psychology is in a very very sad state. It's mostly a collection without organization, this experiment and that experiment, my own personal feeling is that the hottest frontier in social psychology is right this stuff here—organization theory, the theory of work in groups, the management of men in the work situation, all of the questions that are associated with it—the factory you might say—the leadership, personnel policy and so on. I think it's very hot. It's very important.

Well, this is from McGregor *The Human Side of Enterprise* page 6. I'm just reading a few paragraphs from the book. I hope you will be interested enough to pursue it yourself. This is what he said: "Every managerial act" (This is what I think I said in the first meeting of this semester—something of this sort) "Every managerial act rests on assumptions, generalizations and hypotheses, that is to say on theory about human nature and more specifically about motivation in human nature. Our assumptions are frequently implicit, sometimes quite unconscious, often conflicting. Nevertheless they determine our predictions. Theory and practice are inseparable."

Now if I can add my little footnote to that—it is just to be sure that you are sophisticated about this point—don't ever let yourself fall into this very very naive notion that you don't have a philosophy until you take six credits in the philosophy department. A two-year-old child has a philosophy in this sense. That is, we all have all sorts of implicit axioms, truisms which we have learned to take for granted and by which we function, which we take for granted. Sometimes you can see it in the most blatant ways, for instance, driving to school in the morning, to see someone standing in the middle of the road, of a busy automobile road on the white line there, not looking frightened particularly or scared or anything like that, waiting for the traffic to go by. The assumption is nobody wants to kill her. Now she acts on that assumption. If she didn't believe that she certainly wouldn't have put herself in that exposed position. She'd be hiding behind a tree there when traffic came. And this is true. Do we not proceed on that assumption thousands of times a day? We turn our backs to each other and so on. We trust each other in various ways. Well you can add up assumptions of that sort. For instance your assumption let's say that I'm trying to tell you the truth, I'm not trying to fool you. You would assume that to be the case. And so on and so on and so on.

In the work situation there are many assumptions of this same sort which constitute the implicit philosophy which you can pull if you wish: the Weltenschauung, the life outlook, the unspoken philosophy, which not only a two-year-old child has but I'd say that to some extent you could say even a dog has. The assumption that it makes about human beings for instance. Are they going to kick me or are they not going to kick me? It is an assumption. It's a way of looking at life.

Now I mention this because in this realm of history where most of the people are anti-intellectuals and certainly anti-philosophy, anti-theory, this kind of talk—the McGregor kind of talk or the sort of thing I've just been saying is regarded as soft-headed nonsense. It's foolish, it's idiotic, these are the bleeding hearts (that's a characteristic name), the bleeding hearts who want to feed everybody and so on and so on. And the truth is that most factories in this country are still run on this older basis of give them an order or knock them on their head, throw them out if they don't follow it and so on. We certainly have to talk about psychoanalytic resistance because all the facts of life in most factories in this country contradict this. There's a famous example of a manager who came in, the new manager came into this plant (it's a weaving plant), and very pugnaciously went over—his first official act—he went over to one of the workers who was the union representative in this plant and said "Let's get one thing clear here. I'm the boss. What I say goes. Do you understand that?" And this guy just turned around—apparently they were ready for it, he made a signal and every man in the place just stopped the machine and just didn't say anything. O.K. What? Well this is what goes on but don't think that that would change the opinions of that manager particularly. I mean he would go on thinking all these people were crazy or abnormal or psychopathological or think about the good old days or something of the sort, but my experience with these people is that most of them don't change their philosophy. They think something is wrong with the world, rather. However, this kind of philosophy—Theory Y philosophy McGregor calls it—we can call it in our context higher need philosophy, the acceptance of higher needs as part of human nature, that this is very rapidly spreading and within the next decade will spread even more rapidly and it's quite probable that it's becoming kind of an international—this is one of our American exploits you might say. The industrial engineers and industrial experts and so on are now coming to this country to study this kind of stuff so that they can go back to their own countries and try to put it into practice. What happens with production when you make the assumption that people like to be treated respectfully for instance? What happens?

Well back to McGregor. He says this. You can try it for your own situation—for your education situation. Next time you attend a management staff meeting at which a policy problem is under discussion or some action is being considered try a variant on the past time of doodling. Jot down the assumptions, that is the beliefs, convictions, generalizations, the assumptions about human behavior made during the discussion by the participants. Some of these will be explicitly stated. For instance, a man will say "the manager must himself be technically competent in a given field in order to manage professionals within it." Now that's an explicit statement about human nature in this management situation. Many statements will be imperfect but easily inferred. The man says—this is a quote—"We should require the office force to punch time clocks as they do in the factory." And then makes all sorts of assumptions about punctuality and what people will stay away from and go to and so on. Now we make the assumption here, for instance, that in the management of professional personnel you never see any time clocks. I never punch any time clocks. As a matter of fact I don't know any professional person who does and if someone tried to have people punch time clocks there would be revolt immediately. It just—it wouldn't work. Do you see that there is an assumption? It may be that there are time clocks in this place, let's say for the groundkeeping personnel, maybe for the gardeners. I'm not sure. I'd be interested to find out. The assumption would be then that human nature in me is different from human nature in the groundskeeper because somehow he needs a time clock and I don't, or it's good for him and it's not good for me somehow. Well something is implied there. It will not make too much difference whether the problem under discussion is a human problem, or financial, or a technical one. Tune your ear to listen for assumptions of human nature whether they relate to an individual, a particular group or people in general. The length and variety of your list will surprise you.

Now it is possible to have—he goes on—"It is possible to have more or less adequate theoretical assumptions. It is not possible to reach a managerial decision" and, by the way I want to bring this home too: remember each of you are already managers and certainly will be in a very obvious sense when you run your home and you are going to manage children for instance, and in a mutual sense you will be managing your husband or your wife and vice versa. You'll each be managing each other to some extent and this will be based upon assumptions which you now have whether you know it or not. It's the best way to treat a husband. The best way to treat a wife. The best way to treat children. You now have in your blood, in your bones, unconscious—there are many that are conscious, but there are also unconscious ones which you will discover at the proper time—upon which you will act, which will guide your actions. So if he talks about managers here, you apply it to your own situation, please.

The insistence on being practical which is so often made in business and in industry or in the army, or any large organization, what this really means, McGregor says, is "let's accept my theoretical assumption without argument or test." And then he goes on—some of these statements "People need to learn to take responsibility and a manager is supposed to teach his men to do that." Well that's an assumption. It may be true, it may be false. Another one: "Those closer to the situation can make the best decisions." That's a general statement about human nature. The manager says, "I am held responsible, therefore I need to know what is going on in every detail." Another statement explicitly: "Most people can't be trusted." Another one: "They can't really make as good decisions as we can. We've been to college." The assumption of being to college makes better decision making.

And another statement. It's a different kind of thing but it applies to the general social psychological situation and, again, remember what I'm talking about is the application of knowledge of human motivation to these various situations: "In engineering"—this is McGregor again—"In engineering control consists in adjustment to natural law. It does not mean making nature do our bidding ordinarily. We do not for example dig channels in the expectation that water will flow uphill. We do use kerosene to put out a fire. In designing an internal combustion engine we recognize and adjust to the fact that gases expand when heated. We do not attempt to make them behave otherwise. Our control so to speak of nature is not really control in the strict sense. It's adaptation to nature more frequently. With respect to physical phenomena generally control involves the selection of means which are appropriate to the nature of the phenomena. However, in the human field the situation, though it's the same, yet we often dig channels to make water roll uphill. Many of our attempts to control behavior far from representing selective adaptations are in direct violation to human nature. They consist in trying to make people behave as we wish without concern for natural law. Yet we can no more expect to achieve desired results through inappropriate action in this field than in engineering."

For instance, to give you one example—this is an illustration both of good insight and of blindness—it's very obvious that when you are at the lower need level, to put it in our terms in our society, if you're pretty poor, if you have an income—I forget what the income is supposed to be that is poorness—supposing you have an income I think it is $3,000 a year. If you have less than $3,000 a year you are officially considered poor per family. That's not for an individual—family. At that level it's very easy to seduce people, to reward them, to reinforce them, to threaten them, to punish them. The man who has a job—I think for instance our common laborer on the campus gets about $2 an hour which is relatively high. Remember that the minimum wage is $1.25. You can get all the unskilled labor you want to in this country—about 5 percent of the population is unemployed. This is mostly unskilled labor. That's 80 bucks a week. Figuring 50 a year, that's about $4,000 a year—something like that. It's easy at that level to—well, many things happen. It's easier for such a man to be rewarded. That is, you can get him to be dishonest if you want by offering him $10, more easily than you can if his income is $20,000 a year. For the man who gets $10 or $15 or $20,000 a year you offer $10 to be dishonest, to something in some way, it's less likely to happen. That is, the $10 bill is less the motivation. That is, the more money you have, the more the lower need gratifications that you have gratified by money—money is most important for those lower need gratifications—the more gratified you are then, the less value the money has as a motivator. That's clear enough isn't it? That is, the man who is getting two bucks an hour, he's more likely to steal something than the man who is getting twenty bucks an hour, everything else being equal. Well, by the time you get to incomes of $10,000, $12,000, $15,000 or $20,000 where for instance professors are getting to be within the last five years or so—all these people who took the vow of poverty are suddenly getting pretty good salaries unexpectedly, very pleasantly—something happens, something is changed. The old motivators are gone. People are less willing to take on a job and go some place and work for a couple of days at $100 let's say, simply because at those higher need levels, the lower need satisfiers are less important, they're worth less. Well the way things are set up in the minds of these hard headed people are that still they think they can buy anything with money. That is they think that simply by raising a salary or by outbidding someone else in money that they can have the person they want, the personnel policy they want, they can get people to do any jobs they want them to and so on. In spite of the clear finding in this society, that is just not true. It just simply isn't so. As our average income goes up year by year, the society gets more affluent, the people get more affluent, especially the skilled people, you find that—well I would expect for instance—that they become more honest which is to say again that money is less the motivator than it was. Now if money which has been the immemorial motivator to get people to do unpleasant work, if this is no longer a motivator, as it's not when you get to the level of a $15,000 a year, an additional $1,000 isn't going to be of any great importance for you and you won't do anything unpleasant for it, if that's so then the problem arises of how do you? What kind of incentives are there? Let's say the way we are here at Brandeis University. There's a great shortage of psychologists in this country. There's a great shortage of a lot of other kinds of mathematicians for instance—scientists of any kind—physicists, biologists, a great shortage. There's a big oversupply of historians and English professors and so on and so on and it fluctuates from year to year. It's like a market thing. There's a shortage of cabbage in one season and there's a surplus of milk and so on, and to some extent these factors come up. The salaries for professors have gone up in the past five years to the point where you can no longer tempt a man away from another job which he already has by offering him a thousand or two thousand dollars a year more. It doesn't pay. He doesn't have to do it. He's not that desperate for money any more. So he's start figuring all sorts of intangibles: "well my friends are here" or "I have a good boss, I have a good chairman" or "I like my colleagues" or "there's a special lab which I spent so much time setting up I don't want to waste all that time" and so on and so on and so on; "Well, I won't take my kids out of school and interrupt their schooling for the sake of a lousy thousand bucks." What are the incentives at that level? What are the satisfactions? What can you offer to people, if we want psychologists and we are trying to seduce them away from some other place? What we offer them? What can we offer them? It's a question in motivation. In every situation of this sort you'll find some people who will insist that money is the thing and then when people turn them down one after another will not change their philosophy but will keep on thinking of all those people as crazy somehow. They are all crazy. They're just not normal. Now it's funny that in all the social psychological things we can do this, but as McGregor points out "engineers do not do it." We don't talk about "crazy kerosene" or "crazy steel beams." We simply adapt ourselves to their nature. We try to find out what they are like and then use their qualities and their capacities. In industry this is not yet done in many places. All sorts of incentive plans he's talking about here further on in this book, incentive plans are essentially adding more money and then people get astonished by these—bosses will get astonished by the fact that money doesn't seem to have the same pulling power that it used to. And what's happened to everybody.

The last point here that he says, "We can approve our ability to control only if we recognize that control consists in selective adaptation to human nature rather than in attempting to make human nature conform to our wishes. If our attempts to control are unsuccessful, the cause generally lies in our choice of inappropriate means. We will be unlikely to improve our interpersonal competence by blaming people for failing to behave according to our predictions." And remember that's again a problem for us, at your level, of let's say all the predictions that you're going to make about the nature of men and the nature of women, which will carry over into the marriage situation. Men should be treated in such and such a way and most people are apt to hang onto their Weltenschauung let's say, even when it doesn't work, and to say "well, I've got an abnormal man. Something's wrong with him somehow."

I've chosen McGregor because he made kind of the simplest statement and the sharpest, bluntest contrast between, at the extremes, the two philosophies—the unspoken implied philosophies of human motivation by which these two kinds of plants are run. You might say the more authoritarian or lower-need plant or the carrot-and-stick organization, or the lower need motivation kind of situation as over against, this he calls the Theory X, Theory X of human motivation and contrasts this with Theory Y motivation in which in a word implies that human beings have these higher needs which come into action when the lower needs are fulfilled and that incentives, gratifications, motivations and so on have to be focused around these higher needs, after the lower needs have been satisfied. Now here the assumption—this is from McGregor—is about this Theory X: "In this whole realm of industrial psychology, managerial theory and so on, these are the terms that are used very, very widely—Theory X management, Theory Y management. First of all, in Theory X, "Management is responsible for organizing the elements of productive enterprise in the interest of economic ends. That is, management is in control and is totally responsible. With respect to people, this is a process of directing their efforts, of motivating them, that is of giving them motives, controlling their actions, or modifying their behavior." Third, assumption and Theory X: "Without this active intervention by the management people would be passive and even resistant to organizational needs. They must therefore be persuaded, rewarded, punished, controlled, directed." Fourth, the assumption is "The average man is by nature indolent. He works as little as necessary." Five, "He lacks ambition. He dislikes responsibility. He prefers to be led." Six, "He is inherently self-centered, indifferent to organizational needs." Seven, "He is by nature resistant to change." Eight, "He is gullible, that is suggestible. He is not very bright. He is the ready dupe of the charlaton and the demagogue." Theory Y is in general the opposite assumptions plus the positive assumptions that people are motivated by the search for dignity, for self-respect, for appreciation and so on—all these at the esteem levels—for belongingness, groupiness, friendliness, friendship, a warm atmosphere and so on. That at the top they are motivated by various aspects of self-actualization, autonomy, identity, freedom to work out their own talents and capacities.

Memorandum on Salesmen
and Salesmanship

*This is on the grounds that any enterprise which wishes to
endure over a long period of time and to remain in a healthy
and growing state would certainly want a non-manipulative
trusting, relationship with its customers rather than the relationship of the quick fleecing, never to see them again.*

A.H. Maslow, *Maslow on Management*

One characterological difference that seemed to show up very
quickly was that the characteristic salesman was much more
a short-range person, wanting quick results, wanting a steady
and quick flow of rewards and reinforcements. This is a little like saying that he is a more "practical" person, and then it occurred to me
that this contrasts with the more "theoretical" kind of person. And
this contrast, in turn, may possibly be phraseable in terms of short
range in time and space versus long range in time and space. The
"practical" person in this sense has less ability to delay. He needs quick
success and quick wins. This should mean that he works within a
shorter time span, and I think this would be testable. That is, for him
the next few hours, the next few days, constitute the present, in contrast with the more theoretical person for whom the present may
spread over into several years hence.

Then, what I mean by short range or narrow range in space is
something like this: The characteristic salesman type gets his eyes
focused on a particular deal on Thursday afternoon in Philadelphia,
perhaps, with customer Jones and gets eager about consummating that

particular sale. He is less cognizant than a theoretical person would be of the reverberation effects, the echoes, of this one isolated transaction upon what might be happening a year from that time in Philadelphia, in the same place, or in the same space. He cares less about what the effect might be on other parts of the sales organization or of the engineering organization of his enterprise. That is, the practical type is less apt to think of the consequences, of the regularities, of the consistencies and inconsistencies, and of the cause/effect chain at a distance across the country. It's like the holistic way of thinking, not so much in chains of causes and effects, but rather in terms of concentric circles or rings of waves spreading out from center, or of a nest of boxes in the syndrome hierarchy. The more theoretical person is much more aware of all the far consequences both in time and space, of anything he does. The person we call more practical is probably less aware of these reverberating consequences in time and in space.

Perhaps another angle on this, also I think testable, is that the more practical type, the salesmen type, is also more concrete (rather than abstract). He tends to be preoccupied with what's before his nose, with what he can see and touch and feel and what is right here and right now, rather than that which is unseen and which is distant and delayed.

Partly, I suppose, in any society there will be such individual differences in practicality, in concreteness, in here-nowness, and it will be well to use these differences in character for different kinds of purposes. And yet I can't help feeling that the move toward more enlightened management would encourage less rather than more of this particular kind of salesmanship and of practicality and concreteness. That is, I expect the characterological differences would remain but would be diminished. I expect that these characterological differences also would be used, but that extreme practicality would be less usable and less needed. It involves too much cutting off from other people: it involves too much isolation of the person; it involves too much isolation of the particular interpersonal relationship of selling. After all, an enlightened society is more holistic than a nonenlightened society. As a matter of fact, these statements are almost synonyms. Atomistic can describe the nonenlightened society. It's more split up, more dissociated, less bound together, less tied together, less integrated.

There certainly is one useful theoretical point here for characterological descriptions. Our tendency certainly is to contrast in a dichotomous way the practical person and the theoretical person, in the sense that we expect the theoretical person to be not practical. That is, he is all theoretical, he is very high in theory and very low in practicality. But one lesson that we have learned from the study of healthy people is that the healthy person is apt to be *everything*. In this instance the healthy theoretical person would be both healthy and practical, depending upon the particular situation and the objective needs of that situation. Also, the healthy practical person or in this case, the healthy salesman type, would certainly be more practical in the above sense, but not exclusively so. He would also be able to be theoretical when the objective requirements of the situation called for it. These characterological differences would be differences simply in balance and in degree, rather than in all or none, present or absent.

This is all to say that even under enlightened conditions, a salesman type, a practical kind of person, would be needed. The salesman type ought not to be regarded, therefore, as unneeded or useless or pathological. All we have to do is, for enlightened purposes, modify and correct some of the overemphasis, the overdichotomized quality that we now find in what we consider to be the typical salesman, who characteristically is supposed not to give a damn about what happens the day after tomorrow or at a distance from the particular job he is involved in, nor to worry about the far consequences of what he does. This stereotype needs correcting, of course.

One thing that occurs to me, also as testable, is that this kind of here-and-now focus on the present sort of salesman type probably, therefore, is less affected by his past, and particularly by his past successes. For the average person a success of a year ago still is active in bolstering his self-esteem. Probably this is much less so for the here-and-now type of salesman. He needs a continual supply of successes. He's the one who might say in Hollywood, "You're only as good as your last picture." The salesman might say, "You're only as good as your last sale or your last account book" or something of the sort.

I think there *is* something in the picture of the ideal salesman type, whether under good social conditions or under bad social conditions, of the dominance and cockiness and manipulative quality and controlling quality that has been so much mentioned in the literature. A certain amount of self-esteem and self-confidence is a *sine qua non* for a salesman. In order to like the clash of battle, in order to regard a balky customer as a delightful challenge, one would have to have a stable and deep self-confidence and self-esteem, that is, to have the feeling that success is probable. This means on the negative side that the salesman type ought to have few inhibitions and self-doubts. Certainly he ought to have *very* little of the masochistic tendency, of the fear of winning, of the "tendency to be a loser." He mustn't want to bring about his own destruction; he mustn't want to bring about his own punishment; he must not feel guilty about winning; he must not feel exposed to punishment if he wins. This I think is all testable.

It is doubtful that the surface sociability of the salesman type, of the liking for company, of the immersion in groups of people, and so forth, represents any true liking for people. If the phrasing is correct that the salesman type sees himself as a kind of an elk or a moose running out to do battle with other elks, and enjoying the clash of battle but especially enjoying the success in battle, then certainly there must be a rather low impulse to help other people, to be parental, or especially maternal, to be the nursing type, or the doctor or psychotherapeutic type who gets a great kick out of curing other people or of relieving pain, or who gets a great kick out of watching the self-actualization of others. There should be a pretty narrow range of love-identifications, of the circle of brotherhood. There should also be rather less feeling of synergy in the salesman type than in other types of human beings. It all really adds up to a kind of jungle philosophy to some extent, even though the good salesman is apt to see this as a very pleasant jungle, all full of fun and nice battle and sure successes. It is all very pleasing, because he has great confidence in himself and in his ability to overcome the others in the jungle whom he tends to see as weak, not as good as he is, not as bright, not as strong (and perhaps therefore as a little contemptible, as people to be condescended to rather than loved or identified with).

It will be immediately useful in trying to figure out what is a "good" salesman today if we recognize that these are different kinds of people for Theory X and Theory Y. That is, the good Theory X salesman is different from the good Theory Y salesman. And certainly this is important in the selection of personnel and in the training of personnel if the enterprise which the salesman represents is Theory Y rather than Theory X type. A good Theory Y salesman today would certainly be more aware of his ties to his enterprise, more identified with it, more identified with all the people in it. I think he would have a self-image more as a kind of ambassador or representative of the whole enterprise than as a lone wolf, who simply pursues his own interests, or even as an intermediary between the enterprise and the customer. Certainly the elements of manipulation would be less in the Theory Y salesman. For various reasons this would be so, but probably the most important one would be that the best kind of Theory Y salesmanship comes much closer to complete honesty and candor than does Theory X type salesmanship. This is on the grounds that any enterprise which wishes to endure over a long period of time and to remain in a healthy and growing state would certainly want a nonmanipulative, trusting relationship with its customers rather than the relationship of the quick fleecing, never to see them again. This is one of the reasons why a longer range in time is required of a Theory Y salesman than of a Theory X salesman.

Another kind of change needed in the Theory Y salesman is that he would have to regard himself not only as an overcomer and winner and conqueror of the customer, but also as the sense organs of the enterprise for getting feedback from the customers. The Theory Y salesman not only sells, but tries to have good objective factual relationships with the customer, and the salesman in this context should be perceived as a highly valuable source of feedback of information which is absolutely necessary in order to keep on improving the product or to keep on correcting its shortcomings. This kind of conception of the customer and of the salesman requires a different conception of the relationship between them and also the relationship of the salesman to his enterprise. He is part of it, with at least two kinds of specialized functions which only he does, rather than any other members of the enterprise and which he cannot do very well if he regards the customer as a sheep to be fleeced.

I suppose the whole question of mutual good will is involved here. Certainly one can expect from any customer of any type that he will complain when the product is no good. But one can expect only from a customer with good will that he should actively try to pass on information to the salesman and the enterprise which is not a complaint but which is a positive suggestion about improving the product and of expanding the enterprise. What I think of here is the example of the customer going beyond the call of duty, that is actually of taking some trouble to help the salesman and the enterprise. For instance, the local radio station KITT is now announcing that it would like its hearers, if they have any loyalty to the station, to let their advertisers know what they like or dislike about KITT programs. They explain this will make it easier for the radio station to sell advertising time. Well, this is a request beyond the call of duty and would require a very positive feeling for the radio station. This is the kind of example I mean which would be absent from any jungle relationship between the salesman and the customer.

All of this thinking about the long-range and short-range types reminds me that general organismic theory can be used more than it has been in managerial policy. I consider that one of the strongest long-time supports, empirical and theoretical supports, for enlightened management policy is that it is more likely to guarantee maintenance and positive growth in the company if one thinks over a really long-time span of perhaps a century. There are many qualities of enlightened management which become very, very clear and are very easy to understand if one asks the manager, "Do you want this company to grow even after you're dead?" Any man, for instance, who wanted to pass on his privately owned business to his son or to his grandson would certainly function differently from the way he would act if he didn't give a damn about what happened to the whole business when he died or retired. One of the most obvious consequences of a really long-range attitude is the demand it makes for a completely different relationship to the customer. Honesty, candor, good will, nonconcealment, a synergic relationship—all become imperative in such a long-run case.

Something similar is true of a real application of organismic theory, especially in its holistic aspects. That is, if one recognizes the fact that one's enterprise is really related to the community, to the state, to the nation, and to the world, that this is more so under good conditions, then there would be really easily understood consequences of such an attitude. Such an enterprise would behave differently from an enterprise which regarded itself as totally independent and autonomous and beholden to nobody else and really not connected with anybody else, or even *against* everybody else, an enterprise, for instance, involved in swindling some customer who simply passes by on the sidewalk as in a tourist trap or which caters to a transient who will never come by again. Swindling such people is easier for the concrete or short-run kind of person. The fact remains that if one wants a healthy enterprise in the long run and with healthy connections to the whole society, then one cannot be this kind of swindler and let the morrow take care of itself. Again here the example might be the treatment of the Orientals in California from the beginning of the century on, which as can easily be demonstrated, had *some* influence in bringing about Pearl Harbor on the one hand and on the other hand the present Chinese hatred for the United States which may yet help to bring on a war.

All of this discussion about Theory X salesmen and Theory Y salesmen can be compared with the new synergic conception of the law, which it is possible to contrast with the present conception of the law as a kind of duel or trial by combat, or clash between a defense attorney and a prosecuting attorney, in which each one is supposed not to think of justice or truth or anything of the sort, but simply of trying to win under the rules that are available. In a more synergic society, certainly, there would be defendants and prosecutors and so on, but I'm sure it would be far more suitable, far more congruent with such a society that the prosecuting attorney and the defense attorney not only have the obligation to put their client's best foot forward or to make the best case possible, but that this would be embedded in the *larger* duty which they all would have of justice and truth for everybody concerned.

So also, even under enlightened conditions, we are going to want good salesmen (or perhaps we'll call them marketers rather than salesmen to stress the different attitudes and the additional functions). In any case the good marketer will certainly want to put his best foot forward and to stress all the good aspects of his product and not necessarily be totally neutral about it. And let it be stressed that to do this would serve a real function in the society. In any society, by the way, whether socialist or capitalist or anything else, there ought to be someone to point up the best aspects, the great desirability of the particular product. (This is possible in a socialist or a communist society as well as a capitalist for the simple reason that if they ever get really intelligent about it, they are going to decentralize their industries and give a great deal of local autonomy to a particular factory management, and also they are going to retain all of the advantages of competition by having not just one centralized industry turning out bicycles but four or six relatively autonomous factories each of them turning out bicycles, thereby getting the best of both the socialist and capitalist world.)

Theory Y salesmanship would obviously foster less graft and dishonesty in the business world than Theory X management would. This would be not only for moral and ethical reasons (which certainly increase in motivating value as individuals and organizations get healthier), but also in simple pragmatic terms like what was mentioned above in the Theory Y relationship with the salesman to the customer. The building of good will, of trust, of integrity, all have very pragmatic business consequences which are very desirable in relation to customers. I know for myself that if some salesman offers me a crooked deal, I have learned to have nothing to do with him or the enterprise; I simply get away from that situation and have nothing to do with it. It never pays to deal with crooks, especially in the long run and especially if one keeps in mind psychological rewards and punishments as well as financial ones. From this point of view it doesn't pay to swindle on one's income tax or to steal. Taking into account guilt feelings, shame feelings, embarrassment feelings, and inner conflict and the like, this is factually pragmatically true as well as being abstract, ethically desirable—that is to say, it's a practical, hard-headed kind of a statement as well as a soft-headed or tender-minded kind of a statement.

This brings to mind that one consequence of Theory Y salesmanship will be actually to lose some customers, but these will be the bad customers, who I think had better be lost if the enterprise can possibly afford this. These are the customers who would not be loyal anyhow; they would be the ones who would keep on trying to swindle and to lie and to cheat, and so forth. Unless the company badly needs sales at a particular moment, it is really wise, over the course of a century, to have nothing to do with such customers for the sake of momentary profits because in the long run they will be trying to swindle. On the other hand, Theory Y honesty in salesmanship is going to be a positive attraction to the people that we may call *good* customers, the ones who would be loyal, who would stick, who could be trusted, and so forth. Talk here about the theory of the semipermeable membrane which lets the good ones through and keeps the bad ones out.

All of these considerations bring up the question of selection: selection of salesmen by management, selection of customers and salesmen by each other. It raises the question of who is the best selector of men, who would be the best personnel officer to hire and to fire. In general we can say that the healthier people are better selectors because they will select more objectively, that is, in terms of the objective requirements, of the objective situations, in contrast with neurotics who are more apt to pick in terms of a satisfaction of their own neurotic needs. Another way of saying this is that the healthier people are the larger, more widespreading. That is, they can see farther and more objectively in time and space than can less healthy people. This amounts to saying that they are more realistic. This in turn amounts to saying they are more pragmatic, that is to say, more successful, hard-headedly successful, if one takes into account the long range in time and space.

Notes on the Entrepreneur

The main point that I could make in communication in this area would be to point out the difference between the great and the good societies and the regressing, deteriorating societies is largely in terms of the entrepreneurial opportunity and the number of such people in society.

A.H. Maslow, *Maslow on Management*

The entrepreneurial function is too much underplayed and undervalued. The entrepreneurs—the managers, integrators, organizers, and planners—themselves undervalue the worth of their own function and are still apt to think of themselves in the older terms as exploiters, as superficial, as not really working, not really contributing. Therefore, as a group they are apt to feel a little guilty about their rewards.

Partly, I think, this is tied in with the notion of work as *only* sweating and laboring, and partly it is a consequence of misunderstanding of the nature of inventions.

As for inventions, our tendency is to think that they result from a great flash of insight in which in one instant darkness becomes light and ignorance becomes knowledge. This is the notion of the brand-new discovery which never existed before, and it is obviously wrong in most cases, since any invention, however novel, has its history. It should be seen anyway as the product of collaboration and division of labor; that is, invention may result from a sudden integration of previously known bits of knowledge not yet suitably patterned. The flash of discovery is most frequently the closure of a Gestalt rather than the creation of something out of nothing.

If this is so, then the distinction between the invention and the administrative arrangement fails. The administrative arrangement or the managerial invention, for example, the use of interchangeable standard parts at Winchester Arms Company or on Henry Ford's assembly line, and so forth, are also the putting into collocation of pieces of knowledge which were lying there available for anyone but which suddenly become potent and important in this new constellation or pattern.

We might, if we wished, differentiate social inventions from technological inventions, but it does not really matter in principle very much. Discovering a way in which the husband and wife could communicate with each other better is an invention in this sense.

I should say also that the entrepreneurial plan or vision, the recognition of a need which is being unfulfilled and which could be fulfilled to the profit of the entrepreneur and to everyone else's benefit as well, had also better come under the general head of invention.

The main point that I could make in communication in this area would be to point out that the difference between the great and good societies and the regressing, deteriorating societies is largely in terms of the entrepreneurial opportunity and the number of such people in the society. I think everyone would agree that the most valuable 100 people to bring into a deteriorating society like, for instance, Peru, would be not 100 chemists, or politicians, or professors, or engineers, but rather 100 entrepreneurs.

Phrased in this style, the guilt of the self-devaluating entrepreneur can be allayed. He can then see how important he is, even how crucial.

My own opinion is that this need not get tangled up with the question of monetary rewards exclusively. There are other kinds of rewards. It is true that an entrepreneur may be worth huge sums of money to a society, but it is also true that great disparities of income may breed their own problems. If only for theoretical purposes, it is well to recognize that the entrepreneur, the organizer, the spark plug, the active leader upon whom everything depends, can be rewarded in other ways than by money. In the synergic society, like that of the Blackfoot Indians, the leader, or organizer was paid off in public honors of various sorts, in the respect and the regard of everybody in the tribe, in his being welcomed wherever he went, and so forth. The point is that this worked in spite of the fact that this great leader frequently was penniless. That is part of the picture of the great leader—his total generosity. His wealth there was defined in terms of how much he could afford to earn and give away. So also, in England knighthood is considered a great reward. I think we might one day go so far as to single out the great entrepreneur or inventor or leader and honor him by giving him absolute simplicity as in the Catholic church. Conferring a robe of gray monk's cloth perhaps would have the same meaning and the same psychological rewarding power as great sums of money, perhaps even more, depending upon the way in which the society looked at it. If such a man were greatly admired, respected, appreciated, approved, applauded, welcomed, then he would need no money.

It would help keep the point clean and uncontaminated if I were to point out that it holds in principle for any society and for any economic system, whether capitalist, socialist, communist, or fascist. The initiator, spark–plug, coordinator type of person is equally necessary, equally valuable in each of these societies (even though this will conflict with the desire to stagnate and not change, which may exist simultaneously). It is true that other determinants are also involved, for example, is the society synergic or not, exploitative or not, caste-stratified or not, and so forth.

McClelland's work is very important in this connection.[1]

---

[1] D. McClelland, *The Achieving Society* (Princeton, NJ: D. Van Nostrand Co., Inc., 1961).

By-Products of
Enlightened Management

*The man (or woman) who truly is influenced by enlightened
management should become a better husband (or wife) and a
better father (or mother), as well as a better citizen in general.*

A.H. Maslow, *Maslow on Management*

There are plenty of data to indicate that a mother who truly and deeply loves her child can behave in practically any way toward that child, beating it or slapping it or whatever, and yet the child will turn out well. It is as if the basic attitude of love is important and not so much the particular behavior. There are all sorts of data to make this point quite clearly in this relationship at least. Behavior is not a very good index of character or of underlying personality or of attitudes. Anybody who puts on behavior like a cloak, as an actor would, finds that this doesn't work very well. People somehow are able to detect at some conscious or unconscious level that a person is acting and not really feeling deeply the attitude which he is trying to convey through his behavior. So in the same way we have the possible complication that the supervisor who takes all sorts of courses and reads all sorts of books and is trained in various ways and who agrees with the data and who honestly tries to behave like a superior supervisor, may not be able to get the same results if he does not deeply feel democratic, parental, affectionate, and so forth.

This brings up the profound existential question of the difference between *being* something, and *trying to be* something. We are involved here in the paradox that there must be a transition between being something bad and being something good. If a thief becomes conscious of the fact that he is a thief and wants to become an honest man instead, there is no way in which he can do this except by consciously trying not to be a thief and consciously trying to be an honest man. Trying to be an honest man is self-conscious, artificial, not spontaneous, not natural, and may look phony. This is very different from spontaneous honesty which is an expression of deep-lying character attitudes. And yet what else is possible? There is no other way to jump from being a crook to being an honest man except by trying.

This is just as true for the organizational situation. There is no way for an authoritarian supervisor to become a democratic supervisor except by passing through the transitional stage of consciously, artificially, voluntarily *trying* to be a democratic supervisor. This man who is trying to be a democratic supervisor is obviously quite different from the person who is spontaneously a democratic supervisor. We get involved in all sorts of philosophical arguments here which we had better be careful about. It is so easy to despise the "trying" state just because it is not absolutely spontaneous, and therefore it may be rejected, with the person doing the rejecting failing to realize that there is no other possibility than this as a pre-stage to becoming spontaneously and deeply what one is trying to become.

Another way of expressing the above is to say it so: We must try to make a particular kind of people, of personality, of character, of soul one might say, rather than try to create directly particular kinds of behavior. If we talk about creating a particular kind of personality, we at once move over into the explicitly psychological realm of the theory of growth, of personality theory, of the theory of psychotherapy, and take upon ourselves the huge mass of Freudian theory as well, because then we must talk about the unconscious and of various determinants of behavior which are not consciously known to the person. These unconscious determinants of behavior cannot be influenced directly, in general; we must overhaul the personality, create in effect a different kind of human being. (For such a reason as this the term "behavioral science" is not suitable to describe this realm of science.)

This emphasis on the person, and the consequent emphasis on behavior as a by-product of deep-lying personality, is one of the reasons that leads me to feel that the validation of enlightened management and enlightened supervision must come not alone from the behavior in the factory, not alone from the quality and the quantity of the product, but rather must be a test of these aforementioned by-products. Thus I would think that one quite practical test would be what the workers in an enlightened enterprise do when they go back home to their communities. For instance, I would expect that if the management policy were truly growth fostering and truly better-personality producing, that these individuals would, for instance, become more philanthropic in their communities, more ready to help, more unselfish and altruistic, more indignant at injustice, more ready to fight for what they thought to be true and good, and so forth. This can easily enough be measured, at least in principle.

Also, it should be possible to gather data on the change of behavior in the home itself. The man who truly is influenced by enlightened management should become a better husband and a better father, as well as a better citizen in general. Therefore, interviews not only with him but also with his wife and with his children would be a direct technique of validation. I am reminded here of Dick Jones's study[1] in which he tried psychotherapeutic teaching in a high school for a year and then tested for validity of his enterprise by checking the decrease in race prejudice in the girls he had been teaching. He found that there was a decrease in race prejudice, even though he had not even mentioned this topic through the entire year. This is what I mean by measuring the by-product rather than the behavior itself directly. After all it is too easy for passive people or for shrewd people to mimic any behavior or to put on any act which might be necessary for them to keep their job or to get ahead in any particular situation. They might *act* the way management wants them to, but their souls might be totally unchanged.

---

[1] R. Jones, *An Application of Psychoanalysis to Education* (Springfield, IL: Charles C. Thomas, 1960).

Leaders, Pawns, and Power

The following letter to philosopher-editor Henry Geiger offers Maslow's viewpoint on the psychological traits of leadership. Maslow believed that the psychological components of power, power-seekers, authenticity and leadership should be explored in order to help people develop their leadership skills.

Dear Henry:

Last night, I was suffering again from insomnia. I was struggling with all my seemingly contradictory conclusions about self, identity, and intrapsychic concerns on the one hand and social, organizational, and political matters on the other hand. It is rather clear to me now that for individualist psychology, "time wounds all heels" and that virtue pays more often than not. I think that I could prove this hypothesis to be true by using not only clinical material but also orthodox research data as well.

Essentially, I have concluded that over the course of a lifetime— in the proverbial long run—the probability is approximately five to one that evil will be punished. That virtue also will be rewarded seems to have a probability of only about six to five, but it is nevertheless greater than mere chance.

Yet, the real key issue is that punishment and reward are largely intrapsychic, that is, relating to one's sense of happiness, peacefulness, and serenity and to the absence of negative emotions like regret, remorse, or guilt. So as far as external rewards are concerned, these are apt to come in terms of basic-need gratification for belongingness, feeling loved and respected, and generally inhabiting a more platonic world of

Source: A.H. Maslow letter to Henry Geiger (December 1966), reprinted with the permission of Ann R. Kaplan and the *Archives of the History of American Psychology.*

pure beauty, truth, and virtue. That is, our rewards in life are *not* necessarily apt to be in terms of money, power, or social status of the ordinary sort. Thus, we need to more precisely define what we mean by such words as "reward" and "punishment."

In order to sustain a relatively good society, or relatively adequate level of affluence, it definitely seems important that most persons believe in a just outcome regarding reward and punishment for individual behavior. But even for our present society at this time, I believe I could prove my point that evil people are punished in the intrapsychic ways I have suggested above and that good persons get rewarded (although with a much lower probability) in the same ways.

UNDERSTANDING POWER-SEEKERS

Now what has been troubling me as I have been doing exploratory research—that is, "poking" around and thinking continuously—is the matter of power. I am referring specifically to strong and tough persons, those who are power-seekers and power-wielders. These people can be either good or evil, but it is my impression that the very attainment of power tends to tip most individuals over toward becoming evil rather than good. This situation poses a great mystery, and I have no idea why it is so, beyond offering a few unverified guesses. It is certainly true that, in some instances, greater status or power actually ennobles people and makes them live up to their new role or opportunity. The classic example is Harry Truman, who as president of the United States accomplished much more than anyone had expected.

In any case, it definitely seems that power-seekers—who are somewhat more apt to become evil than good—show a tendency to advance upward in the social order and actually attain power. In this context, I remember an old novel titled *The Blood of the Conquerors,* written by Harvey Fergusson (1921/1971). The story recounts how a Mexican American in a small new Mexican town is pitted politically against a hard-bitten "Yankee." The Yankee is an obsessional and relentless power-seeker, subordinating everything in life to its attainment.

Therefore, he finally triumphs over the Mexican, who occasionally stops from the political battle to "smell the daisies" and enjoy the sunshine.

This dichotomy seems to differentiate the truly powerful American figures like John F. Kennedy and Lyndon B. Johnson from those like Adlai Stevenson, who really did not seem to possess the same drive—or personal need—for taking over the reins of government. From the gossip we hear about Stevenson, he insisted on enjoying a good life personally. And of course, to do so takes time and energy away from the relentless pursuit of political power.

Therefore, personages like Stevenson, or even Abraham Lincoln and Thomas Jefferson, are at a disadvantage in the long run in their relationship to those who are ruled by an indomitable drive for power. When these more "benign" figures do achieve power, it is generally because they have been chosen by others and accepted the responsibilities or because they have walked into the power struggle and consciously played the game by its conventional, "no-holds-barred" rules.

Parenthetically, it is precisely this issue that has reconciled me to the necessity for individual mortality. That is, suppose we doubled our present life span. Then, most likely, more of these power-seekers would remain in control of the world for much longer periods of time. For example, Abram Sachar—our president at Brandeis University—is a power-needer and power-seeker. Because of his advancing chronological age, he probably has only another 4, 5, or 10 years to live, and this is a good thing. Like Napoleon, Lyndon B. Johnson, and similar power-persons, Sachar at one point was absolutely necessary—that is, for the original task of building this private university. It was a one-man job, and Sachar performed it beautifully and efficiently. It is quite clear that such a miracle could not have taken place without such a power-wielder at the helm.

But now that the building phase has been completed, what the university requires is a governor—or let's rather say, an "older brother," or a first among equals. We no longer need a dominating, authoritarian boss with all the power in his own hands. Undoubtedly, our next president at Brandeis University will be a milder, more brotherly, and more affectionate man than Sachar. But suppose people like him lived to be 150 years old? What would happen to this educational institution and other social institutions? If it weren't for human mortality, these people would literally control the world.

THE WEAK SELF

Another matter recently became clear to me while I was doing managerial consulting in California: Most people lack a strong sense of self. They do not know what they want or what they are looking for in life. As a result, they are extremely suggestible and will follow a self-confident leader rather than determine their own destinies.

Now, one key aspect about leadership is that effective leaders are unequivocally decisive. They do not exhibit uncertainty, ambivalence, inner conflict, or ambiguity. In essence, they hide their uncertainties and keep them securely contained. The ocean liner captain cannot afford to be a vacillating Hamlet but must always appear strong.

Well, if we accept as a statistical fact that the average American citizen will do whatever the salesperson suggests or will follow a strong leader rather than a thoughtful, complicated one, then another element enters in the subject of leadership: decisiveness. What do I mean? Namely, that there is no more decisive-looking person in the world than a paranoid character. Also, there is no power-seeker more stubborn and persistent than the one who is paranoid. Such persons never relent for a moment. They never stop to laugh, joke, or enjoy the flowers but just press on persistently.

Now for me, this reality offers a solution—or at least a partial solution—to the terribly depressing historical fact that frequently the political leaders who have led the modern world into disaster have been paranoid characters: Hitler, Stalin, and probably Mao Tse-tung as well. In the United States, Senator Joseph McCarthy and Robert Welch (head of the ultraconservative John Birch Society) also have shown this trait. If we examine the annals of political leadership, we often learn that such personages have been paranoid, but unfortunately, we acquire such knowledge only after the damage has already been done. But then the horrifying question arises: Why do such emotionally disturbed people so frequently find it easy to win loyal followers who are thereon led to destruction?

I remember wondering particularly about the right-wing John Birch Society in southern California and came to the same conclusion as Dostoyevsky, Erich Fromm, and other thinkers that many people are afraid of freedom and would prefer to have their decisions made for them.

Long ago, my wife, Bertha, was working as a salesperson in a New York City department store. She was shocked to discover that most of the customers had no idea what they wanted to buy and were requesting almost pathetically to be told. This situation occurred in the gift department, where personal aesthetic taste was important. But in a dismaying percentage of people, this aesthetic sense was utterly lacking. Bertha concluded that it would be possible to sell *anything* at all simply by making a sales pitch. Of course, she never attempted to do so and finally quit the job out of horror for the whole business. But the other salespersons did, as a matter of course, "push" whatever product they needed to dispose of and were generally quite successful at it.

If this phenomenon exists, then it becomes understandable that most people are seeking leaders. And if they are seeking leaders who must appear strong, self-confident, and unshakable, then we can better comprehend why they should flock after paranoid or selfish power-seekers or those who just *have* to control everybody and everything. We also can understand why more thoughtful, rational people—who can see both sides of an issue—would not appeal very much to those seeking absolute decisiveness. Finally, because selfish, narcissistic, and power-driven people find it easier to use others as mere tools for self-advancement, it makes sense why they disproportionally gain power.

In short, I have been developing some explanations for bridging the gap regarding the matter of virtue's rewards in the intrapsychic world and the choices of vicious people in the social, public, and interpersonal world.

AFTER SELF-ACTUALIZATION, WHAT?

In the intrapsychic realm, the first great task is to search for one's identity. Each person must find his or her true, active self, and after that task is accomplished, then life's real problems lie ahead. Clearly, this task is related to finding one's vocation, or calling, or biological destiny. That is, what is the mission that one chooses to love and sacrifice to?

It is as if we had two kinds of intrapsychic psychologies: one involving our daily struggle toward self-actualization and the other involving a completely different psychology or set of rules for living the clean, pure existence of the mystic or sage.

These rules are quite different in various, surprising ways. For instance, there are conventional, classic sorts of research design emphasizing statistics. My graduate students are apt to regard me as inconsistent or even hypocritical when I stress that they must acquire such tools. But now, I have learned to explain that what I am against is the obsessional use of so-called objective tests and statistics *instead* of being guided by one's inner intuitions. I can say that the person who has acquired a sense of self, direction, and vocation can use all of these tools simply as tools. The tools serve rather than boss their user.

For instance, one of my most talented graduate students is completing her dissertation on *peak-experiences* during natural childbirth. She has made many wonderful discoveries but first had to learn data entry, statistical analysis, and the like. It was all for a very good cause. The IBM computer has definitely been her servant and not her boss. In no sense does it rule her. She is now a good person but with stronger muscles.

That is the key point: First you must be a good person and have a strong sense of selfhood and identity. Then immediately, all the forces in the world become tools for one's own purposes. At once, they cease to be forces that cause, determine, and shape but become instruments for the self to use as it wishes. The same principle is true for money. In the hands of a strong and good person, money is a great blessing. But in the hands of weak or immature persons, money is a terrible danger and can destroy them and everyone around them. The identical principle is true for power, both over things and over other people.

In the hands of a mature, healthy human being—one who has achieved full humanness—power, like money or any other instrument, is a great blessing. But in the hands of the immature, vicious, or emotionally sick, power is a horrible danger.

Essentially, if you know who you are, where you are going, and what you want, then it is not hard to deal with inane bureaucratic details, trivialities, and constraints. You can simply disarm them and make them disappear by a simple shrug of your shoulders. I know that I am apt to become impatient with young people today who attribute so much power to social pressures and forces. I point out that all we need to do is pay these influences no attention, and then they vanish. Think of all the millions of dollars spent on television advertising. Such seemingly vast power becomes utterly insignificant before one who purchases products by reading consumer magazines and thereby makes intelligent judgments. The powers of evil in the American establishment suddenly disappear. For such a person, they just cease to exist.

Of course, the whole question of free will and determinism is to some extent resolved by such considerations. To use your own phrase, persons who have achieved their identity are *causers* rather than *caused.* I think it is better to frame this discussion with such words rather than *free will,* which has so many historical accretions that matters get muddled. We might say that such persons are "boss over their determinants" or that they can pick and choose their determinants, selecting those which they like and rejecting those that they dislike.

In a Spinoza-istic sense, such men and women can embrace the determinants of which they approve. Lovingly, they can let themselves be swept away by these forces akin to the manner in which a surfer rides a good wave, which is a very Taoistic activity. Certainly, the surfer does not change the wave in any way. One neither masters, controls, nor fears the wave but makes a nice, harmonious adjustment to it and, therefore, can enjoy and become a part of it.

BECOMING AUTHENTIC

I have been accustomed to say that authentic persons are those who have discovered and accepted their own, biological, temperamental, and constitutional cues, the signals from within. In a sense, this description relates to intuition as well. If you achieve this ability to hear your own impulse voices, then you have attained an inner "supreme court" from which come virtually infallible suggestions and even commands. Such people know what is good and what is bad for them and what they like and dislike.

I remember in one of your lead articles in *MANAS,*[1] you spoke about Ralph Waldo Emerson and how he trusted in his own judgments and intuitions. The verdict of history is that Emerson's judgments and intuitions were very sound and that he, therefore, was right in trusting them. But then you ended your article with a question: "How does one get to become an Emerson?"

This question could be phrased more broadly: "How does one become an identity, a sure person, one who has authentic inner voices and who hears them and has courage to act on them?" Of course, once such persons exist, then they can love themselves and do as they will.

I remember how long ago when I was teaching five psychology courses at Brooklyn College, I was so terribly busy. I was the only clinically oriented professor in the whole place, so I had to invent all

---

[1] This was the name of the late Henry Geiger's avant-garde periodical.

sorts of tricks for providing counseling in just 2 minutes. One trick that I devised when confronted by mothers worried about their children's development was to make a quick judgment: Was the mother emotionally stable, sound, and self-respecting? If apparently so, then I counseled her as follows: "Throw away all your parenting books. Do not listen to your pediatrician. Do not ask any psychologists for advice. Just follow your own intuitions. I guarantee that they will work well on the whole, and in any case, they will work better than any advice you might receive from other people."

But if, in my judgment, the mother was emotionally unstable, neurotic, immature, or deeply confused, then I would give her a list of psychology books to read and would recommend psychotherapy for herself or her child.

Obviously, I was not being inconsistent in my method of counseling. Some people have good intuitions because they have achieved a self. Others have lousy intuitions because they have not attained a self and, therefore, cannot distinguish between the inner voices of authenticity from those of neurosis. Remember the old problem for Christians, and probably other religious believers as well, if a mystic proclaimed he or she had heard the voice of God? It could be quite reasonably asked of such people, "How can you tell whether this is the voice of God or of the devil?" This is indeed a legitimate question.

All right, then, you can say that in a certain sense, the human species is composed of perhaps one percent to three percent of people who have achieved personhood and that the vast majority have not done so and, therefore, must seek for leaders, salespersons, or priests—in a word, anyone who will tell them what to do, what to think, and so on.

EVERYONE A LEADER?

Cross-cultural evidence helps us to clarify the whole issue of leadership. It is possible for the person who is a real self, with real self-trust and self-knowledge, to know that his brother Joe is better at leading the hunting party than he is. Among the Plains Indians with whom I have studied and lived, the leader of a group was always the one who could do best at that particular task involved. They had no such thing as a general, across-the-board leader for *everything*. For this reason, the one who was a good hunter and would become the hunting party leader would quite willingly, and without resentment, subordinate himself in the war party to the one who excelled in that particular activity. Among the Blackfoot tribe, whom I knew best, leadership was determined with good will and in a *synergistic* way: Tribal members accurately knew which individual was best suited for a certain task, and there was no enmity or bitterness about assuming such responsibilities.

As the anthropologist Ruth Benedict has intimated, it seems possible—and important—that we conceptualize, create, and invent social institutions that will either foster or hinder the development of individual self-actualization. The operating principles or "laws" for making a good world are different, to an extent, than for making a good person. At least to the degree that I suggested in the beginning of this long letter to you, intrapsychic rewards and punishments are different from external ones. We must, therefore, have a social psychology along with an individual psychology. Ultimately, both must deal meaningfully with human needs and goods.

This letter has turned out to be an article of sorts, partly because I know we think along the same lines about the topic of leaders, pawns, and power. I have been dictating my comments and will get them transcribed and sent to you. It certainly would be nice if we lived closer to each other, but you are living in Southern California and I am here in the Boston area. Even if by machine, I enjoy talking to you. Moreover, not only do I enjoy it but I also find it useful.

Letter from Chris Argyris

YALE UNIVERSITY
DEPARTMENT OF INDUSTRIAL ADMINISTRATION

NEW HAVEN, CONNECTICUT

103 SHEFFIELD HALL

January 17, 1963

Dr. Abraham H. Maslow
Department of Psychology
Brandeis University
Waltham, Massachusetts

Dear Dr. Maslow:

This morning I had to take a 5:45 A.M. train to New York City. I planned to page through your monograph and then get some sleep. My hope was to then read it when I was more awake. But, it woke me up and before I knew it, I was in New York City. I thoroughly enjoyed it. It is full of ideas and insights. I have no less than 15 references of "points to discuss someday when I meet you." I hope that day will not be too far off.

I am glad to hear of your positive impressions about T groups. Recently, I wrote a book which discusses my views of T groups. It is called <u>Interpersonal Competence and Organizational Effectiveness.</u> If you are interested, and do not have a copy, I should be delighted to send you a copy with my compliments and sincere hopes for any comments. Among other things, I have attempted to relate the value of rationality upon human competence and organizational effectiveness.

You also imply that my concept of leadership is a "be nice" concept. Then you continue to describe how you would view effective leadership and I feel it reads excellently. I thought I said somewhat the same kind of thing when I talked about "reality-centered" leadership. In this connection, I have taken the liberty to send you a somewhat outdated reprint that discusses some of my views of organizational leadership.

In the article, I also discuss briefly my view of organizational health, (which is now expanded in a book form).

By the way, I am not sure that I would agree with your example of the captain who should not share the problems the boat may have had, or is having, if asked. It seems to me that a leader should withhold information when (for personal or organizational reasons) he does not trust himself and/or the other. If, as a passenger you would panic, then he should not tell you. Another possibility, however, is to help you to overcome your panic. Otherwise, is not your anxiety controlling the Captain?

Well, we must get together. I find your work so stimulating and I feel that I have, and continue to learn so much from you.

Sincerely,

Chris Argyris, Professor

CA:AG

Source: Chris Argyris letter to A.H. Maslow, reprinted with the permission of Ann R. Kaplan and the *Archives of the History of American Psychology.*

Communication:
Key to Effective Management

*Maslow spent the last years of his life as a management con-
sultant and scholar in residence for a California corporation
called Saga Foods, Inc. The following speech was given to
Saga senior executives during a retreat for managers.*

The whole series of recent Saga newspapers forces into my consciousness a new subheading under the *eupsychia* and revolution categories, namely, bigness–smallness. One of the clear
issues for the normative social psychologist—and one that I would
now add to my article on utopia—is the necessity for integrating the
advantages of bigness with those of smallness and for avoiding the disadvantages of bigness and those of smallness. This task can definitely
be accomplished—or at least is being attempted—with a fair amount
of success, especially in the business world. We have much to learn
from this important effort now underway. Perhaps I could take as the
simplest model the means by which this issue is being played out in
colleges and universities today.

First, there is the phenomenon exemplified by the University of
California at Berkeley. This is a huge, monstrous, highly centralized,
bureaucratic giant in which feedback and customer satisfaction have
been nearly entirely lost. Communication occurs only downward—
from a handful of top administrators to thousands of students and faculty—and never effectively upward. Such a huge, impersonal, and

Source: A.H. Maslow speech to the executives of Saga Foods, Inc. (June 1969),
reprinted with the permission of Ann R. Kaplan and the *Archives of the History of
American Psychology.*

bureaucratic organization almost inevitably engenders feelings of help-lessness, of not being heard, of having no control over one's fate, and of being a pawn rather than an agent. The same situation was true at Co-lumbia University, where a major student rebellion occurred. Perhaps it was even worse there as its president, trustees, administrators in gen-eral, and faculty lacked the slightest idea of what was occurring among its customers—that is, its student population.

On the national political level, we can take the governments of France and the Soviet Union as examples of bureaucratic monstrosity. In both countries, there has been a nearly total centralization of power, with all sorts of consequent inefficiencies and stupidities leading to feelings of helplessness and rage among its citizens. Here again, the missing element has been the presence of meaningful communication upward—that is, feedback from customers. There has been almost no attention paid to customer satisfaction or wishes.

It is interesting to me that in both countries, the dominant system has broken down completely after *never* working well. What is now being instituted in replacement is almost inevitably a system of greater communication upward, more local control, and more decentraliza-tion and meaningful planning only after receiving feedback from cus-tomers. I think this whole approach can be summarized aptly by one phrase: *individual self-choice.*

An important issue for managers is to retain the advantage of smallness so that the individual is given a choice among alternatives and then is encouraged to express his or her preference by the act of purchasing, registering in a particular course or college, or "voting" with one's feet by migrating to another place, and the like. I hadn't re-alized it fully before, but the whole of the democratic managerial ap-proach—whether we call it *Theory Y management* or *enlightened management*—can be seen from the viewpoint of essentially partici-patory, localized, decentralized democracy, with consequently excel-lent customer feedback and with control being exerted at the individual, personal, and grassroots level.

The present issue of the Saga newspaper has an interesting article on the use of surveys in management. It provides me with an excel-lent example from which I can leap into conceptual generalizations about management, politics, democracy, and societal improvement. That is, the key aspect of Saga's own corporate history is that from the very beginning—when initiating food service at Hobart College back in 1948—Saga circulated surveys among students to obtain their re-actions. This informal method of work-of-mouth, face-to-face evaluation has continued, but it also has been expanded to a larger, more conscious, efficient, and computerized system.

However, it is vital to emphasize that, at bottom, this approach is a matter of *attitude*. An authoritarian person or organization does not ask, listen, or solicit honest feedback. Rather, it tells, orders, or makes pronouncements, without obtaining feedback, evaluation, or assessing customer satisfaction or gaining any real knowledge of how the system is actually working. In contrast, the democratic attitude, which arises from a person's character structure and from societal arrangements, involves a profound respect for other people. I might even describe this attitude as one of compassion, agapean love, or openness to others: a willingness—even an eagerness—to listen. The final consequences of this attitude necessitate a presenting to others of opportunities for true self-choice among real alternatives.

So, if you like human beings; if you like to see them grow; if you think they have a higher nature that can be cultivated; if you experience real satisfaction from the growth, happiness, and self-actualization of other people; if you enjoy their pleasure; if you feel brotherly or sisterly toward them and share their realm of discourse, then you will almost inevitably create certain kinds of social organizations or systems. In contrast, authoritarian "bosses" reject any sense of kinship with the "bossed," with pawns, and with their supposed inferiors.

Another element in the vocabulary for this democratic attitude is *Taoistic respect*. It again arises not from shaping, manipulating, bossing, or controlling other persons but, rather, from respecting them enough to allow and encourage them to affirm their own tastes, preferences, and choices. Taoistic respect in management also involves an active effort to respond to all feedback by improving the alternatives from which self-choice is made.

This idea also can be discussed from the viewpoint of pragmatic consequences (validation, assessment, evaluation, and noting how something works). In private industry, a very efficient form of feedback has come into existence with aspects like profit-and-loss statements, inventory statements, production quantity and quality statements, and the like. All of these constitute a very quick method of cybernetic-like feedback that tells how well the system is functioning and how efficiently it is being run. Of course, when one has such knowledge, then one is armed against catastrophe and breakdown. For example, if there is a red warning light in one part of the system, that indicates there is trouble and then one can immediately go to that part of the sytem to correct and improve it. However, if there is no such feedback mechanism, then any difficulty in any one part of the system remains as it is—to perhaps cure itself but, more likely, to worsen until the total system breaks down.

Also involved here is the general question of the "widsom of the body"—a theory that presupposes the value of self-choice. Here we can cite all the physiological research, such as dealing with food preferences, but, in addition, my own studies on college students' evaluations of their professors' knowledge and competency. For example, I discovered that the students' judgments were just as accurate as those of the professors' own colleagues—a finding that indicated a great deal more student "wisdom" than was generally acknowledged at the time. There is a lot of such data from a variety of subfields in psychology that could be synthesized. Indeed, I believe that it would be useful in the larger strategy of developing a humanistic ethic in social science and management to produce a summary article on all the data on the wisdom, or lack of wisdom, of individual self-choice.

It seems that the core of my outlook—at least so far as humanistic management or politics is concerned—is the notion that everything springs from the individual's own character structure, that is, whether it is essentially democratic or authoritarian. It is also my firm conviction that the humanistic approach really does make people feel happier and more fulfilled, in effect, in being heard and understood and in leading active lives rather than existing like helpless pawns. To feel oneself an agent is precisely the opposite from feeling controlled, shoved around, dominated, and the like.

An authoritarian individual or system produces these latter effects on others. A democratic individual or sytem produces the former effects. It is, therefore, no surprise that given a choice, almost everyone will choose the democratic individual, organization, and society. For to do so is certainly to side with personal pleasure and happiness. We also can add from the viewpoint of self-development that the democratic, compassionate, loving, respecting, and growth-enjoying attitude in the stronger person leads to growth and self-fulfillment in the weaker. In other words, the basic premises of humanistic psychology form the foundation for enlightened management, politics, and social change.

Finally, returning to the theme of the necessity for integrating bigness-smallness, I think it is useful to point out that the problem does not even arise in the small, personal, face-to-face enterprise, school, or social situation. It is only when a successful, one-person business starts becoming much bigger that these problems come up. If we are conscious of the advantages of smallness and customer satisfaction—and have knowledge of what is occurring generally—then we can be forewarned and can arrange to grow larger, as Saga executives have effectively done with their company.

We can institutionalize all the democratic, communicative, respecting, loving, listening, customer-satisfaction kinds of things by using the advantages of technology, in other words, keeping all the benefits of smallness but also capitalizing on the benefits of bigness.

For instance, several articles in this same issue of *Tempo* show the advantages of mass-marketing, mass-purchasing, the division of labor, and being able to hire specialized experts of various kinds in order to improve on what the smaller, face-to-face enterprise does unconsciously and untuitively.

What shall I call this revolutionary new approach? Theory Y management? Enlightened management? *Humanistic management?* Perhaps the latter is the most worthwhile term, because it implies real respect, liking, and understanding of humankind's higher possibilities.

I wish to offer one little addition. The whole system of feedback works best if customers are able to express their opinions—that is, their disapproval, anger, or enthusiasm—immediately. Continuous and instantaneous feedback seems to be the ideal. I have heard that this method has been instituted by Hollywood film companies, in which viewers push "feedback buttons" at the very moment that they are witnessing a particular scene on screen. The more we can emulate such an approach throughout management today, the better our society will become.

Letter from Douglas McGregor

SCHOOL OF INDUSTRIAL MANAGEMENT

ESTABLISHED UNDER A GRANT FROM
THE ALFRED P. SLOAN FOUNDATION, INC.

50 MEMORIAL DRIVE
CAMBRIDGE 39, MASSACHUSETTS

September 26, 1957

Professor Abraham Maslow
Brandeis University
Waltham, Massachusetts

Dear Professor Maslow:

I am filling the stereotype of the absent-minded professor! In a talk which I gave here at MIT last spring I drew heavily on your ideas about motivation. At the time I made a mental note to be sure to send you a copy of the talk when it appeared. Now I cannot remember whether I did or not!

If I did send you the enclosed reprint, please forgive me for doing so again. If I did not, please forgive the lapse of time.

In any event, I hope you will approve in general of the way I have used your thinking to strengthen some of my own. The implications of your theory of motivation for management philosophy and policy in industry are indeed significant. My observation is that everyday happenings on a wide scale bear out the truth of your point that satisfied needs are not motivators.

Are there any data beyond those you cite in <u>Motivation and Personality</u> in support of your principle of self-actualization? I would be most interested in learning whether the research you mention there has been carried forward and with what results?

Sincerely yours,

Douglas McGregor

DM:fab

encl

Source: Douglas McGregor letter to A.H. Maslow reprinted with the permission of Ann R. Kaplan and the *Archives of the History of American Psychology.*

The Dynamics of
American Management

Maslow gave the following speech to Saga Foods executives in November 1969. In this speech he expounds upon his ideas regarding enlightened management and the application to American industry. Maslow recalled his time at Saga as heaven, and he became an important advisor to then CEO, Bill Laughlin. Andy Kay, CEO of Kaypro at the time, introduced Laughlin to Maslow, after Maslow had spent the summer observing the behavior of the managers and employees at Kaypro. Maslow's work at Kaypro resulted in his classic book on workplace behavior, Eupsychian Management.

Perhaps, the best service I can provide is to compare your managerial group with others. Of course, brief impressions can be unreliable. This is just one particular observational experience. But I wanted to offer my overall impressions about you as a group and then compare this organizational setup with that of others.

So first, let's talk about organizational setups. It is going to sound very corny and "square," but what I have witnessed here in the last couple of days just would not happen anywhere on the face of the earth except in the United States. That fact is well-known. This kind of advanced management is absolutely American, and it is sweeping the whole world. There is a lot of talk about "American imperialism" nowadays, but the truth is that American workers simply are more

Source: A.H. Maslow speech to the executives of Saga Foods, Inc. (November 1969), reprinted with the permission of Ann R. Kaplan and the *Archives of the History of American Psychology.*

efficient, desirable, and accomplished wherever they go. They just do a better job than other nationalities.

Half of this reality is due to the financial strength and vast natural resources of the United States. But the other half is due to American management, and this *managerial skill is essentially a by-product of democratic rather than aristocratic feeling.* In other places in the world, most of you would not have a chance of becoming managers at a national company like Saga, because you would not have achieved the necessary, prior promotions. There are only a few exceptions, such as Scandinavia, England, France, West Germany, and Italy, where such advancement might be possible.

I am an example of this same American dynamic. I have a high post and high status in my field. You might say that I have received many promotions and have attained the top level of my field. I am very conscious of the fact that this could not have happened in any other country in the world. My father was an immigrant. I was brought up in the slums of New York City. I am a sidewalk boy who has gone on to a marvelous vocation. I got to exactly the spot for which I was born—and that thought was running through my mind as our group talked earlier.

I do not know where you have individually come from, but the fact is that it could be anyplace. None of you needs any "pull," you do not need a well-placed relative, you do not need any hereditary privileges, you do not have to be a member of the clan, and you do not have to attend a particular school. It all depends on your own capability and talents.

I think that it might be helpful for this group—as it has been personally helpful for me—simply to become more aware of our good fortune and our plain luck in being part of this American dynamic. Why? Because individually, we do not "deserve" our heritage of freedom, vast natural resources, national political maturity, or managerial skill.

I feel grateful and privileged to be an American, and I suggest that you do too. Of course, that awareness carries with it various responsibilities and obligations.

THE OPENNESS TO EXPERIMENT

If we are indeed the lucky ones, we could regard what we are doing at the Saga Corporation as a kind of "test tube" experiment for the rest of the world. For there is hardly any other society on earth that is affluent enough to afford to take its workers away from their workplace and sit them down just to talk with each other for a couple of days. This practice simply is not done anywhere else. And your group has made excellent use of this opportunity through your personal openness, your willingness to discuss things, and your open ear. To allocate all this time for a retreat definitely costs money, and Saga is paying a hell of a lot of money to get feedback from you as managers.

If you understand this fact, it can't help but support your self-esteem. It must make you feel good that you can affect things and that you are not a helpless pawn of fate or controlled by huge, external, impersonal forces. Each of you has an opinion about something, and so Saga is paying for the privilege of hearing you say it. For this reason, psychologists would expect you to gain in self-esteem, maturity, and emotional health.

It has been suggested that only about 5 percent of the general population are active agents. They are the ones who run themselves and the world. It is very clear to me that every single member of this group is one of those active agents.

You are not among the 95 percent who are helpless and lack direction.

Before I go into specific aspects of what I have observed, I would like to make a few general comments. First, what you have experienced the last couple of days during your retreat is true democratizing of the workplace, and it is still atypical for most organizations. As I have already mentioned, this approach of *enlightened management* hardly exists anywhere outside the United States. Even within this country, no more than 5 percent of companies have yet embraced the democratic ethos by really trusting their employees. So in a very real way, your group represents a great revolution in humankind's history. This principle is definitely post-Marxian. It is truly a new thing. It is as revolutionary as the ideas of Galileo, Darwin, or Freud were in their own day. It is a new way of working together.

Now with the Marxian approach to the workplace, there are inevitably adversarial conflict, struggle, and class haggles. The bosses are out to squeeze as much sweat out of the workers as possible, and the workers are out to retaliate as best as they can. That is a Marxian relationship. But we are in a different kind; we are post-Marxian because we are working together with good will and good faith. We share the assumption that it is desirable for you to do a good job—even for your own sake—in the sense that you do not think of your next level of supervisors as your innate enemies or anything like that. You have to get along with them.

This attitude shows itself in the fact that you have not behaved like a group of enemies or real rivals, in the sense of trying to "stab" or cut each other down. You have behaved like a group of colleagues, akin to U.S. senators, generals, or sovereign entities. This fact is unusual; it is definitely unusual. We can afford to be self-conscious about it. You can enjoy this self-awareness.

In short, I see your managerial retreat as a very advanced "scouting" or "pilot experiment" for all of humankind. If this workplace experiment is successful, then humankind has a very different future than that envisioned by the Marxists with their images of inevitable class warfare and strife. For my part, I feel a sense of gratitude and good fortune about all of such developments.

MANAGEMENT STYLES (THEORY X AND THEORY Y)

I don't know how familiar you are with the recent literature on managerial and organizational styles. To put it succinctly, *Theory Y* assumes that if you give people responsibilities and freedom, then they will like to work and will do a better job. Theory Y also assumes that workers basically like excellence, efficiency, perfection, and the like.

Theory X, which still dominates most of the world's workplace, has a contrasting view. It assumes that people are basically stupid, lazy, hurtful, and untrustworthy and, therefore, that you have got to check everything constantly because workers will steal you blind if you don't.

Well, the last few days provide a marvelous example of Theory Y in action. You are all being trusted and you are all on your own, and it shows. Psychologists like myself would think that every person in this group is solid, reliable, trustworthy, and substantial. In relationship to your managerial position at Saga, you are concerned and involved, and you identify with the overall organization. It is a very lucky thing for people to enjoy their work and to identify with the entire organization, rather than to view it as a pack of enemies. I can report back to you that your group showed much greater openness and courage than most. There would not be one percent of employees I have ever seen who would be able to speak so openly with one another.

EXPRESSION OF AGGRESSION

Your group displayed a certain amount of "caginess," but it was much less than I have seen elsewhere. Your relationship toward your supervisors is more open, direct, and courageous. There was not a single person who avoided the whole situation through "camouflage," as I typically would expect to see.

For example, in most situations in which I am invited to speak or observe, I have aroused considerable suspicion and defensiveness. Typically, two people are chatting to each other at the water-cooler. Then I approach, and they freeze. I have not seen that kind of anxious response here. Of course, defensiveness can emerge in all sorts of ways that psychologists can see, but essentially, you are confining it to yourselves.

The healthy means of handling aggression is to not be afraid of it. Furthermore, we must learn not to be afraid of our own aggression. It is helpful to think of it as similar to the gasoline in your automobile. Yes, it is very powerful, but it can be used productively. To deal with aggression in this manner means to be able to offer criticism: to be capable of saying, "I don't like this," or "I don't like that," or "I recommend that you do such and such" or "I recommend that you *not* do such and such."

In many places of the world, to utter such statements would result in family feuds, tribal fighting, and even death. For instance, in Japan, people do not dare to speak bluntly to one another. Everything is cloaked in politeness, indirection, and the like. Well, I would say that from my clinical viewpoint, you handled aggressive feelings very well and openly—and that sort of behavior is the mark of strong, healthy people.

OPENNESS AND DIRECTION WITH YOUR SUPERVISOR

Your relationship with your supervisor seems to be a healthy one. Admittedly, "John" [not his real name] is a tough-minded guy and he comes on strong. If he were my boss, I think that I would be a little fearful and worried about what I would say to him. Well, I think that you handled yourselves very well—without losing your sense of dignity and autonomy in the face of a forceful character who also has power over you. This behavior I can say is unusual. It usually does not happen this way.

Generally, when there is a strong boss, everybody is involved in fawning and flattering, figuring out pleasing things to say—"kissing ass," in other words. But your supervisor asked you to talk straight to him, and you did.

Now, I am sure that you also "put your best foot forward" and engaged in a certain amount of censoring and diplomacy in your words with John. But relative to other situations, you were fairly blunt and absolutely straightforward and honest. This also means that you were strong. I would say that you were certainly among the top five percent in your ability to handle such workplace relationships.

Remember, handling aggression is a problem for many people in our society. The healthy way to do so is to become involved with people who are not afraid of one another and who know their own minds and what they want.

HANDLING OUR FEELINGS OF AFFECTION

Especially for men in our society, another major problem is the expression of affection. We do not do this very well as a society. Others generally are more successful than ours in handling love, friendship, and physical contact. It is always possible to make judgments about how strangulated people are regarding this particular quality.

I would rate your group as above average, somewhere around the 75th percentile, in dealing with affectionate feelings. I must be honest, you are not tops! Sometimes I witnessed open displays of affection, but it was too often couched defensively—like in making jokes to cover it up. For instance, you meet your best friend and you like him. But instead of putting your arm around him, you punch him or call him an "old son of a bitch." Of course, you do not display that behavior except with your closest friends, but it is nevertheless a roundabout way of expressing affection.

Frankly, I do not know how important this issue is in your relationships. It is my view that because the workplace is structured hierarchically—that is, you have more powerful superiors and weaker subordinates—there could be warmer, more affectionate, expressive relationships in both directions. So that if you like someone or feel friendly, then you just show it. After all, organizational development groups and *t-groups* are supposed to help us develop more ability in expressing affection and friendliness.

However, your group definitely did not show *fearfulness*. You were not a strangulated group. For example, Lutheran ministers constitute perhaps the most emotionally frozen group I have observed in American society. Why this is so, I am not sure. They study texts proclaiming that "God is love," but they are unable to express any affection, or any openness, at all toward each other. Certainly, I do not get the impression that yours is a strangulated group in that sense.

Now, I have been studying the psychological characteristics of workplace executives in American society—the top executives—and this research brings up another aspect of the problem of showing affection. That is, our whole society "undersells" itself by claiming to be merely materialist. Actually, the United States is the most unmaterialist superpower that has ever existed. Yet, we keep putting on a camouflage. Our citizens—especially figures like corporate executives—are afraid of appearing corny or "square," of getting sentimental, of crying in the movies, and of looking soft.

Well, I can tell you as a psychologist that the strongest people in our society are maybe the softest—in the sense of being altruistic and idealistic. They think in terms that they would never dare to verbalize in public but that are essentially the "boy scout oath" to the highest power. Part of the American difficulty with affection, love, and sentiment is mixed up with our never-ceasing effort to look tough, strong, and invulnerable. It is as if mature adults are trying to cloak themselves in the whole adolescent interpretation of masculinity. I remember recently seeing a teenage antiwar protester on the television news. He was carrying a placard saying, "I am a man." Then, he began throwing rocks into storefront windows! Well, men do not throw rocks into windows. Only kids do.

Anyway, if I were offering recommendations to our entire society, I would advise its members to be more like Italians or Mexicans, who are a little more openly expressive of affection.

MANLINESS

The definition of adult masculinity—of what a fully grown, mature man is like—certainly includes softness, that is, the ability to become sentimental and affectionate. It is only the adolescent male who does not dare to show his affection. You know, adolescents today find it very hard to display affection because that behavior appears weak. So unfortunately, they miss out on many good things.

Well, your group expressed plenty of positive remarks here. When someone had something good to express, it was clearly stated. That is a mature, psychologically healthy attitude. It is typical of the man who feels authentically self-confident and who can, therefore, be tender. But if you lack self-confidence, then you have to act tough all the time and consequently to overdo tough behavior.

OUR INNER PICTURE OF PEOPLE

One thing that I can recommend for you, especially if you are seeking promotions and greater responsibilities, is that your judgments about people could be improved by becoming more varied, that is, deeper and fuller. Unfortunately, your statements in this regard were rather skimpy.

For instance, your group had a role-playing exercise in which you were invited to make statements about one another. Well, from a psychological perspective, your comments generally were shallow. People are so complicated, so rich, and so varied! My impression is that you feel restrained in expressing interpersonal relationships or making interpersonal judgments. If I can make a recommendation here, it is that you can be more successful simply by looking more carefully and persistently at people. Try to make a richer, more complex picture than the one you have made. Of course, any brief picture—for example, "Describe someone you know by using only two words"—may be wrong. That is where feedback comes in.

Now, I do not know whether your shortcoming in this respect relates more to a problem in expression or in your inner portraits of one another. My hunch is that it is the former.

As managers, you have to deal with people all the time. If you did not do this task well, then you would quickly be out of a job. So, my guess is that you are intuitive, perceptive, and diplomatic in interpersonal relationships far more than you are able to articulate or discuss. But it is very desirable to be able to talk these feelings out because you must write down your estimates and judgments of people. Because talking about your perceptions also causes them to become more *conscious* rather than *unconscious,* I would advise you to initiate more discussions.

SIMILARITIES AND DIFFERENCES

The similarities among each of you are greater than the differences. I will say it again: By comparison with others, your group is composed of people who are very much alike in the characteristics that I have mentioned. That is, each one of you gives me the impression of strength, solidity, reliability, and dependability. My conjecture is that you do your job well. For instance, I have gotten the definite feeling that I could really rely on each of you—without exception—in an emergency.

Of course, individual differences exist among you. But as far as your work is concerned, what I have just said indeed applies. My impression is that you each have all the necessary qualities for placing at the top 5th percentile of leadership in this society or any other society. It is this top 5 percent, you know, who get necessary things done and who keep a society going effectively. It is this same 5 percent who are the most responsible and who, in effect, lead and support the other 95 percent of citizens. So far as your work at Saga is concerned, your individual differences are less significant.

OUR PROFESSIONALISM

For what it is worth—because it is just my impression—I think you would benefit from reading more about the intellectual backdrop to your job. As I have been saying today, "You are leaders not only for America, but for the entire world." We are sort of the pilots for other nations because they lack the money, the time, and the efficiency to accomplish what we have learned about management right here in this retreat. So, I recommend that you do more reading in the rich literature of managerial theory.

If I had one book to suggest, it would be Douglas McGregor's (1960) *The Human Side of Enterprise.* It usually serves as the introduction to a whole line of thinking. A more recent, excellent book by McGregor (1967) is *The Professional Manager.* Such volumes would help to provide a conceptual framework—a wider context—for your daily work at Saga, with all its details. By reading such books, you would not only become effective managers but also improve your promotability. So there is another example of *synergy* at work!

Here we have the merging of self-interest and altruism, of self-interest and other-interest. In the best situations, this synergy always occurs. For instance, if you get along well with your spouse in a marriage, you eventually realize that narrow self-interest ceases to exist. You are one person, but you are inevitably also part of a team. There is a pooling of interests.

Well, in the field of enlightened management—enlightened industry—this same merging of interests takes place. If you do a good job at Saga, then you are benefiting yourself, the company, the country, and ultimately the entire world. If America could fulfill the American dream a little more fully, we could help fulfill a world dream.

Our country has sometimes been criticized badly in the international press, but the American dream still beckons. You know, if the doors to our country were completely opened, then probably 98 percent of humankind would want to enter. That is a kind of voting with one's feet! So the American dream still beckons.

If you do your own job better, and I think you all can, and if you are more Olympian—gazing down as though from a great height at your daily routine—then you gain a better perspective of how everything fits together. By reading stimulating books, you can attain some of that wider outlook.

Of course, reading generally will help you to get along better with other people. That is good for you personally and for the entire world. So I really recommend that you read more.

CONCLUSION

Thanks for allowing me to observe your managerial retreat. Your willingness to do so is itself a sign of maturity, for many groups would have refused my attendance. Its members would have become tense and ill at ease in the presence of a psychologist. People tend to run away from psychologists due to deluded fears about our X-ray eyes or our ability to "read minds."

In this context, I would like to end with a humorous anecdote. I was recently attending a big party when a young woman walked into the room. She was stunning physically, and I found myself staring at her beauty. I was momentarily overwhelmed by her physical attractiveness. Suddenly, the young woman noticed me staring at her and strode right over. Stepping close, she said, "I know what you're thinking!"

Taken aback, I awkwardly managed to stammer, "You do?" "Yes," she smiled triumphantly. "I know that you're a psychologist, and so you're trying to psychoanalyze me!"

And I laughed and replied, "Well, that's *not* what I was thinking of!"

So, I take your willingness to allow my presence here during retreat to be a sign of self-confidence, lack of fear, and emotional healthfulness. To accept me, as a psychologist, in your midst is significant, and I personally appreciate it. For me, it has been a very interesting and inspiring couple of days.

SCHOOL OF INDUSTRIAL MANAGEMENT

ESTABLISHED UNDER A GRANT FROM   50 MEMORIAL DRIVE

THE ALFRED P. SLOAN FOUNDATION, INC.   CAMBRIDGE 39, MASSACHUSETTS

November 16, 1956

Professor Abraham Maslow
Department of Psychology
Brandeis University
Waltham, Massachusetts

Dear Professor Maslow:

Thanks for the two reprints you sent along recently. As usual, I found them provocative.

You might be interested to know that I used your <u>Motivation and Personality</u> with a group of seventeen senior executives in a seminar here at MIT this fall. I assigned selected chapters amounting to about half the book, and their response was genuinely enthusiastic. We had a long discussion of the implications of your self-actualization concept and it was quite clear that the whole idea not only made sense but fired their imagination because of its implications in industry.

I wish you'd give me a ring when you are going to be around Cambridge so that we might have lunch together some day. It seems to be characteristic that one never sees one's nearby colleagues.

Sincerely yours,

Douglas McGregor

DM:fab

Source: Douglas McGregor letter to A.H. Maslow, reprinted with the permission of Ann R. Kaplan and the *Archives of the History of American Psychology.*

Theory Z

In 1968, Maslow hoped to break new ground in the field of management theory with Theory Z which presupposed that people, once having reached a level of economic security, would strive for a life steeped in values, a work life where the person would be able to create and produce.

I have recently found it more and more useful to differentiate between two kinds (or better, degrees) of self-actualizing people, those who were clearly healthy, but with little or no experiences of transcendence, and those in whom transcendent experiencing was important and even central. As examples of the former kind of health, I may cite Mrs. Eleanor Roosevelt, and, probably, Truman and Eisenhower. As examples of the latter, I can use Aldous Huxley, and probably Schweitzer, Buber, and Einstein.

It is unfortunate that I can no longer be theoretically neat at this level. I find not only self-actualizing persons who transcend, but also *non*healthy people, non–self-actualizers who have important transcendent experiences. It seems to me that I have found some degree of transcendence in many people other than self-actualizing ones as I have defined this term. Perhaps it will be found even *more* widely as we develop better techniques and better conceptualizations. After all, I am reporting here my impressions from the most preliminary of explorations. In any case, it is my tentative impression that I am more likely to find cognizing of transcendence not only in self-actualizing but also in highly creative or talented people, in highly intelligent people, in very strong characters, in powerful and responsible leaders

Source: A.H. Maslow paper (1968), reprinted with the permission of Ann R. Kaplan and the *Archives of the History of American Psychology.*

and managers, in exceptionally good (virtuous) people and in "heroic" people who have overcome adversity and who have been strengthened by it rather than weakened.

To some as yet unknown extent the latter are what I have referred to as "peakers" rather than "nonpeakers," and Yea-sayers rather than Nay-sayers, life-positive rather than life-negative (in Reich's sense), eager for life rather than nauseated or irritated by it.

The former are more essentially practical, realistic, mundane, capable, and secular people, living more in the here-and-now world, that is, what I have called the D-realm for short, the world of deficiency-needs and of deficiency-cognitions. In this *Weltanschauung,* people or things are taken essentially in a practical, concrete, here-now, pragmatic way, as deficiency-need suppliers or frustrators; that is, as useful or useless, helpful or dangerous, personally important or unimportant.

"Useful" in this context means both "useful for survival" *and* "useful for growth toward self-actualization and freedom from basic deficiency-needs." More specifically, it means a way of life and a world view generated not only by the hierarchy of basic needs (for sheer physical survival, for safety and security, for belongingness, friendship, and love, for respect, esteem, and dignity, for self-esteem and feelings of worth), but also by the need for the actualization of one's personal, idiosyncratic potentialities (that is, identity, Real Self, individuality, uniqueness, self-actualization). That is, it refers to the fulfillment not only of one's specieshood, but also of one's *own* idiosyncratic potentialities. Such people live in the world, coming to fulfillment in it. They master it, lead it, use it for good purposes, as (healthy) politicians or practical people do. That is, these people tend to be "doers" rather than meditators or contemplators, effective and pragmatic rather than aesthetic, reality-testing and cognitive rather than emotional and experiencing.

The other type (transcenders?) may be said to be much more often aware of the realm of Being (B-realm and B-cognition), to be living at the level of Being; that is, of ends, of intrinsic values; to be more obviously metamotivated; to have unitive consciousness and "plateau experience" (Asrani) more or less often; and to have or have had peak experiences (mystic, sacral, ecstatic) with illuminations or insights or cognitions which changed their view of the world and of themselves, perhaps occasionally, perhaps as a usual thing.

It may fairly be said of the "merely-healthy" self-actualizers that, in an overall way, they fulfill the expectations of McGregor's Theory Y.

But of the individuals who have transcended self-actualization we must say that they have not only fulfilled but also transcended or surpassed Theory Y. They live at a level which I shall here call Theory Z for convenience and because it is on the same continuum as Theories X and Y and with them forms a hierarchy.

Obviously, we are dealing here with extraordinarily intricate matters, and as a matter of fact, with philosophies of life in general. Extended and discursive treatment would lead to volumes and sets of volumes.

It occurred to me, however, that condensed beginning could be achieved with the aid of Table 1. Using Keith Davis' very convenient summary table as a base, I have extended it in the ways indicated by italicizing. It can hardly be said to be light reading, but I do think that anyone who is really curious or interested can catch something of what I am trying to communicate. More extended treatment may be found in the various items listed in the bibliography.

One final caution: It should be noted that this hierarchical arrangement by levels leaves open the difficult and, as yet, unsolved problem of the degrees of overlap or correlation between the following progressions or hierarchies:

1. The hierarchy of needs (which can be taken either as coming to crises in a chronological progression à la Erickson *or* with age held constant).

2. A progression of basic-need gratifications from infancy through childhood, youth, adulthood, to old age, but at any time.

3. Biological, phyletic evolution.

4. From illness (diminution, stunting) to health and full humanness.

5. From living under bad environmental conditions to living under good conditions.

6. From being constitutionally or generally a "poor specimen" (in the biologist's sense) to being a "good specimen" in the zoo keeper's sense.

Of course all these complexities make the concept "psychological health" even more moot than it usually is and strengthen the case for using instead the concept of "full humanness," which applies well to all these variations without difficulty. Conversely, we can then use the one concept "stunting or diminution of humanness" instead of immature, unlucky, sick, born defective, underprivileged. "Diminution of humanness" covers them all.

DIFFERENCES (IN DEGREE) BETWEEN TRANSCENDERS AND MERELY HEALTHY PEOPLE

Nontranscending and transcending self-actualizers (or Theory-Y and Theory-Z people) share in common all the characteristics described for self-actualizing with the one exception of presence or absence or, more probably, greater or lesser number and importance of peak experiences and B-cognitions and what Asrani has called plateau experiences (serene and contemplative B-cognitions rather than climactic ones).

But it is my strong impression that the nontranscending self-actualizers do *not* have the following characteristics or have less of them than do the transcenders.

1. For the transcenders, peak experiences and plateau experiences become *the* most important things in their lives, the high spots, the validators of life, the most precious aspect of life.

2. They (the transcenders) speak easily, normally, naturally, and unconsciously the language of Being (B-language), the language of poets, of mystics, of seers, of profoundly religious men, of men who live at the Platonic-idea level or at the Spinozistic level, under the aspect of eternity. Therefore, they should better understand parables, figures of speech, paradoxes, music, art, nonverbal communications, and so forth. (This is an easily testable proposition.)

3. They perceive unitively or sacrally (that is, the sacred within the secular), or they see the sacredness in all things *at the same time* that they also see them at the practical, everyday D-level. They can sacralize everything at will; that is, perceive it under the aspect of eternity. This ability is in *addition* to—not mutually exclusive with—good reality testing within the D-realm. (This is well described by the Zen notion of "nothing special.")

4. They are much more consciously and deliberately metamotivated. That is, the values of Being, or Being itself seen both as fact

and value, for example, perfection, truth, beauty, goodness, unity, dichotomy-transcendence, B-amusement, and so forth are their main or most important motivations.

5. They seem somehow to recognize each other, and to come to almost instant intimacy and mutual understanding even upon first meeting. They can then communicate not only in all the verbal ways but also in the nonverbal ways as well.

6. They are *more* responsive to beauty. This may turn out to be rather a tendency to beautify all things, including all the B-Values, or to see the beautiful more easily than others do, or to have aesthetic responses more easily than other people do, consider beauty most important, or to see as beautiful what is not officially or conventionally beautiful. (This is confusing, but it is the best I can do at this time).

7. They are *more* holistic about the world than are the "healthy" or practical self-actualizers (who are also holistic in this same sense). Mankind is one and the cosmos is one, and such concepts as the "national interest" or "the religion of my fathers" or "different grades of people or of IQ" either cease to exist or are easily transcended. If we accept as the ultimate political necessities (as well as today the most urgent ones), to think of all men as brothers, to think of national sovereignties (the right to make war) as a form of stupidity or immaturity, then transcenders think this way more *easily,* more reflexively, more naturally. Thinking in our "normal" stupid or immature way is for them an *effort,* even though they can do it.

8. Overlapping this statement of holistic perceiving is a strengthening of the self-actualizer's natural tendency to synergy—intrapsychic, interpersonal, intraculturally and internationally. This cannot be spelled out fully here because that would take too long. A brief—and perhaps not very meaningful—statement is that synergy transcends the dichotomy between selfishness and unselfishness and includes them both under a single superordinate concept. It is a transcendence of competitiveness, of zero-sum of win-lose gamesmanship. The reader who is interested enough is referred to what has already been written on the subject.

9. Of course there is more and easier transcendence of the ego, the Self, the identity.

10. Not only are such people lovable as are all of the most self-actualizing people, but they are also more awe-inspiring, more "unearthly," more godlike, more "saintly" in the medieval sense, more

easily revered, more "terrible" in the older sense. They have more often produced in me the thought, "This is a great man."

11. As one consequence of all these characteristics, the transcenders are far more apt to be innovators, discovers of the new, than are the healthy self-actualizers, who are rather apt to do a very good job of what has to be done "in the world." Transcendent experiences and illuminations bring clearer vision of the B-Values, of the ideal, of the perfect, of what *ought* to be, what actually *could* be, what exists *in potentia*—and therefore of what might be brought to pass.

12. I have a vague impression that the transcenders are less "happy" than the healthy ones. They can be more ecstatic, more rapturous, and experience greater heights of "happiness" (a too weak word) then the happy and healthy ones. But I sometimes get the impression that they are *as* prone and maybe more prone to a kind of cosmic-sadness or B-sadness over the stupidity of people, their self-defeat, their blindness, their cruelty to each other, their shortsightedness. Perhaps this comes from the contrast between what actually is and the ideal world that the transcenders can see so easily and so vividly, and which is in principle so easily attainable. Perhaps this is a price these people have to pay for their direct seeing of the beauty of the world, of the saintly possibilities in human nature, of the non-necessity of so much of human evil, of the seemingly obvious necessities for a good world; for example, a world government, synergic social institutions, education for human goodness rather than for higher IQs or greater expertness at some atomistic job, and so forth. Any transcender could sit down and in five minutes write a recipe for peace, brotherhood, and happiness, a recipe absolutely within the bounds of practicality, absolutely attainable. And yet he sees all this *not* being done; or where it is being done, then so slowly that the holocausts may come first. No wonder he is sad or angry or impatient at the same time that he is also "optimistic" in the long run.

13. The deep conflicts over the "elitism" that is inherent in *any* doctrine of self-actualization—they are after all superior people whenever comparisons are made—is more easily solved—or at least managed—by the transcenders than by the merely healthy self-actualizers. This is made possible because they can more easily live in both the D- and B-realms simultaneously, they can sacralize everybody so much more easily. This means that they can reconcile more easily the absolute necessity for some form of reality-testing, comparing, elitism in

the D-world (you *must* pick a good carpenter for the job, not a poor carpenter; you *must* make some distinction between the criminal and the policeman, the sick man and the physician, the honest man and the fake, the intelligent man and the stupid one) on the one hand, and on the other hand, the transfinite and equal, noncomparable sacredness of everybody. In a very empirical and necessary sense, Carl Rogers talks about the "unconditional positive regard" that is *a priori* necessary for effective psychotherapy. Our laws forbid "cruel and unusual" punishment; that is, no matter *what* crime a man has committed, he must be treated with a dignity not reducible below a certain point. Seriously religious theists say that "each and every person is a child of God."

This sacredness of every person and even of every living thing, even of nonliving things that are beautiful, and so forth, is so easily and directly perceived in its reality by every transcender that he can hardly forget it for a moment. Fused with his highly superior reality-testing of the D-realm, he could be the godlike punisher, the comparer, non-contemptuous, *never* the exploiter of weakness, stupidity, or incapability even while he realistically recognized these gradable qualities in the D-world. The way of phrasing this paradox that I have found useful for myself is this: The factually-superior transcending self-actualizer acts always to the factually-inferior person as to a brother, a member of the family who must be loved and cared for no matter what he does because he is after all a member of the family. But he can still act as stern father or older brother, and not only as an all-forgiving mother or motherly father. This punishment is quite compatible with godlike transfinite love. From a transcendent point of view, it is easy to see that even for the good of the transgressor himself it may be better to punish him, frustrate him, to say "No," rather than to gratify him or please him now.

14. My strong impression is that transcenders show more strongly a positive correlation—rather than the more usual inverse one—between increasing knowledge and increasing mystery and awe. Certainly by most people scientific knowledge is taken as a *lessener* of mystery and therefore of fear, since for most people mystery breeds fear. One then pursues knowledge as an anxiety-reducer.

But for peak-experiencers and transcenders in particular, as well as for self-actualizers in general, mystery is *attractive* and challenging rather than frightening. The self-actualizer is somewhat apt to be bored by what is well known, however useful this knowledge may be. But this is especially so for the peaker for whom the sense of mystery of reverence and of awe is a reward rather than a punishment.

In any case, I have found in the most creative scientists I have talked with that the more they know, the *more* apt they are to go into an ecstasy in which humility, a sense of ignorance, a feeling of smallness, awe before the tremendousness of the universe, or the stunningness of a hummingbird, or the mystery of a baby are all a part, and are all felt subjectively in a positive way, as a reward.

Hence the humility and self-confessed "ignorance" and yet also the happiness of the great transcender-scientist. I think it a possibility that we *all* have such experiences, especially as children, and yet it is the transcender who seems to have them more often, more profoundly, and values them most as high moments in life. This statement is meant to include both scientists and mystics as well as poets, artists, industrialists, politicians, mothers, and many other kinds of people. And in any case, I affirm as a theory of cognition and of science (for testing) that at the highest levels of development of humanness, knowledge is positively rather than negatively correlated with a sense of mystery, awe, humility, ultimate ignorance, reverence, and a sense of oblation.

15. Transcenders, I think, should be less afraid of "nuts" and "kooks" than are other self-actualizers, and thus are more likely to be good selectors of creators (who sometimes look nutty or kooky). I would guess that self-actualizers would generally value creativeness more and therefore select it more efficiently (and therefore should make the best personnel managers or selectors or counselors) and yet to value a William Blake type takes, in principle, a greater experience with transcendence and therefore a greater valuation of it. Something like this should be true at the opposite pole: A transcender should also be more able to screen out the nuts and kooks who are *not* creative, which I suppose includes most of them.

I have no experience to report here. This follows from theory and is presented as an easily testable hypothesis.

16. It follows from theory that transcenders should be more "reconciled with evil" in the sense of understanding its occasional inevitability and necessity in the larger holistic sense, that is, "from above," in a godlike or Olympian sense. Since this implies a better understanding of it, it should generate *both* a greater compassion with it *and* a less ambivalent and a more unyielding fight against it. This sounds like a paradox, but with a little thought can be seen as not at

all self-contradictory. To understand more deeply means, at this level, to have a stronger arm (not a weaker one), to be more decisive, to have less conflict, ambivalence, regret, and thus to act more swiftly, surely and effectively. One can *compassionately* strike down the evil man if this is necessary.

17. I would expect another paradox to be found in transcenders: Namely, that they are more apt to regard themselves as *carriers* of talent, *instruments* of the transpersonal, temporary custodians so to speak of a greater intelligence or skill or leadership or efficiency. This means a certain particular kind of objectivity or detachment toward themselves that to nontranscenders might sound like arrogance, grandiosity, or even paranoia. The example I find most useful here is the attitude of the pregnant mother toward herself and her unborn child. What is self? What is not? How demanding, self-admiring, arrogant does she have a right to be?

I think we would be just as startled by the judgment, "I am the best one for his job and therefore I demand it," as by the equally probable judgment, "You are the best one for this job and therefore it is your duty to take it away from me." Transcendence brings with it the "transpersonal" loss of ego.

18. Transcenders are in principle (I have no data) more apt to be profoundly "religious" or "spiritual" in either the theistic or nontheistic sense. Peak experiences and other transcendent experiences are in effect also to be seen as "religious or spiritual" experiences if only we redefine these terms to exclude their historical, conventional, superstitious, institutional accretions of meaning. Such experiences could indeed be seen as "antireligious" from the merely conventional point of view or as religion-surrogates, or religion-replacements or as a "new version of what *used* to be called religion or spirituality." The paradox that some atheists are far more "religious" than some priests can be easily enough tested and thus given operational meaning.

19. Perhaps another quantitative difference that may show up between these two kinds of self-actualizers—I am not at all sure of it—is that the transcenders, I suspect, find it easier to transcend the ego, the self, the identity, to go beyond self-actualization. To sharpen what I think I see: Perhaps we could say that the description of the healthy ones is more exhausted by describing them *primarily* as strong identities, people who know who they are, where they are going, what they want, what they are good for, in a word, as strong

Selves, using themselves well and authentically and in accordance with their own true nature. And this of course does not sufficiently describe the transcenders. They are certainly this; but they are also more than this.

20. I would suppose—again as an impression and without specific data—that transcenders, because of their easier perception of the B-realm, would have more end experiences (of suchness) than their more practical brothers do, more of the fascinations that we see in children who get hypnotized by the colors in a puddle, or by raindrops dripping down a windowpane, or by the smoothness of skin, or the movements of a caterpillar.

21. In theory, transcenders should be somewhat more Taoistic, and the merely healthy somewhat more pragmatic. B-cognition makes everything look more miraculous, more perfect, just as it *should* be. It therefore breeds less impulse to *do* anything to the object that is fine just as it is, less needing improvement, or intruding upon. There should then be more impulse simply to stare at it and examine it than to do anything about it or with it.

22. A concept that adds nothing new but which ties all the foregoing in with the whole rich structure of Freudian Theory is the word "postambivalent" that I think tends to be more characteristic of all self-actualizers and *may* turn out to be a little more so in some transcenders. It means total wholehearted and unconflicted love, acceptance, expressiveness, rather than the more usual mixture of love and hate that passes for "love" or friendship or sexuality or authority or power, and so forth.

23. Finally I call attention to the question of "levels of pay" and "kinds of pay" even though I am not sure that my two groups differ much, if at all, in this regard. What is crucially important is the fact itself that there are many kinds of pay other than money pay, that money as such steadily recedes in importance with increasing affluence and with increasing maturity of character, while higher forms of pay and metapay steadily *increase* in importance. Furthermore, even where money pay continues to *seem* to be important, it is often so not in its own literal, concrete character, but rather as a symbol for status, success, self-esteem with which to win love, admiration, and respect.

This is an easily researched subject. I have been collecting ads for some time now which seek to attract professional, administrative, or executive employees, ads for Peace Corps and VISTA-type work, and sometimes even for less skilled, blue collar employees in which the attractions that are set forth to lure the applicant are not only money but also higher-need gratifications and metaneed gratifications, for example, friendly co-workers, good surroundings, a secure future, challenge, growth, idealistic satisfactions, responsibility, freedom, an important product, compassion for others, helping mankind, helping the country, a chance to put one's own ideas into effect, a company of which one can be proud, a good school system, even good fishing, beautiful mountains to climb, and so forth. The Peace Corps goes so far as to *stress* as an attraction low money wages and great hardships, self-sacrifice, and so forth, all for the sake of helping others.

I assume that greater psychological health would make these kinds of pay more valuable especially with sufficient money and with money held constant as a variable. Of course, a large proportion of self-actualizing people have probably fused work and play anyway; that is, they love their work. Of them, one could say, they get paid for what they would do as a hobby anyway, for doing work that is intrinsically satisfying.

The only difference I can think of, that further investigation may turn up between my two groups, is that the transcenders may actively seek out jobs that make peak experiences and B-cognition more likely.

One reason for mentioning this in this context is my conviction that it is a theoretical necessity in planning the Eupsychia, the good society, that leadership must be separated from privilege, exploitation, possessions, luxury, status, power-over-the-people, and so forth. The only way that I can see to protect the more capable, the leaders and managers from *ressentiment,* from the impotent envy of the weak, of the underprivileged, of the less capable, of those who need to be helped, that is, from the Evil Eye, from overturn by the underdog, is to pay them, *not* with more money, but with less, to pay them rather with "higher pay" and with "metapay." It follows from the principles so far set forth here and elsewhere that this would please both the self-actualizers and the less psychologically developed, and would abort the development of the mutually exclusive and antagonistic classes or castes that we have seen throughout human history. All we need to do to make practical this post-Marxian, post-historical possibility is to learn not to pay too much for money, that is, to value the higher rather than the lower. Also it would be necessary here to desymbolize money; that is, it must *not* symbolize success, re-spectworthiness, or loveworthiness.

These changes should in principle be quite easily possible since they already accord with the preconscious or not-quite-conscious value-life of self-actualizing people. Whether or not this *Weltanschauung* is or is not more characteristic of transcenders remains to be discovered. I suspect so, mostly on the grounds that mystics and transcenders have throughout history seemed spontaneously to prefer simplicity and to avoid luxury, privilege, honors, and possessions. My impression is that the "common people" have therefore mostly tended to love and revere them rather than to fear and hate them. So perhaps this could be a help in designing a world in which the most capable, the most awakened, the most idealistic would be chosen and loved as leaders, as teachers, as obviously benevolent and unselfish authority.

24. I cannot resist expressing what is only a vague hunch; namely, the possibility that my transcenders seem to me somewhat more apt to be Sheldonian ectomorphs while my less-often-transcending self-actualizers seem more often to be mesomorphic. (I mention this only because it is in principle easily testable.)

Epilogue

Because it will be so difficult for so many to believe, I must state explicitly that I have found approximately as many transcenders among businessmen, industrialists, managers, educators, political people as I have among the professionally "religious," the poets, intellectuals, musicians, and others who are *supposed* to be transcenders and are officially labeled so. I must say that each of these "professions" has different folkways, different jargon, different personae, and different uniforms. Any minister will talk transcendence even if he hasn't got the slightest inkling of what it feels like. And most industrialists will carefully conceal their idealism, their metamotivations, and their transcendent experiences under a mask of "toughness," "realism," "selfishness," and all sorts of other words which would have to be marked off by quotes to indicate that they are only superficial and defensive. Their more real metamotivations are often not repressed but only suppressed, and I have sometimes found it quite easy to break through the protective surface by very direct confrontations and questions.

I must be careful also not to give any false impressions about numbers of subjects (only three or four dozen who have been more or less carefully talked with and observed, and perhaps another hundred or two talked with, read, and observed but not as carefully or in depth), or about the reliability of my information (this is all exploration or investigation or reconnaissance rather than careful final research, a first approximation rather than the normally verified science which will come later), or the representativeness of my sample (I used whomever I could get, but mostly concentrated on the *best* specimens of intellect, creativeness, character, strength, success, and so forth).

At the same time, I must insist that it is an empirical exploration and reports what I have *perceived,* rather than anything I dreamed up. I have found that it helps to remove scientific uneasiness about my freewheeling explorations, affirmations, and hypotheses if I am willing to call them prescientific rather than scientific (a word which for so many means verification rather than discovery). In any case, every affirmation in this paper is in principle testable, provable or disprovable.

PART THREE

CREATIVITY AND INNOVATION

The key question isn't what fosters creativity? But it is why in God's name isn't everyone creative? Where was the human potential lost? How was it crippled? I think therefore a good question might be not why do people create but why do people not create or innovate? We have got to abandon the sense of amazement in the face of creativity, as if it were a miracle if anybody created anything.

A.H. Maslow, *Maslow on Management*

INTRODUCTION

During Maslow's lifetime, he became known as the "father of creativity and innovation." Today, throughout corporate boardrooms around the world, leadership teams and consultants are attempting to manage for creativity and innovation. Yet, if we believe as Maslow did, that it is human nature to create and innovate, our search for the answers takes us down a very different path.

Maslow correlated creativity with a person's ability to withstand the lack of structure, the lack of a predictable future, the lack of control, and a high tolerance for ambiguity and plans that change quickly (or planlessness). In my experience with Silicon Valley companies, these very factors are quite apparent. Lack of clear and delineated structure often appears as chaos in the organizational makeup of these companies. Yet, if we believe Maslow's work, these factors may well be at the heart of the creativity and innovation taking place within the firms themselves.

For the past decade, leading business thinkers have been challenging others to become comfortable with change and ambiguity and to forgo control in unpredictable markets. Although such advice was not based on spurring innovation and creativity, it may very well be an important factor.

Some of Maslow's most important published and unpublished papers on creativity and innovation follow.

The Creative Attitude

This excerpt is from an undated and unpublished manuscript found in the Maslow papers. Maslow discusses the need for developing people into types that can deal with uncertainty; "who don't need to do what their daddies did" and who can face a tomorrow with confidence that they will be able to improvise in situations that have never existed before. In the "new economy" Maslow's words and thoughts, written decades ago, seem timeless.

My feeling is that the concept of creativeness and the concept of the healthy, self-actualizing, fully human person seem to be coming closer and closer together, and may perhaps turn out to be the same thing.

Another conclusion I seem to be impelled toward, even though I am not quite sure of my facts, is that creative art education, or better said, Education-Through-Art, may be especially important not so much for turning out artists or art products, as for turning out better people. If we have clearly in mind the educational goals for human beings that I will be hinting at, if we hope for our children that they will become full human beings, and that they will move toward actualizing the potentialities that they have, then, as nearly as I can make out, the only kind of education in existence today that has any faint inkling of such goals is art education. So I am thinking of education through art not because it turns out pictures but because I think it may be possible that, clearly understood, it may become the paradigm for all other education. That

Source: A.H. Maslow excerpt from the manuscript, "The Creative Attitude" (undated), reprinted with the permission of Ann R. Kaplan and the *Archives of the History of American Psychology.*

is, instead of being regarded as the frill, the expendable kind of thing which it now is, if we take it seriously enough and work at it hard enough and if it turns out to be what some of us suspect it can be, then we may one day teach arithmetic and reading and writing on this paradigm. So far as I am concerned, I am talking about all education. This is why I am interested in education through art—simply because it seems to be good education in potential.

Another reason for my interest in art education, creativeness, psychological health, and so forth, is that I have a very strong feeling of a change of pace in history. It seems to me that we are at a point in history unlike anything that has ever been before. Life moves far more rapidly now than it ever did before. Think, for instance, of the huge acceleration in the rate of growth of facts, of knowledge, of techniques, of inventions, of advances in technology. It seems very obvious to me that this requires a change in our attitude toward the human being, and toward his relationships to the world. To put it bluntly, we need a different kind of human being. I feel I must take far more seriously today than I did twenty years ago, the Heraclitus, the Whitehead, the Bergson kind of emphasis on the world as a flux, a movement, a process, not a static thing. If this is so and it is obviously much more so than it was in 1900 or even in 1930—if this is so, then we need a different kind of human being to be able to live in a world which changes perpetually, which doesn't stand still. I may go so far as to say for the educational enterprise: What's the use of teaching facts? Facts become obsolete so darned fast! What's the use of teaching techniques? The techniques become obsolete so fast! Even the engineering schools are torn by this realization. M.I.T. for instance, no longer teaches engineering *only* as the acquisition of a series of skills, because practically all the skills that the professors of engineering learned when they were in school have now become obsolete. It's no use today learning to make buggy whips. What some professors have done at M.I.T., I understand, is to give up teaching of the tried and true methods of the past, in favor of trying to create a new kind of human being who is comfortable with change, who enjoys change, who is able to improvise, who is able to face with confidence, strength, and courage a situation of which he has absolutely no forewarning.

Even today *everything* seems to be changing: international law is changing, politics are changing, the whole international scene is changing. People talk with each other in the United Nations from across different centuries. One man speaks in terms of the international law of the nineteenth century. Another one answers him in terms of something else entirely, from a different platform in a different world. Things have changed that fast.

To come back to my title, what I'm talking about is the job of trying to make ourselves over into people who don't need to staticize the world, who don't need to freeze it and to make it stable, who don't need to do what their daddies did, who are able confidently to face tomorrow not knowing what's going to come, not knowing what will happen, with confidence enough in ourselves that we will be able to improvise in that situation which has never existed before. This means a new type of human being. Heraclitian, you might call him. The society which can turn out such people will survive; the societies that *cannot* turn out such people will die.

You'll notice that I stress a great deal improvising and inspiration, rather than approaching creativeness from the vantage point of the finished work of art, of the creative work. As a matter of fact, I won't even approach it today from the point of view of completed products at all. Why is this? Because we're pretty clearly aware now from our psychological analysis of the process of creativeness and of creative individuals, that we must make the distinction between primary creativeness and a secondary creativeness. The primary creativeness or the inspirational phase of creativeness must be separated from the working out and the development of the inspiration. This is because the latter phase stresses not only creativeness, but also relies very much on just plain hard work, on the discipline of the artist who may spend half a lifetime learning his tools, his skills, and his materials, until he becomes finally ready for a full expression of what he sees. I am very certain that many, many people have waked up in the middle of the night with a flash of inspiration about some novel they would like to write, or a play or a poem or whatever and that most of these inspirations never came to anything. Inspirations are a dime a dozen. The difference between the inspiration and the final product, for example, Tolstoy's *War and Peace,* is an awful lot of hard work, an awful lot of discipline, an awful lot of training, an awful lot of finger exercises and practices and rehearsals and throwing away first drafts and so on. Now the virtues which go with the secondary kind of creativeness, the creativeness which results in the actual products, in the great paintings, the great novels, in the bridges, the new inventions, and so on, rest as heavily upon other virtues—stubbornness and patience and hard work and so on—as they do upon the creativeness of the personality. Therefore, in order to keep the field of operation clean, you might say, it seems necessary to me to focus upon improvising on this first flash and, for the moment, not to worry about what becomes of it, recognizing that many of them do get lost. Partly for this reason, among the best subjects to study for this inspirational phase of creativeness are young children, whose inventiveness and creativeness very frequently cannot be defined in terms of product. When a little boy discovers the decimal system for himself this can be a high moment of inspiration, and a high creative moment, and should not be waved aside because of some *a priori* definition which says creativeness ought to be socially useful or it ought to be novel, or nobody should have thought of it before, and so forth.

For this same reason I have decided for myself not to take scientific creativeness as a paradigm, but rather to use other examples. Much of the research that's going on now deals with the creative scientists, with people who have proven themselves to be creative, Noble prize winners, great inventors, and so on. The trouble is, if you know a lot of scientists, that you soon learn that something is wrong with this criterion because scientists as a group are not nearly as creative generally as you would expect. This includes people who have discovered, who have created actually, who have published things which were advances in human knowledge. Actually, this is not too difficult to understand. This finding tells us something about the nature of science rather than about the nature of creativeness. If I wanted to be mischievous about it, I could go so far as to define science as a technique whereby noncreative people can create. This is by no means making fun of scientists. It's a wonderful thing it seems to me, for limited human beings, that they can be pressed into the service of great things even though they themselves are not great people. Science is a technique, social and institutionalized, whereby even unintelligent people can be useful in the advance of knowledge. That is as extreme and dramatic as I can make it. Since any particular scientist rests so much in the arms of history, stands on so many shoulders of so many predecessors, he is so much a part of a huge basketball team, of a big collection of people, that his own shortcomings may not appear. He becomes worthy of reverence, worthy of great respect through his participation in a great and respect-worthy enterprise. Therefore, when he discovers something, I have learned to understand this as a product of a social institution, of a collaboration. If he didn't discovery it, somebody else would have pretty soon. Therefore, it seems to me that selecting our scientists, even though they have created, is not the best way to study the theory of creativeness.

I believe also that we cannot study creativeness in an ultimate sense until we realize that practically all the definitions that we have been using of creativeness, and most of the examples of creativeness that we use are essentially male or masculine definitions and male or masculine products. We've left out of consideration almost entirely the creativeness of women by the simple semantic technique of defining only male products as creative and overlooking entirely the creativeness of women. I have learned recently (through my studies of peak experiences) to look to women and to feminine creativeness as a good field of operation for research, because it gets less involved in products, less involved in achievement, more involved with the process itself, with the going-on process rather than with the climax in obvious triumph and success.

This is the background of the particular problem I am talking about.

★ ★ ★ ★

The puzzle that I'm now trying to unravel is suggested by the observation that the creative person, in the inspirational phase of the creative furor, loses his past and his future and lives only in the moment. He is all there, totally immersed, fascinated and absorbed in the present, in the current situation, in the here-now, with the matter-in-hand. Or to use a perfect phrase from *The Spinster* by Sylvia Ashton-Warner, the teacher absorbed with a new method of teaching reading to her children says, "I am utterly lost in the present."

This ability to become "lost in the present" seems to be a *sine qua non* for creativeness of any kind. But also certain *prerequisites* of creativeness—in whatever realm—somehow have something to do with this ability to become timeless, selfless, outside of space, of society, of history.

It has begun to appear strongly that this phenomenon is a diluted, more secular, more frequent version of the mystical experience that has been described so often as to have become what Huxley called *The Perennial Philosophy.* In various cultures and in various eras, it takes on somewhat different coloration—and yet its essence is always recognizable—it is the same.

It is always described as a loss of self or of ego, or sometimes as a transcendence of self. There is a fusion with the reality being observed (with the matter-in-hand, I shall say more neutrally), a oneness where there was a twoness, an integration of some sort of the self with the non-self. There is universally reported a seeing of formerly hidden truth, a revelation in the strict sense, a stripping away of veils, and finally, almost always, the whole experience is experienced as bliss, ecstasy, rapture, exaltation.

Little wonder that this shaking experience has so often been considered to be superhuman, supernatural, so much greater and grander than anything conceivable as human that it could only be attributed to trans-human sources. And such "revelations" often serve as basis, sometimes the *sole* basis, for the various "revealed" religions.

And yet even this most remarkable of all experiences has now been brought into the realm of human experience and cognition. My researches on what I call peak experiences, and Marghanita Laski's on what she calls ecstasies, done quite independently of each other, show that these experiences are quite naturalistic, quite easily investigated and, what is to the point right now, that they have much to teach us about creativeness as well as other aspects of the full functioning of human beings when they are most fully realizing themselves, most mature and evolved, most healthy, when, in a word, they are most fully human.

One main characteristic of the peak experience is just this total fascination with the matter-in-hand, this getting lost in the present, this detachment from time and place. And it seems to me now that much of what we have learned from the study of these peak experiences can be transferred quite directly to the enriched understanding of the here-now experience, of the creative attitude.

It is not necessary for us to confine ourselves to these uncommon and rather extreme experiences, even though it now seems clear that practically all people can report moments of rapture if they dig around long enough in their memories, and if the simplest version of the peak experience, namely fascination, concentration, or absorption in *anything* which is interesting enough to hold this attention completely. And I mean not only great symphonies or tragedies; the job can be done by a gripping movie or detective story, or simply becoming absorbed with one's work. There are certain advantages in starting from such universal and familiar experiences which we all have, so that we can get a direct feeling or intuition or empathy, that is, a direct experiential knowledge of a modest, moderate version of the fancier "high" experiences. For one thing we can avoid the flossy, high-flying, extremely metaphorical vocabulary that is so common in this realm.

Well then, what are some of the things that happen in these moments?

Giving Up the Past. The best way to view a present problem is to give it all you've got, to study *it* and its nature, to perceive *within* it the intrinsic interrelationships, to discover (rather than to invent) the answer to the problem within the problem itself. This is also the best way to look at a painting or to listen to a patient in therapy.

The other way is merely a matter of shuffling over past experiences, past habits, past knowledge to find out in what respects this current situation is similar to some situation in the past, that is, to classify it, and then to use *now* the solution that once worked for the similar problem in the past. This can be likened to the work of filing clerk. I have called it "rubricizing." And it works well enough to the extent that the present *is* like the past.

But obviously it *doesn't work* in so far as the matter-in-hand is different from the past. The file-clerk approach fails then. This person confronting an unknown painting hurriedly runs back through his knowledge of art history to remember how he is supposed to react. Meanwhile of course he is hardly looking at the painting. All he needs is the name or the style or the content to enable him to do his quick calculations. He then enjoys it if he is supposed to, and doesn't if he is *not* supposed to.

In such a person, the past is an inert, undigested foreign body which the person carries about. It is not yet the person himself.

More accurately said: The past is active and alive only insofar as it has re-created the person, and has been digested into the present person. It is not or should not be something *other* than the person, something alien to it. It has now become Person (and has lost its own identity as something different and other), just as past steaks that I have eaten are now me, *not* steaks. The digested past (assimilated by intussusception) is different from the undigested past. It is Lewin's "ahistorical past."

Giving Up the Future. Often we use the present not for its own sake but in order to prepare for the future. Think how often in a conversation we put on a listening face as the other person talks, secretly however preparing what we are going to say, rehearsing, planning a counterattack perhaps. Think how different your attitude would be right now if you knew you were to comment on my remarks in five minutes. Think how hard it would be then to be a good, total listener.

If we are totally listening or totally looking, we have thereby given up this kind of "preparing for the future." We don't treat the present as merely a means to some future end (thereby devaluating the present). And obviously, this kind of forgetting the future is a prerequisite to total involvement with the present. Just as obviously, a good way to "forget" the future is not to be apprehensive about it.

Of course, this is only one sense of the concept "future." The future which is within us, part of our present selves, is another story altogether.

Innocence. This amounts to a kind of "innocence" of perceiving and behaving. Something of the sort has often been attributed to highly creative people. They are variously described as being naked in the situation, guileless, without *a priori* expectations, without "shoulds" or "oughts," without fashions, fads, dogmas, habits, or other pictures-in-the-head of what is proper, normal, "right," as being ready to receive whatever happens to be the case without surprise, shock, indignation, or denial.

Children are more able to be receptive in this undemanding way. So are wise old people. And it appears now that we *all* may be more innocent in this style when we become "here-now."

Narrowing of Consciousness. We have now become much less conscious of everything other than the matter-in-hand (less distractible). *Very* important here is our lessened awareness of other people, of their ties to us and ours to them, of obligations, duties, fears, hopes, and so forth. We become much more free of other people, which in turn, means that we become much more ourselves, our Real Selves (Horney), our authentic selves, our real identity.

This is so because *the* greatest cause of our alienation from our real selves is our neurotic involvements with other people, the historical hangovers from childhood, the irrational transferences, in which past and present are confused, and in which the adult acts like a child. (By the way, it's all right for the *child* to act like a child. His dependencies on other people can be very real. *But,* after all, he *is* supposed to outgrow them. To be afraid of what daddy will say or do is certainly out of place if daddy has been dead for twenty years.)

In a word, we become more free of the influence of other people in such moments. So, insofar as these influences have affected our behavior, they no longer do so.

This means dropping masks, dropping our efforts to influence, to impress, to please, to be lovable, to win applause. It could be said so: If we have no audience to play to, we cease to be actors. With no need to act we can devote ourselves, self-forgetfully, to the problem.

Loss of Ego: Self-Forgetfulness, Loss of Self-Consciousness. When you are totally absorbed in non-self, you tend to become less conscious of yourself, less self-aware. You are less apt to be observing yourself like a spectator or a critic. To use the language of psychodynamics, you become less dissociated than usual into a self-observing ego and an experiencing ego; that is, you come much closer to being *all* experiencing ego. (You tend to lose the shyness and bashfulness of the adolescent, the painful awareness of being looked at, and so forth.) This in turn means more unifying, more oneness and integration of the person.

It also means less criticising and editing, less evaluating, less selecting and rejecting, less judging and weighing, less splitting and analyzing of the experience.

This kind of self-forgetfulness is one of the paths to finding one's true identity, one's real self, one's authentic nature, one's deepest nature. It is almost always felt as pleasant and desirable. We needn't go so far as the Buddhists and Eastern thinkers do in talking about the "accursed ego"; and yet there *is* something in what they say.

Inhibiting Force of Consciousness (of Self). In some senses consciousness (especially of self) is inhibiting in some ways and at some times. It is sometimes the locus of doubts, conflicts, fears, and so forth. It is sometimes harmful to full-functioning creativeness. It is sometimes an inhibitor of spontaneity and of expressiveness (*but* the observing ego is necessary for therapy).

And yet it is also true that some kind of self-awareness, self-observation, self-criticism—that is, the self-observing ego—*is* necessary for "secondary creativeness." To use psychotherapy as an example, the task of self-improvement is partly a consequence of criticizing the experiences that one has allowed to come into consciousness. Schizophrenic people experience many insights and yet don't make therapeutic use of them because they are too much "totally experiencing" and not enough "self-observing-and-criticizing." In creative work, likewise, the labor of disciplined construction succeeds upon the phase of "inspiration."

Fears Disappear. This means that our fears and anxieties also tend to disappear. So also our depressions, conflicts, ambivalence, our worries, our problems, even our physical pains. Even—for the moment—our psychoses and our neuroses (that is, if they are not so extreme as to prevent us from becoming deeply interested and immersed in the matter-in-hand).

For the time being, we are courageous and confident, unafraid, unanxious, unneurotic, not sick.

Lessening of Defenses and Inhibitions. Our inhibitions also tend to disappear. So also our guardedness, our (Freudian) defenses, and controls (brakes) on our impulses as well as the defenses against danger and threat.

Strength and Courage. The creative attitude requires both courage and strength and most studies of creative people have reported one or another version of courage: stubbornness, independence, self-sufficiency, a kind of arrogance, strength of character, ego-strength, and so forth; popularity becomes a minor consideration. Fear and weakness cast out creativeness or at least make it less likely.

It seems to me that this aspect of creativeness becomes somewhat more understandable when it is seen as a part of the syndrome of here-now self-forgetfulness and other-forgetfulness. Such a state intrinsically implies less fear, less inhibition, less need for defense and self-protection, less guardedness, less need for artificiality, less fear of ridicule, of humiliation and of failure. All these characteristics are *part of* self-forgetfulness and audience-forgetfulness. Absorption casts out fear.

Or we can say in a more positive way, that becoming more courageous makes it easier to let oneself be attracted by mystery, by the unfamiliar, by the novel, by the ambiguous and contradictory, by the unusual and unexpected, and so forth, instead of becoming suspicious, fearful, guarded, or having to throw into action our anxiety-allaying mechanisms and defenses.

Acceptance: The Positive Attitude. In moments of here-now immersion and self-forgetfulness we are apt to become more "positive" and less negative in still another way, namely, in giving up criticism (editing, picking and choosing, correcting, skepticism, improving, doubting, rejecting, judging, evaluating). This is like saying that we accept. We don't reject or disapprove or selectively pick and choose.

No blocks against the matter-in-hand means that we let it flow in upon us. We let it wreak its will upon us. We let it have its way. We let it be itself. Perhaps we can even approve of its being itself.

This makes it easier to be Taoistic in the sense of humility, non-interference, receptivity.

Trust vs. Trying, Controlling, Striving. All of the foregoing happenings imply a kind of trust in the self and a trust in the world which permits the termporary giving up of straining and striving, of volition and control, of conscious coping and effort. To permit oneself to be determined by the intrinsic nature of the matter-in-hand here-now necessarily implies relaxation, waiting, receiving. The common effort to master, to dominate and to control are antithetical to a true coming-to-terms with or a true perceiving of the materials (or the problem, or the person, and so forth). Especially is this true with respect to the future. We *must* trust our ability to improvise when confronted with novelty in the future. Phrased in this way, we can see more clearly that trust involves self-confidence, courage, lack of fear of the world. It is also clear that this kind of trust in ourselves-facing-the-unknown-future is a condition of being able, to turn totally, nakedly, and wholeheartedly to the present.

(Some clinical examples may help. Giving birth, urination, defecation, sleeping, floating in the water, sexual surrender are all instances in which straining, trying, controlling, have to be given up in favor of relaxed, trusting, confident letting things happen.)

Taoistic Receptivity. Both Taoism and receptivity mean many things, all of them important, but also subtle and difficult to convey except in figures of speech. All of the subtle and delicate Taoistic attributes of the creative attitude which follow have been described again and again by the many writers on creativeness, now in one way or another. However, everyone agrees that in the primary or inspirational phase of creativeness, some degree of receptivity or noninterference or "let-be" is descriptively characteristic and also theoretically and dynamically necessary. Our question now is how does this receptivity or "letting things happen" relate to the syndrome of here-now immersion and self-forgetfulness?

For one thing, using the artist's respect for his materials as a paradigm, we may speak of this respectful attention to the matter-in-hand as a kind of courtesy or deference (without intrusion of the controlling will) which is akin to "taking it seriously." This amounts to treating it as an end, something *per se,* with its own right to be, rather than as a means to some end other than itself; that is, as a tool for some extrinsic purpose. This respectful treatment of its being implies that it is respect-worthy.

This courtesy or respectfulness can apply equally to the problem, to the materials, to the situation, or to the person. It is what one writer (Follett) has called deference (yielding, surrender) to the authority of the facts, to the law of the situation. I can go over from a bare *permitting* "it" to be itself, to a loving, caring, approving, joyful, *eagerness* that it be itself, as with one's child or sweetheart or tree or poem or pet animal.

Some such attitude is a *priori* necessary for perceiving or understanding the full concrete richness of the matter-in-hand, in *its* own nature and in *its* own style, without our help, without our imposing ourselves upon it, in about the same way that we must hush and be still if we wish to hear the whisper from the other.

This cognition of the Being of the other (B-cognition) is fully described in Chapter 9.

Integration of the B-Cognizer (vs. Dissociation). Creating tends to be the act of a whole man (ordinarily); he is then *most* integrated, unified, all of a piece, one-pointed, totally organized in the service of the fascinating matter-in-hand. Creativeness is therefore systemic; that is, a whole—or Gestalt—quality of the whole person; it is not added-to the organism like a coat of paint, or like an invasion of bacteria. It is the opposite of dissociation. Here-now-allness is less dissociated (split) and more one.

Permission to Dip into Primary Process. Part of the process of integration of the person is the recovery of aspects of the unconscious and preconscious, particularly of the primary process (or poetic, metaphoric, mystic, primitive, archaic, childlike).

Our conscious intellect is too exclusively analytic, rational, numerical, atomistic, conceptual and so it misses a great deal of reality, especially within ourselves.

Aesthetic Perceiving rather than Abstracting. Abstracting is more active and interfering (less Taoistic); more selecting-rejecting than the aesthetic (Northrop) attitude of savoring, enjoying, appreciating, caring, in a noninterfering, nonintruding, noncontrolling way.

The end product of abstracting is the mathematical equation, the chemical formula, the map, the diagram, the blueprint, the cartoon, the concept, the abstracting sketch, the model, the theoretical sytem, all of which move further and further from raw reality ("the map is *not* the territory"). The end product of aesthetic perceiving, of non-abstracting is the total inventory of the percept, in which everything in it is apt to be equally savored, and in which evaluations of more important and less important tend to be given up. Here greater richness of the percept is sought for rather than greater simplifying and skeletonizing.

For many confused scientists and philosophers, the equation, the concept, or the blueprint have become more real than the phenomenological reality itself. Fortunately now that we can understand the interplay and mutual enrichment of the concrete and the abstract, it is no longer necessary to devalue one or the other. For the moment we intellectuals in the West who have heavily and exclusively overvalued abstractness in our picture of reality, even to the point of synonymizing them, had better redress the balance by stressing concrete, aesthetic, phenomenological, nonabstracting, perceiving of *all* the aspects and details of phenomena, of the full richness of reality, including the useless portions of it.

Fullest Spontaneity. If we are fully concentrated on the matter-in-hand, fascinated with it for its own sake, having no other goals or purposes in mind, then it is easier to be fully spontaneous, fully functioning, letting our capacities flow forth easily from within, of themselves, without effort, without conscious volition or control, in an instinct-like, automatic, thoughtless way; that is, the fullest, least obstructed, most organized action.

The one main determinant of the organization and adaptation to the matter-in-hand is then most apt to be the intrinsic nature of the matter-in-hand. Our capacities then adapt to the situation most perfectly, quickly, effortlessly, and change flexibly as the situation changes; for example, a painter continuously adapts himself to the demands of his developing painting; as a wrestler adapts himself to his opponent; as a pair of fine dancers mutually adapt to each other; as water flows into cracks and contours.

Fullest Expressiveness (of Uniqueness). Full spontaneity is a guarantee of honest expression of the nature and the style of the freely functioning organism, and of its uniqueness. Both words, spontaneity and expressiveness, imply honesty, naturalness, truthfulness, lack of guile, nonimitativeness, and so forth, because they also imply a noninstrumental nature of the behavior, a lack of willful "trying," a lack of effortful striving or straining, a lack of interference with the flow of the impulses and the free "radiating" expression of the deep person.

The only determinants now are the intrinsic nature of the matter-in-hand, the intrinsic nature of the person and the intrinsic necessities of their fluctuating adaptation to each other to form a fusion, a unit; for example, a fine basketball team, or a string quartet. Nothing outside this fusion situation is relevant. The situation is not a means to any extrinsic end; it is an end in itself.

Fusion of the Person with the World. We wind up with the fusion between the person and his world which has so often been reported as an observable fact in creativeness, and which we may now reasonably consider to be a *sine qua non.* I think that this spider web of interrelationships that I have been tearing apart and discussing can help us to understand this fusion better as a natural event, rather than as something mysterious, arcane, esoteric. I think it can even be researched if we understand it to be an isomorphism, a molding of each to each other, a better and better fitting together or complementarity, a melting into one.

It has helped me to understand what Hokusai meant when he said, "If you want to draw a bird, you must become a bird."

Moments of Creativeness

Maslow described experiences that happen in moments of creativeness.

1. *Giving Up the Past*—"The past is active and alive only in so far as it has re-created the person, and has been digested into the present person. It is not or should not be something *other* than the person. It has now become Person, and has lost its own identity as something different and other."

2. *Giving Up the Future*—"We don't treat the present as merely a means to some future end thereby devaluating the present. This kind of forgetting the future is a prerequisite to total involvement with the present."

3. *Innocence*—Being naked in the situation, without "shoulds" or "oughts," without fashions, dogmas, habits, as being ready to receive whatever happens to be the case without surprise, shock, indignation or denial.

4. *Narrowing of Consciousness*—"This means dropping masks, efforts to influence, to impress, to please, to win applause. If we have no audience to play to, we cease to be actors."

5. *Loss of Ego: Self-Forgetfulness, Loss of Self-Consciousness*—"When you are totally absorbed in non-self, you tend to become less conscious of yourself, less self-aware."

6. *Inhibiting Force of Consciousness (of Self)*—"In some senses consciousness (especially of self) is inhibiting in some ways at some times—it sometimes is the locus of doubts, conflicts and fears. It is sometimes an inhibitor of spontaneity and of expressiveness." (It is also true that the self-observing ego *is* necessary for "secondary creativeness.")

7. *Fears Disappear*—"For the time being, we are courageous and confident, unafraid, unanxious, not sick."

8. *Lessening of Defenses and Inhibitions*

9. *Strength and Courage*—"Becoming more courageous makes it easier to let oneself be attracted by mystery, by the unfamiliar, by the unusual and unexpected, etc. . . . "

10. *Acceptance: The Positive Attitude*—Giving up criticism (editing, correcting, skepticism, evaluating)—this is like saying that we accept.

11. *Trust vs. Trying, Controlling, Striving*—"To permit oneself to be determined by the intrinsic nature of the matter-in-hand here-now necessarily implies relaxation, waiting, receiving."

(continued)

(Continued)

12. *Taoistic Receptivity*—". . . in the primary or inspirational phase of creativeness, some degree of receptivity or non-interference or "let-be" is descriptively characteristic and also theoretically and dynamically necessary." ". . . using the artist's respect for his materials as a paradigm, we may speak of this respectful attention to the matter-in-hand as a kind of courtesy or deference which is akin to 'taking it seriously.' This amounts to treating it as an end with its own right to be, rather than as a means to some end other than itself."

13. *Integration of the B-Cognizer (vs. Dissociation)*—"Creating tends to be the act of a whole man; he is then *most* integrated, totally organized in the service of the fascinating matter-in-hand."

14. *Permission to Dip into Primary Process*—"Part of the process of integration of the person is the recovery of aspects of the unconscious and preconscious . . ."

15. *Esthetic Perceiving Rather than Abstracting*—"Abstracting is more active and interfering (less Taoistic); more selecting-rejecting than the esthetic (Northrop) attitude of savoring, enjoying, appreciating, caring, in a non-interfering, non-intruding, non-controlling way."

16. *Fullest Spontaneity*—"If we are fully concentrated on the matter-in-hand, fascinated with it for its own sake, then it is easier to be fully spontaneous, fully-functioning . . ."

17. *Fullest Expressiveness (of uniqueness)*—"Both words, spontaneity and expressiveness, imply honesty, naturalness, truthfulness, lack of guile, non-imitativeness, etc. because they also imply a non-instrumental nature of the behavior, a lack of willful 'trying,' a lack of effortful striving . . ."

18. *Fusion of the Person with the World*—"I think that this spider web of inter-relationships that I have been teasing apart and discussing can help us to understand this fusion better as a natural event, rather than as something mysterious, arcane, esoteric."

    "I think it can even be researched if we understand it to be an isomorphism, a molding of each to each other . . . a melting into one."

Source: A.H. Maslow paper (undated), reprinted with the permission of Ann R. Kaplan and the *Archives of the History of American Psychology.*

A Holistic Approach
to Creativity

"What is the cause of creativity?" "What is the most important single thing we can do?" "Shall we add a three-credit course in creativity to the curriculum?" I half expect to hear someone ask soon, "Where is it localized?" or try implanting electrodes with which to turn it on or off. In the consultations I've had with Research and Development people in industry, I also get the strong impression that they keep looking for some secret button to push, like switching a light on and off.

A.H. Maslow

It has been interesting for me to compare the present–day situation in the field of creativeness with the situation about twenty or twenty-five years ago. First of all I want to say that the amount of data that has been accumulated—the sheer amount of research work— is far beyond what anybody could reasonably have expected then.

My second impression is that, in comparison with the great accumulation of methods, of ingenious testing techniques, and of sheer quantity of information, theory in this realm has not advanced very much. I want to raise the theoretical questions, that is, what disturbs me about the conceptualizations in this field of research, and the bad consequences of these disturbing conceptualizations.

I think the most important thing that I would like to communicate is my impression that the thinking and the research in the field of creativeness tends to be too atomistic and too *ad hoc,* and that it is not as holistic, organismic, or systemic as it could be and should be.

Source: A.H. Maslow paper (undated), reprinted with the permission of Ann R. Kaplan and the *Archives of the History of American Psychology.*

Now of course I don't want to make any foolish dichotomies or polarizations here. That is, I don't want to imply any piety about holism or antagonism to dissection or atomism. The question for me is how to integrate them best, rather than choosing between them. One way of avoiding such a choosing up of sides is to use Pearson's old discrimination between a general factor ("G") and specific or special factors ("S"), both of which enter into the makeup not only of intelligence, but also of creativeness.

It seems to me terribly impressive, as I read the creativeness literature, that the relationship with psychiatric health or psychological health is so crucial, so profound, so terribly important, and so obvious and yet it is not used as a foundation on which to build. For instance, there has been rather little relationship between the studies, let's say in the field of psychotherapy on the one hand, and of creativeness on the other. One of my graduate students, Richard Craig, has published what I consider to be a very important demonstration that there *is* such a relationship. We were very much impressed with the table in Torrance's book, *Guiding Creative Talent*, in which he pulled together and summarized the evidence of all the personality characteristics that have been demonstrated to correlate with creativeness. There are perhaps thirty or more characteristics that he considered sufficiently valid. What Craig did was to put down these characteristics in a column and then in another column beside them to list the characteristics that I have used in describing self-actualizing people (which overlaps considerably with the lists many other people have used in describing psychological health, for example, Rogers' "Fully Functioning Person" or Jung's "Individuated Person" or Fromm's "Autonomous Person," and so on).

The overlap was almost perfect. There were two or three characteristics in that list of thirty or forty which had not been used to describe psychologically healthy people, but were simply neutral. There was no single characteristic which went in the other, opposite direction, which makes, let's say arbitrarily, nearly forty characteristics or perhaps thirty-seven or thirty-eight which were the same as psychological health—which added up to a syndrome of psychological health or self-actualization.

It cite this paper as a good jumping-off point for discussion because it is my very powerful conviction (as it was a long time ago) that the problem of creativeness is the problem of the creative person (rather than of creative products, creative behaviors, and so forth). In other words, he is a particular or special kind of human being, rather than just an old-fashioned, ordinary human being who now has acquired new extrinsic possessions, who has now got a new skill like ice skating, or accumulated some more things that he "owns" but which are not intrinsic to him, to his basic nature.

If you think of the person, the creative person, as being the essence of the problem, then what you are confronted with is the whole problem of transformation of human nature, the transformation of the character, the full development of the whole person. This in turn necessarily involves us in the question of the *Weltanschauung,* the life philosophy, the way of living, the code of ethics, the values of society, and so on. This is in sharp and direct contrast with the *ad hoc,* causal, encapsulated, atomistic conception of theory, research, and training which I have heard implied so often, for example, "What is *the* cause of creativity?" "What is *the* most important *single* thing we can do?" "Shall we add a three-credit course in creativity to the curriculum?" I half expect to hear someone ask soon, "Where is it localized?" or try implanting electrodes with which to turn it on or off. In the consultations I've had with Research and Development people in industry, I also get the strong impression that they keep looking for some secret button to push, like switching a light on and off.

What I would propose in trying to achieve the creative person is that there could be hundreds and almost literally thousands of determinants of creativeness. That is, anything that would help the person to move in the direction of greater psychological health or fuller humanness would amount to changing the whole person. This more fully human, healthier person would then, epiphenomenally, generate and spark off dozens, hundreds, and millions of differences in behaving, experiencing, perceiving, communicating, teaching, working, and so forth, which would *all* be more "creative." He would then be simply another *kind* of person who would behave in a different way in *every* respect. And then instead of the single secret push button or trick or three-credit course which will presumably, *ad hoc,* produce more creativeness, *ad hoc,* this more holistic, organismic point of view would suggest the more likely question: "And why should not *every* course help toward creativeness?" Certainly this kind of education *of the person* should help create a better *type* of person, help a person grow bigger, taller, wiser, more perceptive—a person who, incidentally, would be more creative as a matter of course in *all* departments of life.

I give you just one example which pops into my head. One of my colleagues, Dick Jones, did a doctoral dissertation which I thought was terribly important from a philosophical point of view, but which has not been noticed enough. What he did was to run a kind of a group-therapy course with high school seniors, and then found that at the end of the year racial and ethnic prejudice had gone down, in spite of the fact that for one full year he had made it his business to avoid ever mentioning these words. Prejudice is not created by pushing a button. You don't have to train people to be prejudiced, and you can't really directly train them to be "unprejudiced." We have tried, and it doesn't work very well. But this "being unprejudiced" flies off as a spark off the wheel, as an epiphenomenon, as a by-product, simply from becoming a better human being, whether from psychotherapy, or from any other influence that improves the person.

About twenty-five years ago my style of investigation of creativeness was very different from the classical scientific (atomistic) method. I had to invent holistic interviewing techniques. That is, I tried to get to know one single person after another as profoundly and as deeply and as fully as I could (as unique, individual persons) to the point where I felt I understood them as a whole person. It was as if I were getting very full case-histories of whole lives and whole people *without* having particular problems or questions in mind, that is, without abstracting one aspect of the person rather than another, that is, I was doing it idiographically.

And yet it is *then* possible to be nomothetic, to *then* ask particular questions, to do simple statistics, to come to *general* conclusions. One can treat each person as an infinity, and yet infinities can be added, percentages made, just as transfinite numbers can be manipulated.

Once you get to know a sample of people profoundly and deeply, and individually in this way, then certain operations become possible that are not possible in typical classical experiments. I had a panel of about 120 people with each of whom I had spent an awful lot of time just simply getting to know them in general. Then, *after* the fact, I could then ask a question, go back to the data and answer it, and this could have been done even if all the 120 people had died. This contrasts with the *ad hoc* experimentation on a single problem in which one variable would be modified and all others presumably "held constant" (although of course we know very well that there are thousands of variables which are presumably, but not actually, controlled in the classical experimental paradigm and which are very far from being held constant).

If I may be permitted to be bluntly challenging, it is my firm opinion that the cause-effect way of thinking which works pretty well in the nonliving world and which we have learned to use more or less well to solve human problems, is now dead as a general philosophy of science. It shouldn't be used any more because it just tends to lead us into *ad hoc* thinking, that is, of one cause producing one specific effect, and of one factor producing one factor, instead of keeping us sensitive to *systemic* and organismic changes of the kind that I've tried to describe, in which any single stimulus is conceived to change the whole organism, which then, as a changed organism, emits behavior changed in *all* departments of life. (This is also true for social organizations, large and small.)

For instance, if you think of physical health, and if you ask the question, "How do you get people's teeth to be better?" "How do you get their feet to be better?" or their kidneys, eyes, hair, and so forth, any physician will tell you that the best thing to do is to improve the general systemic health. That is, you try to improve the general (G) factor. If you can improve the diet and the mode of living and so on and so on, then these procedures, in one single blow, will improve their teeth and their kidneys and their hair and their liver and their intestines and *everything else;* that is, the whole system will be improved. In the same way general creativeness, holistically conceived, emanates from the whole system, generally improved. Furthermore, any factors that would produce a more creative person would also make a man a better father, or better teacher, or better citizen, or a better dancer, or a better anything, at least to the extent that the "G" factor is strengthened. To this is then added of course the specific (S) contributions that differentiate the good father from the good dancer or good composer.

A pretty good book on the sociology of religion is Glock and Stark and I would recommend it as a rather intelligent and competent picture of this type of atomistic and *ad hoc* thinking. *Ad hoc* thinkers, S-R thinkers, cause-effect thinkers, one-cause-to-one-effect thinkers, going into a new field start the way these writers do. First of course they feel they must define religion, and of course they have to define this in such a way that it is pure and discrete, that it is not anything else. So they then proceed to isolate it, cut it away and dissect it away from everything else. So they wind up with the Aristotelian logic "A" and "Not A." "A" is all "A" and nothing but "A." It's just pure "A"; and "Not A" is pure everything else and so they have no overlap, no melting, no merging, no fusing, and so on. The old possibility (taken very seriously by all profoundly religious people) that religious attitudes can be one aspect or characteristic of practically *any* behavior—indeed of *all* behaviors—is lost on the very first page of the book. This enables them to go ahead and get into an absolute and total chaos, as beautiful a chaos as I have ever seen. They get into a blind alley—and stay there—in which religious behavior is separated off from all other behavior so that all they deal with through the whole book is the external behavior—going to church or not going to church, and saving or not saving little pieces of wood, and bowing or not bowing before this or that or the other thing, thereby leaving out of the whole book what I might call small "r" religion entirely, that is, the religious people who have nothing to do with institutions or with supernaturals or with idolatry. This is a good example of atomistic thinking, but I've got plenty of others. One can think atomistically in any department of life.

We can do the same with creativeness if we want to. We can make creativeness into a Sunday behavior also, which occurs in a particular room, in a particular building, such as a classroom, and at a particular separated-off time, for example, on Thursdays. It's just creativeness and nothing else there in that room and at that time and at no time or place else. And only certain areas have to do with creativeness, painting, composing, writing, but not cooking or taxi driving or plumbing. But I raise the question again of creativeness being an aspect of practically any behavior at all, whether perceptual or attitudinal or emotional, conative, cognitive, or expressive. I think if you approach it in that way you get to ask all sorts of interesting questions which wouldn't occur to you if you approached it in this other dichotomized way.

It's a little like the difference in the ways you would try to learn to be a good dancer. Most people in an *ad hoc* society would go to the Arthur Murray School where you first move your left foot and then your right foot three paces and bit by bit you go through a lot of external, willed motions. But I think we would all agree, and I might even say that we *know* that it is rather characteristic of successful psychotherapy that there are *thousands* of effects among which might very well be good dancing, that is, being more free about dancing, more graceful, less bound up, less inhibited, less self-conscious, less appeasing, and so on. In the same way I think that psychotherapy, where it is good (and we all know there is plenty of bad psychotherapy too) and is successful, then psychotherapy, in my experience, can be counted on to enhance the creativity of a person without your ever trying to or without your ever mentioning the word.

I can also mention a relevant dissertation one of our students has done, which turned up most unexpected kinds of things. This started out to be a study of peak experiences in natural childbirth, ecstacies from motherhood and so on. But it shifted considerably because what Mrs Tanzer has been finding out is that all sorts of other miraculous changes come about when childbirth is a good or great experience. When it's a good experience, many things in life change for the woman. It may have some of the flavor of the religious conversion experience, or of the great illumination effect, or the great success experience which changes radically the woman's self-image, and therefore changes all her behaviors.

I would like to say also that this general approach seems to be a much better, a more fruitful way to talk about "climate." I have tried to pin down the Nonlinear Systems organizational setup and what was the cause of all the good effects there. All I can say is that the whole place was a climate of creative atmosphere. I couldn't pick one main cause as over against another. There was freedom of a *general* kind, atmospheric, holistic, global, rather than a little thing that you did on Tuesday—one particular, separable thing. The right climate, the *best* climate for enhancing creativeness would be a Utopia, or Eupsychia, as I prefer to call it, a society which was specifically designed for improving the self-fulfillment and psychological health of all people. That would be my general statement, the "G" statement. Within and against that background, we could *then* work with a particular "figure," with a particular *ad hoc,* the "S," or specific factors that make one man a good carpenter and another a good mathematician. But without that general societal background, in a bad society (which is a general systemic statement), creativeness is just less likely, less possible.

I think that the parallel from therapy can also be useful to us here. We have much to learn from the people who are interested in this realm of research and thinking. For instance, we must face their problem of what identity means, of what is the real Self, and of what therapy does and what education does, by way of helping people move toward identity. On the other hand we have a model of some kind of real Self, some kind of characteristic which is conceived biologically to some extent. It is constitutional, temperamental, "instinctoid." We are a species and we are different from other species. If this is so, if you can accept this instead of the *tabula rasa* model, the person as pure clay which is to be molded or reinforced into any predesigned shape that the arbitrary controller wants, then you must also accept the model of therapy as uncovering, unleashing, rather than the model of therapy as molding, creating, and shaping. And this would be true also for education. The basic models generated by these two different conceptions of human nature would be different—teaching, learning, everything.

Is then creativeness part of the general human heritage? It does very frequently get lost, or covered up, or twisted or inhibited, or whatever, and then the job is of uncovering what all babies are, in principle, born with. Well, I think that this is a very profound and very general philosophical question that we are dealing with, a very basic philosophical stance.

Finally, I would like to make one last point which is an "S" point, not a "G" point. I would like to ask, when do we *not* want creativeness? Sometimes creativeness can be a horrible nuisance. It can be a troublesome, dangerous, messy thing, as I learned once from a "creative" research assistant who gummed up a research that I had been working at for over a year. She got "creative" and changed the whole thing in the middle of it without even telling me about it. She gummed up all the data, so that a year's work was lost, messed up. On the whole we want the trains to run on time, and generally we want dentists *not* to be creative. A friend of mine had an operation a couple of years ago, and he still remembers feeling uneasy and afraid until he met his surgeon. Fortunately, he turned out to be a nice obsessional type of man, very precise, perfectly neat with a little hairline mustache, every hair in place, a perfectly straight, controlled, and sober man. My friend then heaved a sigh of relief—this was not a "creative" man. Here was a man who would do a normal, routine, pedestrian operation, not play any tricks or try any novelties or experiments or do any new sewing techniques or anything like that. This is important, I think, not only in our society, where, with our division of labor, we ought to be able to take orders and to carry through a program and be predictable. But also it is important for each of us not only in our capacity as creative workers, but also as students of creativeness, with a tendency to deify the one side of the creative process, the enthusiastic, the great insight, the illumination, the good idea, the moment in the middle of the night when you get the great inspiration, and of underplaying the two years of hard and sweaty labor that then are necessary to make anything useful out of the bright idea.

In simple terms of time, bright ideas really take a small proportion of our time. Most of our time is spent on hard work. My impression is that our students don't know this. It may be that these dead cats have been brought to my door more because my students so frequently identify with me, because I have written about peak experiences and inspirations and so on, that they feel that this is the only way to live. Life without daily or hourly peak experiences, that's no life, so that they can't do work that is boring.

Some student tells me, "No, I don't want to do that because I don't enjoy it," and then I get purple in the face and fly up in a rage—"Damn it, you do it, or I'll fire you"—and he thinks I am betraying my own principles. I think also that in making a more measured and balanced picture of creativeness, we workers with creativity have to be responsible for the impressions we make upon other people. Apparently one impression that we are making on them is that creativeness consists of lightning striking you on the head in one great glorious moment. The fact that the people who create are good workers tends to be lost.

Blocks to Creativeness

One *let's* one's self be healthy—creative by not being afraid of one's depths. This means a) to find out what one really is; b) to accept it without loss of self-esteem or fear of the disapproval of others, even likes it and is proud of it; c) to let it freely express itself. Then creativity is an automatic by-product because the person has then become himself (idiosyncratic, unique); he has become integrated and unitary (whole; and he has become uninhibited, undeadened; un-controlled allowing the dynamic processes within him free expression (alive; and he has become easy and effortless), play. This development towards self-actualization also automaticly permits the person to be perceptive in relation to the true nature of reality and flexible in relationship to its perpetual changing. Such a man can then more easily see reality as *it* is, and therefor permits him to transcend Ego and Self-consciousness and to B-cognize the other. Acceptance of self and therefore *being* self automatically permits B-cognition (freely accepted experience). One can hardly seek B-cognition directly. It is mostly epiphenomenon, an unsought-for reward for being healthy.

Such a person then cannot help being creative, because he is then growing, self-actualizing, being, rather than defending or trying to win others.

This whole thesis can be put in another way, in reverse, to make clearer what I mean. Only healthy or fully functioning people can truly perceive reality *per se* (without personal motivational abstracting or clarifying or condemnation by personal purpose). And clearly in order to solve a problem, one must be able to perceive the problem as it really is; in order to relate one's self creatively to one's self, to others, or to nature, one must be able to perceive their intrinsic nature and only healthy people can do this as a usual thing. The only way to meet the demands of "what-ness," is by being a "who-ness") (L. Frank).

This implies also the point (e.g., Tumin) that one aspect of the definition of creativeness is to stress intrinsic work satisfactions rather than extrinsic, expression rather than coping (purposeful motivated goal oriented, designed). The satisfaction comes from within rather than from without. So also does the activity itself spring from within rather than from without. It is un-motivated (at least so far as deficiency motivations are concerned). It is serendipitous rather than forced or planned.

It *must* then be novel (at least in the person's own history) without even trying to be novel, but otherwise it is not necessary or desirable to include novelty in the definition of creativeness, because it is creative when the person discovers it for himself even if it has been discovered before by others. Creativeness is a spontaneous act much more frequently than it is a consciously formulated program. ("So also in the great creative cultures of the past." Fuelop-Miller.)

★ ★ ★ ★

The conception of healthy regression must be clearly understood because it is so essentially involved in this system of thought. Health creativeness comes essentially out of the unconscious or the real self or the depths. For the person who denies his depths or is afraid of them (as in the classical compulsive obsessive neurosis) is much less often creative in this sense. The path to health-creativeness involves an ability to regress, to be childish, to give up reality, to play with thoughts, to let the psyche rule, to let one's self be controlled by the deeper forces within which are ordinarily controlled by the necessity for adaptation to external reality.

★ ★ ★ ★

One important suggestion I have for helping one's own creativeness as well as making the world safe for other people's creativeness is to find out empirically what these creative people are actually like, what their characteristics are. For instance, people tend to be unconventional, "queer," unrealistic, undisciplined, inexact, "unscientific," childish, irresponsible, wild, stubborn, speculative, "drunk," uncritical, irregular, uncontrolled, emotional. This sounds like a description of a bum or a bohemian but it should be stressed that the creative person is *capable* of being wild in this way when it is called for. He is *not* this way all the time. One way to say it is that he is not regressed all the time (that would be insanity) but he can easily and gracefully and happily regress to the unconscious when he wants to. This is a kind of controlled or permitted or willed regression. Kris calls it "regression in the service of the ego." Such a person can first regress and then come back to "reality" and become more controlled, critical, responsible, and so forth.

This recognition has important consequences for practice. Our culture tends to approve of the anal character rather than the oral, of the compulsive, obsessive rather than the hysterical, the administrator rather than the creator, of the practical man rather than the poet. Even our conception of science as a creative effort is in its roots uncreative, for science tends to be defined not in terms of wildness but in terms of order and discipline. (This kind of science may actually be seen as a refuge for uncreative people who want to be fruitful rather than creative.)

(continued)

(Continued)

Now if one recognizes and accepts these un-expected characteristics as a cultural aspect of creativeness than when they come up in one's self, they will be encouraged rather than feared. Also we will be more apt to recognize creativeness in other people, and then be able to encourage it and foster it instead of killing it. This will be especially true if we are courageous enough to recognize that the creative person's ability to be wild need not be identified with the complete inability to control of the schizophrenic. It will be seen as play rather than as breakdown. It will be seen as normal rather than abnormal. It can be understood to be absolutely compatible with a good adaptation to reality.

This is all essentially an empirical and scientific job, i.e., to study the actual characteristics of actually creative people.

★ ★ ★ ★

Essential creativeness comes out of the real self (or the unconscious, or the id). It rests on primary processes in the psychoanalytic sense. It is akin to fantasy, to poetry and other creativeness seen ordinarily in the dream.

In contrast the unconscious is essentially an adjustment to reality. Rote learning, and adjustment are based upon acceptance of reality as it is. Creativeness is essentially a revolt against reality, a declaration of independence of reality. For if it involves something new, this means it *is* dissatisfaction with what is old or what already exists. The conscious is practical rather than impractical. It involves problem centering versus means and technique centering.

★ ★ ★ ★

Rubricising. The Einstellung experiments. The Agassiz story.

★ ★ ★ ★

Practical in the main involves a repudiation of femaleness whether in himself or in woman. The I.Q. is a male concept. Thinking as ordinarily defined is a male kind of thinking. Ordinary science is a male product.

★ ★ ★ ★

The concept of closeness to the unconscious.

★ ★ ★ ★

Universal clinical experience agrees that psychoanalysis or psychotherapy or self-analysis enhances and uncovers creativeness.

★ ★ ★ ★

Safety needs first gratified then comes growth, then we find creativeness as a by-product. Creativeness is "sticking your neck out."

★ ★ ★ ★

While I think of creativity as primarily an epiphenomenon of health, of a found self, and an expression of it, yet it can also be taught and encouraged ad hoc, from the top, so to speak, rather than the bottom. Most fruitful of all techniques is a particular kind of art education. Creative education in general—dance therapy. Rhythm and music therapy. Poetry. Self-analysis (especially gestalt therapy). The right graduate education. The growth colleges (Bennington, Sarah Lawrence). Progressive education. General semantics. *Any* technique of find *any* aspect of the self. Any process of facing the unconscious (as in dream interpretation). Any process of self-confrontation. The study of the creative process and of creative people and their character and their ways. The improvement of external conditions of all sorts. (Educational, family, economic, political, religious, philosophical, cultural, childishness, feminine play, learn to be uncritical *first, then* critical, emotion, craziness.)

★ ★ ★ ★

Source: A.H. Maslow MIT notes (June 27, 1956), reprinted with the permission of Ann R.Kaplan and the *Archives of the History of American Psychology.*

Creative Keys

In innocense, i.e., to the innocent everything is equally probable; everything is equally important; everything is equally interesting. The best way to try to understand this is to see it through the eyes of the child. To the child the word importance doesn't mean anything at first. That which catches the eye, anything that glitters or happens to strike the eye by accident is as important as anything else. There seems to be no structuring of the environment to that which comes forward as figured and that which recedes into the background as ground, as relatively unimportant; as undifferentiated, unstructured.

If one expects nothing, if one has no anticipations, or apprehensions, if in a certain sense there is no future, because the child is moving totally here—now, there can be no surprise, no disappointment. One thing is as likely as another to happen. This is "perfect waiting," without any demand that one thing happen rather than another. There is no prognosis. And also no prediction means no worry.

Any child's reaction to pain, for instance, is total, without inhibition, without control of any kind. The whole organism goes into a yell of pain and rage. Partly this can be understood as concrete reaction to the concrete here now moment. This is possible because there is no expectation of the future, hence no preparation for the future, no rehearsal or anticipation. Neither is there any eagerness ("I can't wait"). There is certainly no impatience.

In the child there is a total unquestioning acceptance of whatever happens.

Since there is also very little memory, very little leaning on the past, there is little tendency in the child to bring the past into the present, or into the future. The consequence is that the child is totally here now, or totally innocent, one could say, or totally without the past and future. These are all ways of defining further concrete perception, B-cognition (of the child). And occasional B-cognition of the sophisticated adult who has managed to achieve the "second naivety."

I should add also that this is all related to my conception of the creative personality as one is totally here now, one who lives without the future and one is giving up his past. I guess a new way of saying this would be that the creative person is an innocent. An innocent could be defined as a grown person who can perceive or think, or react as a baby. It is this innocense that is recovered in the "second naivety," or perhaps I will call it the "second innocense" of the wise old man who has managed to recover the ability to be childlike.

I must put in here someplace the notion of innocense as the direct perception of the B-values. As in the Andersen fable of the child who was able to see that the King has no clothes on, when all the adults had been fooled into thinking so just as in Asch's experiment (put one of these copies in the creative file, put the other in the B-cognition file).

Source: A.H. Maslow paper (August 3, 1961), reprinted with the permission of Ann R. Kaplan and the *Archives of the History of American Psychology.*

Emotional Blocks
to Creativity

In the late 1940s, Maslow began studying creativity as an academic pursuit and interest. Nearly 20 years later, industry took a keen interest in his research on the subject. He was called on to consult and to speak to various industries on the subject. The following chapters are his original papers on creativity and innovation.

I am a little startled to find myself in this situation, because ten or fifteen years ago when I started research with this problem of creativity it was entirely an academic and professorial one. I've been amazed to be plucked at in the last couple of years by big industries of which I know nothing, or organizations like yourself whose work I don't really know at all, and I find myself a little uneasy, like many of my colleagues, on this score, because I am not sure what I can deliver exactly.

I am not sure whether the work that I have done, the conclusions that I have come to, and what we "know" about creativity today are quite usable in its present form in large organizations. All I can present here are essentially paradoxes, problems, and riddles and, at this moment, I don't know how they're going to be solved.

The management of creative personnel is fantastically difficult and important. How we are going to deal with this problem I don't quite know. The kind of creative people that I've worked with are people who are apt to get ground up in an organization? apt to be afraid of

Source: A.H. Maslow lecture to U.S. Army Engineers, Ft. Belvoir, VA, reprinted with the permission of Ann R. Kaplan and the *Archives of the History of American Psychology*.

it? and apt generally to work off in a corner or an attic by themselves. The place of the "lone wolf" in a large organization, is a major problem in today's society.

How does one reconcile the revolutionary with the stable society? The people I've studied are essentially revolutionary in the sense of both turning their backs on what already exists, and of being dissatisfied with what is now the case.

During the last ten years or so we have found that, primarily, the sources of creativeness of the kind that a large organization would be interested in, that is, the generation of really new ideas, are in the depths of human nature. We don't even have a vocabulary for it yet that's very good. You can talk in Freudian terms if you like, that is you can talk about the unconscious. Or in the term of another school of psychological thought, you may prefer to talk about the real self. But in any case it's a *deeper* self. It is deeper in an operational way, in the sense that you have to dig for it. As ore is deep, so is this deeper self. It's deep in the ground. You have to struggle to get at it thru surface layers.

Most people don't know about this new frontier. Not only do we not know about it but we are afraid to know about this new frontier. There is resistance to knowing about it. Primary creativeness comes out of the unconscious, the source of new discovery, of real novelty, of ideas which depart from what exists at this point. Secondary creativity is the kind of productivity demonstrated in some recent researches by Anne Roe who demonstrated a peculiar paradox in group after group of well-known people—of capable, fruitful, functional, famous people. In one research she studied all the starred biologists in the American Men of Science; in another, every paleontologist in the country. She found that to a certain degree, many good scientists are what the psychopathologist would call, rather rigid, rather constricted people, people who are afraid of their unconscious, in the sense that I have mentioned. And you may then arrive at a peculiar conclusion that I've come to and that is that science can be defined as a technique whereby uncreative people can create and discover, by working along with a lot of other people, by standing upon the shoulders of people who have gone before them, by being cautious and careful. This I will call secondary science and as mentioned earlier secondary creativity.

The primary creativeness which comes out of the unconscious is probably a heritage of every human being. It is common and universal. Certainly it is found in all healthy children. It is the kind of creativeness that any healthy child had and which is then lost by most people as they grow up. If you dig in a psychotherapeutic way, into the unconscious layers of the person, you find it there. We have probably all had the experience that we can be more creative in our dreams than we are in waking life. We can be wittier, bolder, more original, and more clever. With the lid, the controls, the repressions and defenses taken off, we find generally more creativeness than appears to the naked eye. The universal conclusion of psychoanalysts is that general psychotherapy may normally be expected to release creativeness which did not appear before the psychotherapy took place. This will be difficult to prove, but that is the impression they all have. Call it expert opinion if you like. Psychotherapy can help people who would like to write but who are blocked. It can help them to release, to get over this block, and to get started writing again. Getting down to these deeper layers which are ordinarily repressed, will release a common heritage—something that we all have had—and that was lost.

A certain form of neurosis from which we can learn a great deal in breaking into this problem is the compulsive–obsessive neurosis.

These rigid and tight people are people who cannot play very well. They try to control their emotions and so look rather cold and frozen in the extreme case. They are tense; they are constricted. These are the people who in a normal state generally tend to be very orderly, very neat, very punctual, very systematic, and very controlled. They make excellent bookkeepers, for instance, and so on. In psychodynamic terms these people can be briefly described as "sharply split," possibly more sharply split than most of the rest of the population, as between what they are conscious of, what they know about themselves, and what's concealed from themselves, what is unconscious or repressed. As we learn more about these people and about the reasons for the repressions, we are also learning that these reasons obtain for all of us in a lesser degree. Again we've learned from the extreme case something about the more average and the more normal. These people *have* to be this way. They have no alternative. They have no choice. The only way such a person can achieve safety, order, security, lack of anxiety, is, via orderliness, predictability, control, and mastery. These desirable goals are all made possible for him by these particular techniques. The "new" is threatening for such a person; but nothing new can happen to him if he can order it to his past experience, if he can freeze the world of flux, if he can make believe nothing is changing. If he can proceed into the future on the basis of "well tried" laws and rules, habits, modes of adjustment which have worked in the past, and which he will insist on using in the future, then he feels safe and he doesn't feel anxious.

Why does he have to do this? Of what is he afraid? The answer of the dynamic psychologist is—in very general terms—that he is afraid of his emotions, or of his deepest instinctual urges, or his deepest self, which he desperately represses. He's *got* to! Or else he feels he will go crazy. This internal drama of fear and defense is within one man's skin. But it tends by this man to be generalized, projected outward; he is then apt to see the whole world in this fashion. What he's really fighting off are dangers within himself. Anything in the external world that reminds him of or resembles these dangers within himself, he fights. He fights against his own impulses to disorderliness by becoming extra orderly. And he will be threatened by disorderliness in the world because it reminds him or threatens him with this revolution from the suppressed, from within. Anything that endangers this control; anything that strengthens either the hidden, to him dangerous impulses, anything that weakens the defensive walls, will frighten and threaten this kind of person.

Much is lost by this process. Such a man can gain a kind of equilibrium. Such a man can live his life out without cracking up. He can, by a desperate effort, hold things under control. A good deal of his energy is taken up with this effort and so he is apt to become fatigued just simply controlling himself. But he can manage. He can get along by protecting himself against the dangerous portions of his unconscious, or against his unconscious self, or his real self, which he has been taught to regard as dangerous. Everything that is unconscious must be walled off. There is a fable of an ancient tyrant who was hunting somebody who had insulted him. He knew this someone had walled up in a certain town so he ordered every man in that town to be killed, just to be sure that the one person wouldn't get away. The compulsive obsessive does something like that. He kills off and walls off everything unconscious in order to be sure that the dangerous portions of it don't get out.

Out of this unconscious, this deeper self, this portion of ourselves of which we are generally afraid and trying to keep under control, comes the ability to play, to enjoy, to fantasize, to laugh, to loaf, to be spontaneous. And, what's most important for us here, creativity, a kind of intellectual play, a kind of permission to be ourselves, to fantasize, to let loose, and to be crazy, privately. (Every really new idea looks crazy, at first.) The compulsive-obsessive gives up his primary creativeness. He gives up the possibilities for being artistic. He gives up his poetry. He gives up his imagination. He drowns all his healthy childishness. Furthermore, this applies not only to the neurotic but also to what we call a good adjustment, and to what Ross Mooney describes as being able to fit into the right harness, that is, getting along well in the world, using common sense, being realistic, being mature, taking on responsibility. Certain aspects of these adjustments involve turning one's back upon what is threatening to the good adjustment. These dynamic efforts to make peace with the world and with the necessities of common sense, with the necessities of physical, biological, and social realities, are generally made at the cost of giving up a portion of our deeper selves. It is not as dramatic in us as in the case I've described. It is becoming more and more apparent, however, that what we call a normal adult adjustment involves denying that which would threaten us as well. And what does threaten us is softness, fantasy, emotion, "childishness." In creative men, (and uncreative men too) is the horrible fear of anything that the person himself would call "femininity," "femaleness," which we immediately call "homosexual." If he's been brought up in a tough environment, "feminine" means practically everything that's creative: Imagination, fantasy, color, poetry, music, tenderness, languishing, being romantic. In general, these are walled off as dangerous to one's picture of one's own masculinity. Everything that's called "weak" tends to be repressed in the normal masculine adult adjustment. And many things are called weak which are not weak at all.

These unconscious processes can be separated into "primary processes" and "secondary processes."

Primary processes, the unconscious processes of cognizing, of perceiving the world and of thinking, are very, very different from the laws of common sense, of good logic, of what the psychoanalyst calls the "secondary processes" in which we are logical, sensible, and realistic. When "secondary processes" are walled-off from the primary processes, both processes suffer. At the extreme, the walling off of or the complete splitting off of logic, common sense, and rationality from the deeper layers of the personality produces the compulsive obsessive person, the compulsively rational person, the person who cannot live in the world of emotion, who doesn't know whether he is in love or not because love is illogical, who can't even permit himself to laugh frequently because laughing, too, is not logical, rational, and sensible. When this is walled off, when the person is split, we have a diseased rationality and also diseased primary processes. These secondary processes, walled off and dichotomized, can be considered largely as an organization generated by fears and by frustration. It is a system of defenses, repressions and controls, of appeasement, and of cunning underhanded negotiations with a frustrating and dangerous physical and social world which is the only source of gratification of needs and which makes us pay dearly for whatever gratifications we get from it. Such a sick conscious, or ego, or conscious self becomes aware of and then lives only by what it perceives to be the laws of nature and of society. This is blindness. The compulsive obsessive person not only loses much of the pleasures of living, but also he becomes cognitively blind to much of himself, much in other people, and even in nature. There is much he is blind to in nature even as a scientist. Such people *can* get things done, but *at what cost* to himself?, (because he's not a happy person). And, secondly, what things does he get done? Are they worthy of doing?

One of my old professors was a man who characteristically saved things. All the newspapers that he had ever read were bound by weeks. Each week was bound with a little red string; all the papers of the month were tied together with a yellow string. He had a regular breakfast every day—Monday orange juice, Tuesday oatmeal, Wednesday prunes, and so on. God help his wife if there were prunes on Monday. He saved all his old razor blades and packaged them nicely with labels. When he first came into his laboratory, he labeled everything. He had everything organized, and then put little stickers on them. He spent hours trying to get a label on a little probe of the sort that didn't have any space for a label at all. The lid of the piano in his laboratory carried the label "piano." This kind of man is in real trouble. He is himself extremely unhappy. The kind of things that this fellow did are pertinent to the question I raised above. These people get things done but which things? Are they worth while? Sometimes they are, sometimes they are not. Many of our scientists are of this type. In this kind of work, such a *poking* character can be very very useful. Such a man can spend twelve years in *poking* at the microdissection of the nucleus of a one-celled animal. It takes that kind of patience, persistence, stubborness, and need-to-know that all people have. Society can most often use that sort of person.

Primary processes then in this dichotomized walled off, feared sense, this is sick. But it *needn't* be sick. Deep down, we look at the world through our wishes, fears, and gratifications. A really young child looks at the world, at itself, and at other people. It is logical in the sense of having no negative, no contradictions, no separate identities, no opposites, no mutual exclusions. Aristotle doesn't exist for the primary processes. It is independent of control, taboos, discipline, inhibitions, delays, planning, calculations of possibility or impossibility. It has nothing to do with time and space or with sequence, casualty, order, or with the laws of the physical world. This is a world quite other than the physical world. When it is placed under the necessity of disguising itself from conscious awareness to make things less threatening, it can condense several objects into one as in a dream. It can displace emotions from their true objects to other harmless ones. It can obscure by symbolizing. It can be omnipotent, ubiquitous, omniscient. Everything I've said holds for the dream. It has nothing to do with action. It can make things come to pass without doing or without acting, simply by fantasy. For most people it is preverbal, very concrete, closer to raw experiencing and usually visual. It is prevaluational, premoral, pre-ethical, pre-cultural. It is prior to good and evil. In most civilized people just *because it has been walled off* by this dichotomizing, it tends to be childish, immature, crazy, dangerous, frightening. The person who has completely suppressed the primary processes, completely walled off the unconscious, is sick in the particular way which I have described.

The person in whom the secondary processes of control, reason, order, logic, have completely crumbled is a schizophrenic. He's a very, very sick man, too.

The healthy person, especially the healthy person who creates, has somehow managed a fusion and a synthesis of both primary and secondary processes; both conscious and unconscious; both of deeper self and of conscious self. And he manages to do this gracefully and fruitfully. It is *possible* to do even though it is not very common. It is certainly possible to help this process along by psychotherapy; deeper and longer psychotherapy can be even better. In this fusion both the primary processes and the secondary processes, partake of each other, then change in character. The unconscious doesn't become frightening any more. This is the person who can live with his unconscious; live with, let's say, his childishness, his fantasy, his imagination, his wish fulfillment, his femininity, his poetic quality, his crazy quality. He is the person, as one psychoanalyst said, "who can regress in the service of ego." This is *voluntary* regression. This person is the one who has that kind of creativeness at his disposal, readily available, that I think we're interested in.

The compulsive-obsessive kind of man that I mentioned earlier, in the extreme instance, *cannot* play. He cannot let go. Such a man tends to avoid parties because he's so sensible and you're supposed to be a little silly at a party. He is afraid to get a little tight because then his controls loosen up too much; for him this is a great danger. He has to be in control all the time. Such a person will probably make a horrible subject for hypnosis. He will probably get frightened by being anesthesized, or by any other loss of full consciousness. These are people who try to be dignified, orderly, conscious, rational at a party where you are not supposed to be. The person who is comfortable enough with his unconscious is able to let go that much anyhow—a little crazy in this party sense; to be silly, to play along with a gag and to enjoy it; and to enjoy being nutty for a little while anyhow—"in their service of the ego" as the psychoanalyst has said. This is like a conscious, voluntary regression—instead of trying to be dignified and controlled at all times.

Psychotherapy, self-therapy, self-knowledge is a difficult process because, as things stand now for most of us, the conscious and the unconscious are walled off from each other. How do you get these two worlds, the psychic world and the world of reality to be comfortable with each other? In general, the process of psychotherapy, is a matter of slow confrontation, bit by bit, with the help of a technician, with the uppermost layers of the unconscious. They are exposed, tolerated, and assimilated. They turn out to be not so dangerous, not so horrible after all. Then comes the next layer, and then the next. In this same process of getting a person to face something of which he is terribly afraid and then when he does face it, finding that there was nothing to fear in the first place. He has been afraid of it because he has been looking at it through the eyes of the child that he used to be. This is childish misinterpretation. What the child was afraid of and therefore repressed, was beyond the reach of common sense learning and experience and growing up. It has to stay there until it's dragged out by some special process. The conscious must become strong enough to dare friendliness with the enemy.

A fair parallel can be found in the relations between men and women throughout history. Men have been afraid of women and have therefore dominated them, unconsciously, for very much the same reasons that they have been afraid of their primary processes. The dynamic psychologists are apt to think that much of the relationship of men to women is determined by the fact that women will remind men of their own unconscious, that is of their own femaleness, their own softness, their own tenderness. And therefore fighting women, trying to rule or to derogate them has been part of this effort to *control* these unconscious forces which are within everyone of us. Between a frightened master and a resentful slave no true love is possible. Only as men become strong, self-confident, and integrated can they tolerate and finally enjoy self-actualizing women, women who are full human beings. But no man fulfills himself without such a woman, in principle. Therefore strong men and strong women are the condition of each other. Neither can exist without the other. They are the cause of the other. Women grow men and men grow women. They are the reward of each other. If you are a good enough man that's the kind of woman you'll get and that's the kind of woman you'll deserve. Therefore, going back to our parallel, healthy, primary processes and healthy secondary processes, that is healthy fantasy and healthy rationality, need each other in order to fuse into a true integration.

Chronologically, our knowledge of primary processes was derived first from studies of dreams, fantasies, and neurotic processes, and later of psychotic, insane processes. Little by little this knowledge has been freed of its taint of pathology, irrationality, immaturity, and primitiveness, in the bad sense. Only recently have we become fully aware, from our studies of healthy people, of the creative process, of play, of aesthetic perception, of the meaning of healthy love, of healthy growing and becoming, of healthy education, that every human being is both poet and engineer, both rational and nonrational, both child and adult, both masculine and feminine, both in the psychic world and in the world of nature. Only slowly have we learned what we lose by trying daily to be *only* and *purely* rational, *only* "scientific," *only* logical, *only* sensible, *only* practical, *only* responsible. The integrated person, the fully evolved human, the fully matured person, must be available to himself at both these levels, simultaneously. It is now obsolete to stigmatize this unconscious side of human nature as sick rather than healthy. That is the way Freud thought of it originally but we are learning differently now. We are learning that complete health means being available to yourself at all levels. We can no longer call this side "evil" rather than "good," lower rather than higher, selfish rather than unselfish, beastly rather than human. Throughout human history, the history of Western civilization, and more especially the history of Christianity there has tended to be this dichotomy. No longer can we dichotomize ourselves into a cave man and a civilized man, into a devil and a saint. We can now see this as an illegitimate dichotomy, an illegitimate "either/or," in which by the very process of splitting and dichotomizing we create a sick "either" and a sick "or," that is to say a sick conscious and a sick unconscious, a sick rationality, and sick impulses.

Once we transcend and resolve this dichotomy, once we can put these together into the unity in which they are originally, for instance, in the healthy child, in the healthy adult, or in specially creative people, we can recognize that the dichotomizing or the splitting is itself a pathological process. And then it becomes possible for your civil war to end. This is precisely what happens in self-actualizing people, psychologically healthy people. It is *exactly* what we find in such people. When we pick out from the population the healthiest one percent or fraction of one percent, these people have in the course of their lifetime, sometimes with the benefit of therapy, sometimes without, been able to put together these two worlds, and to live comfortably in both of them. I've described the healthy person as having a healthy childlikeness. It's hard to put it into words because the word "childlikeness" customarily means the opposite of maturity. The most mature human beings living are also childlike. That sounds like a contradiction but actually it is not. The most mature people are the ones that can have the most fun. These are people who can regress at will, who can become childish and play with children and be close to them. It is no accident that children generally tend to like them and get along with them. They can regress to that level. Involuntary regression is of course a very dangerous thing. Voluntary regression, however, apparently is characteristic of very healthy people.

Now as for practical suggestions about achieving this fusion I don't quite know. The only really practicable one that I know in ordinary practice for making this fusion within the person is psychotherapy. And this is certainly not a practicable or even a welcome suggestion.

There are possibilities, of course, of self-analysis and self-therapy. Any technique which will increase self-knowledge in depth should in principle increase one's creativity by making available to oneself these sources of fantasy, play with ideas, being able to sail right out of the world and off the earth; getting away from common sense. Common sense means living in the world as it is today, but creative people are people who don't want the world as it is today but want to make another world. And in order to be able to do that, they have to be able to sail right off the surface of the earth, to imagine, to fantasy, and even to be crazy, and nutty. The suggestion that I have to make, the practical suggestion for you people who manage creative personnel, is simply to watch out for such people as they already exist and then to pluck them out and hang on to them.

I think I was able to be of service to one company by making this recommendation. I tried to describe to them what these primary-creative people are like. They are precisely the ones that make trouble in an organization, usually. I wrote down a list of some of their characteristics that would be guaranteed to make trouble. They tend to be unconventional; they tend to be a little bit queer; unrealistic; they are often called undisciplined; sometimes inexact; "unscientific," that is, by a specific definition of science. They tend to be called childish by their more compulsive colleagues, irresponsible, wild, crazy, speculative, uncritical, irregular, emotional. This sounds like a description of a bum or a Bohemian or an eccentric. And it should be stressed, I suppose, that in the early stages of creativeness, you've got to be a bum, and you've got to be a Bohemian, you've got to be crazy. People who have already successfully been creative have let themselves "brainstorm" in the early stages of thinking. They let themselves be completely uncritical. They allow all sorts of wild ideas to come into their heads. And in great bursts of emotion and enthusiasm, they may scribble out the poem or the formula or the mathematical solution or work up the theory, or design the experiment. Then, and only then, do they become secondary, become more rational, more controlled and more critical. If you try to be rational and controlled and orderly in this first stage of the process, you'll never get to it. Now the brainstorming technique, as I remember it, consisted in just this—in not being critical—letting yourself play with ideas—free association—letting them come out on the table, in profusion, and then only later on, tossing away those ideas which are bad, or useless, and retaining the ones which are good. If you are afraid of making this kind of crazy mistake then you'll never get any of the bright ideas either.

This kind of Bohemian business is not necessarily uniform or continued. I am talking about people who are able to be like that *whey they want to be* (regression in the service of the ego; voluntary regression; voluntary craziness; voluntary going into the unconscious.) These same people can afterwards put on their caps and gowns and become grown up, rational, sensible, orderly, and so on, and examine with a critical eye what they produced in a great burst of enthusiasm, and creative fervor. Then they can say sometimes, "It felt wonderful while it was being born, but it's no good," and toss it away. A truly integrated person can be both secondary and primary; both childish and mature. He can regress and then come back to reality, becoming then more controlled and critical in his responses.

I mention that this was of use to one company or at least to this one person in the company who was in charge of creative personnel, because it was precisely this sort of person he'd been firing. He had laid very great stress on taking orders well and on being well adjusted to the organization.

I don't know how an organization manager is going to work these things out. I don't know what would happen to morale. This is not my problem. I don't know how it would be possible to use such characters in the middle of an organization which has to do the orderly work that ensues upon the idea. An idea is just the beginning in a very complex process of working out. That's a problem that we'll be working out in this country more than any other place on the face of the earth, I guess, during the next decade or so. We've got to face it. Huge sums of money now are going into research and development. The management of creative personnel becomes a new problem.

The standard of practice which has worked well in large organizations, absolutely needs modification and revision of some sort. We'll have to find some way of permitting people to be individualistic in an organization. It will have to be a practical kind of working out, just simply trying out this and trying out that and trying out the other, and finally coming to kind of an empirical conclusion. It would be a help to be able to spot these as characteristics, not only of craziness, but also of creativeness. (By the way I don't want to put in a good recommendation for everybody who behaves like this. Some of them actually *are* crazy.) Now we've got to learn to distinguish. It's a question of learning to respect or at least to look with an open eye on people of this sort and trying somehow to fit them into society. Customarily today such people are lone wolves. You will find them, I think, more in the academic situation than you will in large organizations or large corporations. They tend to be more comfortable there because they're permitted to be as crazy as they like. Everybody expects professors to be crazy, anyhow, and it doesn't make much difference to anyone. They're not beholden to anyone else except for their teaching, perhaps. But the professor has time enough ordinarily to go off into his attic or his basement and dream up all sorts of things, whether they are practical or not. In an organization you've got to give out, ordinarily. I don't know how you can put these necessities together in your situation. It's like a story I heard recently. Two psychoanalysts met each other at a party. One analyst walked up to the other analyst and slapped him in the face without any warning. The analyst who was slapped looked startled for a moment and then shrugged his shoulder and said, "That's *his* problem."

The Need for
Creative People

The rate of acceleration of accumulation of new scientific facts, of new inventions, of increased affluence presents every human being today with a situation different from any that has happened before. We must develop people who are capable of coping with the inevitable rapid obsolescence of any new product or any old way of doing things. They must be people who will not fight change but will anticipate it and enjoy it.

A. Maslow, *Archives of the History of American Psychology*

The question is, Who is interested in creativity? And my answer is that practically everybody is. This interest is no longer confined to psychologists and psychiatrists. Now it has become a question of national and international policy as well. People in general, and especially the military, the politicians, and the thoughtful patriots, all must soon come to the following realization: there is a military stalemate and it looks as if there will continue to be. The function of the army today is essentially to prevent war rather than to make war. Therefore the continuing struggle between the large political systems, that is, the cold war, will continue to be waged, but in a nonmilitary fashion. That system will prevail which will appeal to other neutral people. Which turns out a better kind of person, more brotherly, more peaceable, less greedy, more lovable, more respect-worthy? Who will attract the African and Asian people?, and so forth and so on.

In general, then, the more psychologically healthy (or more highly evolved) person is a political necessity. He has to be a person who is not

Source: A.H. Maslow paper (undated), reprinted with the permission of Ann R. Kaplan and the *Archives of the History of American Psychology.*

hated, a person who can get along and be friendly, deeply friendly with anybody, including Africans and Asians, who are very quick to detect any condescension or prejudice or hatred. Certainly one of the characteristics that is necessary is that the citizen of the country which will lead and win out must not have race prejudice. He must feel brotherly, he must feel like helping, he must be a trustworthy leader rather than someone who is mistrusted. In the long run he must not be authoritarian, not sadistic, and so forth.

UNIVERSAL NEEDS

But in addition to this, there is another, possibly more immediate necessity for any viable political, social, economic system, and that is to turn out more creative people. This is the same kind of consideration that weighs so heavily with our great industries, because they are all so aware of possible obsolescence. They are all aware that however rich and prosperous they may be at this moment, they may wake up tomorrow morning to find that some new product has been invented which makes them obsolete. What will happen to the automobile manufacturers if someone comes out with a cheap, personal-travel technique of some kind, one which could sell at half the price of an automobile? As a consequence, every rich corporation that can afford it pours back a very large percentage of its money into research and development of *new* products, as well as into the improvement of the old ones. The parallel on the international scene is the armament race. It is perfectly true that there is a careful balance now of deterrent weapons and bombs and bombers, and so forth But supposing something happened next year of the kind that happened when the Americans invented the atom bomb?

Therefore there is also a huge amount of research and development now going on, under the head of defense or military expenditures in all the large countries. Each must try to discover first that new weapon which will make all present weapons obsolete. I think that the rulers of the powerful countries are beginning to realize that the people who are capable of discovering such things are that peculiar breed to whom they have always been reflexly antagonistic, that is, the creative persons. Now they will have to learn about the management of creative personnel, the early selection of creative persons, the education and fostering of creative persons, and the like.

In essence, this is why I think so many more of our leaders today are interested in the theory of creativeness. The historical situation with which we are confronted helps to create an interest in creativeness among thoughtful people, among social philosophers, and many other kinds of people. Our era is more in flux, more in process, more rapidly changing than any previous one in history. The rate of acceleration of accumulation of new scientific facts, of new inventions, of new technological developments, of new psychological happenings, of increased affluence, presents every human being today with a situation different from any that has ever happened before. Among other things, this new lack of continuity and stability from past to the present into the future makes all sorts of changes necessary which many people don't realize yet. For instance, the whole process of education, especially of technical and professional education, has changed entirely in the last few decades. To make it simple, there is little use in learning facts; they become obsolete too fast. There is little use in learning techniques; they become obsolete almost overnight. It is of little use, for instance, for professors of engineering to teach their students all the techniques that they themselves learned back in *their* school days; these techniques are almost useless now. In effect, we are confronted in practically every area of life with obsolescence of old facts and theories and methods. We are all a bunch of buggy-whip makers whose skills are now useless.

New Teaching Concepts

What is then the correct way of teaching people to be, for example, engineers? It is quite clear that we must teach them to be creative persons, at least in the sense of being able to confront novelty, to improvise. They must not be afraid of change but rather must be able to be comfortable with change and novelty, and if possible (because best of all) even be able to *enjoy* novelty and change. This means that we must teach and train engineers not in the old and standard sense, but in the new sense, that is, "creative" engineers.

This, in general, is also true of executives, leaders, and administrators in business and industry. They must be people who are capable of coping with the inevitably rapid obsolescence of any new product, or of any old way of doing things. They must be people who will not fight change but who will anticipate it, and who can be challenged enough by it to enjoy it. We must develop a race of improvisers, of "here-now" creators. We must define the skillful person or the trained person, or the educated person in a very different way than we used to (that is, *not* as one who has a rich knowledge of the past so that he can profit from past experiences in a future emergency). Much that we have called learning has become useless. Any kind of learning which is the simple application of the past to the present, or the use of past techniques in the present situation has become obsolete in many areas of life. Education can no longer be considered essentially or only a learning process; it is now also a character training, a person-training process. Of course this is not *altogether* true, but it is very largely true, and it will become truer and truer year by year. (I think this is perhaps the most radical and blunt and unmistakable way of saying what I am trying to say.) The past has become almost useless in some areas of life. People who depend too much upon the past have become almost useless in many professions. We need a new kind of human being who can divorce himself from his past, who feels strong and courageous and trusting enough to trust himself in the present situation, to handle the problem well in an improvising way, without previous preparation, if need be.

All of this adds up to increased emphasis on psychological health and strength. It means an increased valuing of the ability to pay the fullest attention to the here-now situation, to be able to listen well, to be able to see well in the concrete, immediate moment before us. It means that we need people who are different from the average kind of person who confronts the present as if it were a repetition of the past, and who uses the present simply as a period in which he prepares for future threats and dangers, which he doesn't trust himself enough to meet unprepared when the time comes. This new kind of human being that we would need even if there were no cold war, and even if we were all united in a brotherly species, is needed simply to confront the new kind of world in which we live.

The cold war considerations that I have talked about above, as well as the new kind of world we are now confronting, force certain other necessities upon our discussion of creativeness. Since in essence we are talking about a kind of person, a kind of philosophy, a kind of character, then the stress shifts away from stress on created products, and technological innovations and aesthetic products and innovations, and so forth. We must become more interested in the creative process, the creative attitude, the creative person, rather than in the creative product alone.

Therefore it seems to me a better strategy to turn more attention to the inspiration phase of creativeness rather than to the working-out phase of creativeness, that is, to "primary creativeness" rather than to "secondary creativeness."

We must, more often, use as our example not the finished work of art or science which is socially useful, but rather we must focus our attention on improvising, on the flexible and adaptable, efficient confronting of any here-now situation which turns up, whether it is important or unimportant. This is so because using the finished product as a criterion introduces too many confusions with good work habits, with stubbornness, discipline, patience, with good editing abilities, and other characteristics which have nothing directly to do with creativeness, or at least are not unique to it.

All of these considerations make it even *more* desirable to study creativeness in children rather than in adults. Here many of the confounding and contaminating problems are avoided. For instance, here we can no longer stress social innovation or social usefulness or the created product. Also we can avoid confusing the issue by avoiding preoccupation with great inborn talent (which seems to have little connection with the universal creativeness that we are all heir to).

These are some of the reasons why I consider nonverbal education so important, for example, through art, through music, through dancing. I am not particularly interested in the training of artists because in any case this is done in a different way. Neither am I much interested in the children having a good time, nor even in art as therapy. For that matter I am not even interested in art education, *per se*. What I am really interested in is the new kind of education which we must develop which moves toward fostering the new kind of human being that we need, the process person, the creative person, the improvising person, the self-trusting, courageous person, the autonomous person. It just happens to be a historical accident that the art educators are the ones who went off in this direction first. It could just as easily be true of mathematical education and I hope it will be one day.

Certainly mathematics or history or literature are still taught today in most places in an authoritarian, memorizing way (although already, this is not true for the very newest kind of education for improvising, for guessing, for creativeness, for pleasure that J. Bruner has been writing about, and that the mathematicians and physicists have created for the high schools). The question again is how to teach children to confront the here-now, to improvise, and so forth, that is, how to become creative people, able to assume the creative attitude.

The new education-through-art movement with its stress on nonobjectivity is one subject in which right and wrong are much less involved, in which correctness and incorrectness can be pushed aside, and in which therefore the child can be confronted with himself, with his own courage or anxiety, with his stereotypes or his freshness, and so forth. A good way to say this is that where reality has been withdrawn, we have a good projective test situation, and we therefore have a good psychotherapeutic or growth situation. This is exactly what is done both in projective testing and in insight therapy; that is, reality, correctness, adaptability to the world, physical and chemical and biological determiners are all removed, so that the psyche can reveal itself more freely. I might even go so far as to say that in this respect, education through art is a kind of therapy and growth technique, because it permits the deeper layers of the psyche to emerge, and therefore to be encouraged, fostered, trained, and educated.

Notes on Creativeness

Creativeness is correlated with the ability to withstand the lack of structure, the lack of future, the lack of predictability, of control, the tolerance for ambiguity, for planlessness.

A.H. Maslow, *Maslow on Management*

We can learn from the T-group experiences that creativeness is correlated with the ability to withstand the lack of structure, the lack of future, lack of predictability, of control, the tolerance for ambiguity, for planlessness.

Here-now creativeness is dependent on this kind of ability to forget about the future, to improvise in the present, to give full attention to the present, for example, to be able fully to listen or to observe.

This general ability to give up future, structure, to give up control and predictability, is also characteristic of loafing, or of the ability to enjoy—to say it in another way—which itself is also essentially unmotivated, purposeless, without goal, and therefore without future. That is to say, in order to be able to listen totally, in order to be able to immerse oneself, to be all there in the here-now, one must be able to give up the future in the sense of being able to enjoy, to loaf, to saunter instead of purposefully walking, to take one's ease, in a word—to play.

Note, also, that the self-actualizing subjects can enjoy mystery, futurelessness, ambiguity, lack of structure. They can be contrasted with Kurt Goldstein's brain-injured subjects as well as with the obsessional neurotics in whom there is such a tremendous and compulsive need for control, for prediction, for structure, for law and order, for an agenda, for classifying, for rehearsing, for planning. In other words, it is as if these people were afraid of the future and also mistrusted their own ability to improvise in the face of an emergency, of something that would come up unexpectedly. This is then a combination of a lack of trust in one's self, a kind of fear that one does not have the ability or the capacity to face anything which is unexpected, which is not planned for, which is not controllable and predictable, and so on. Give the examples here of the geometrizing of time and space of the brain-injured people.[1] I think I can also use my article, "Emotional Blocks to Creativity" for good obsessional examples.

Point out that these are all safety mechanisms, all fear and anxiety mechanisms. They all represent lack of courage, lack of confidence in the future, lack of confidence in one's self. It takes a certain kind of courage, which is simultaneously a kind of justified trust in one's self and a justified trust in the goodness of the environment and of the future, to be able to face an unexpected, an unknown, unstructured situation without any guards or defenses, and with an innocent faith that one can improvise in the situation. Perhaps, for communication purposes some simpler examples may be necessary, for instance, like pointing out to an audience how commonly in a conversation, when the other person is talking, they are not really listening but are rather planning and rehearsing what they are going to say as a response. Then point out how this means lack of confidence in their ability to improvise, that is, to think up words to say without preparing beforehand, without planning.

I think another good example might be actual motion pictures of the way in which a little toddler or perhaps an infant shows in actual behavior total trust in the mother or the father. Get pictures of a kid jumping off a height into his father's arms with total fearlessness and total trust. Or into a swimming pool.

I think that it would be useful to add this to my discussion of safety science contrasted with growth science or self-actualizing science.[2] Compare with Kurt Goldstein's brain-injured patients[3] and with the symptoms of the obsessional neurotics. Let's compare, in a parallel column, B. F. Skinner's stress again and again and again in his lectures and written papers on predictability, on control, lawfulness, structure, and so forth. Then make an actual count of how infrequently the words

---

[1] E. Strauss in Rollo May, et al. (Eds.), *Existence* (New York: Basic Books, 1958).
[2] Forthcoming book on *Psychology of Science*.
[3] Kurt Goldstein, *The Organism* (Boston: Beacon Press, 1963).

creativeness, improvising, spontaneity, expressiveness, autonomy, and the like, occur. Then do the same for Carl Rogers or for other similar, "humanistic" writers. It occurs to me that this would make a very nice experiment that even an undergraduate student could do easily enough. It would make the point I'm trying to make very neatly and easily and unmistakably. In any case this would also make the parallel with two kinds of psychopathology and at the very least dramatize the point that I am trying to make that these words may be psychopathological. (Of course, it's also necessary to stress that they can be quite healthy. But then, the question is how to make the differentiation between neurotic need for predictability and the normal pleasure in predictability, control, lawfulness, orderliness in the world, and so on.)

I guess here it would be useful, especially for the laymen, to make a little discussion of just what the differences are between the neurotic needs and normal or healthy needs. At the moment I can think of the facts that the neurotic needs are uncontrollable, inflexible, compulsive, irrational, independent of good or bad circumstances; that their gratification does not bring real pleasure but only momentary relief; that their frustration brings, very quickly, tension, anxiety, and finally hostility and anger. Furthermore, they are ego-dystonic rather than ego-syntonic; that is, they are felt as alien or as something overcoming one, rather than as one's own autonomous self-willed coming-from-within desires or impulses. The neurotic person is apt to say, "Something comes over me," or "I don't know what came over me," or "I have no control over it."

Run through all of this creativeness stuff and apply it to the managerial situation, the leadership and fellowship situation. In every discussion about these things in any enterprise of any kind whatsoever, there is certainly going to come up from those who need more structure, whether for good reasons or bad, the questions about anarchy and chaos and the like. It is necessary to meet these not only on a rational level but also to understand them as possibly neurotic or irrational or deeply emotional. Sometimes the proper way to handle this is not to argue logically but to interpret psychoanalytically. It's very easy to point out without too much offense in such groupings that this is a demand for a set of laws and rules and principles which are all written down in the book, that this is a demand for controlling the future and for anticipating anything that might come up in the future. Since this latter is realistically impossible, that is, since the future is, after all, unpredictable to some extent, then trying to make a "book of rules" which will anticipate any possible contingency in the future is a futile effort; and then one can go on to ask, Why can't we trust ourselves to be able to handle these unexpected contingencies in the future? Why must we prepare for them so? Can't we handle exceptions; don't we trust ourselves to have good judgment, even in an unanticipated situation? Why can't we wait until we have experiences piling up in the situations and *then* make whatever rules are necessary as a kind of formulation of actual experience in the actual situation. In this way one comes to a minimum of rules rather than to a maximum of rules. (But it may be necessary to concede, as I have had to do in the past, that in extremely large organizations like the Army and the Navy it is necessary to have a Book of Rules.)

Addition to the Notes
on the Creative Person

It is as if these people were afraid of the future and also mis-
trusted their own ability to improvise in the face of something
that would come up unexpectedly. This is then a combination
of a lack of trust in ones' self, a kind of fear that one does not
have the ability or the capacity to face anything which is un-
expected, unpredictable.

A.H. Maslow, *Maslow on Management*

Since so much of the trouble with mechanical and authoritarian organization, and with old-fashioned treatment of the worker as an interchangeable part, seems to be the inability to shift and change, the obsessional need for a planned-out future, for schedules, for sameness, and the like, it seems to me that it would be basically quite important for the philosophy of democratic management to study more carefully the psychodynamics of creativeness.

It is desirable to stress, in this context particularly, the ability to be imprecise. The creative person is able to be flexible; he can change course as the situation changes (which it always does); he can give up his plans, he can continuously and flexibly adapt to the law of the changing situation and to the changing authority of the facts, to the demand character of the shifting problem.

This means, to say it in a theoretical way, that he is able to face a changing future; that is, he does not need a fixed and unchanging future. He seems not to be threatened by unexpectedness (as the obsessional and rigid person is). For the creative person who is able to improvise, plans are definitely no more than heuristic scaffoldings and can be cast aside easily without regret and without anxiety. He tends not to feel irritated when plans change or schedules change or the future changes. On the contrary, my impression is that he is sometimes apt to show *increased* interest, alertness, and engagement with the problem. Self-actualizing people are attracted to mystery, to novelty, change, flux, and find all of these easy to live with; as a matter of fact, these are what make life interesting. These people, that is, the self-actualizing people and also the creative people and the good improvisors tend, on the contrary, to be easily bored with monotony, with plans, with fixity, with lack of change.

Of course, this is all seen from another angle—the ability of the matured personality, the strong personality to be *all there,* to be totally here and now, to be able to pour himself totally into the current situation, to be able to listen perfectly and to see perfectly, and so forth. This, I have pointed out, can be phrased in terms of giving up the past and the future, or of pushing them aside from the present situation. That is, the person viewing a present problem does not see it merely as a matter of shuffling over every problem he has ever had in the past to see which past solutions fit this present problem. Nor does he use the problematic situation as a period in which to prepare himself for the future, to rehearse what he is going to say, to plan his attack or counterattack, and so forth. He is totally immersed in the here and now, thereby implying considerable courage and trust in himself, the calm expectation of being able to improvise when the time comes for him to solve new problems. This means a particular kind of healthy self-respect, self-trust. It also implies freedom from anxiety and from fear. This, in turn, means a certain appraisal of the world, of reality, of environment, which permits him to trust it, not to see it as overwhelmingly dangerous and powerful. He feels that he is able to manage it. He is not afraid of it. It does not look monstrous or frightening. Self-respect means that the person thinks of himself as a prime mover, as the responsible one, as autonomous, the determiner of his own fate.

Our Aesthetic Needs:
Exploratory Notes

The following essay, written in January 1950, highlights the importance of the aesthetic needs of the individual. Today, in product development as well as in workspace and environment, aesthetic needs play a vital role—one Maslow always regarded as imperative to success.

Very little is known empirically about our aesthetic pleasures, needs, impulses, creativeness, or, indeed, anything aesthetic at all. And yet, aesthetic experiences can be so poignant and aesthetic hunger can be so desperate that we are irresistibly tempted to postulate concepts that correspond to these subjective matters. It would be important to offer a theory to explain these acute experiences. There is only one thing we cannot do with our aesthetic impulses and that is to leave them alone!

It would be easily possible to scrape together out of common knowledge bits and scraps of evidence to support the postulation of aesthetic needs, just as we have done concerning the existence of cognitive needs. If nothing else, such bibliographic research would justify my theoretical effort and demonstrate the existence of an unsolved problem—a gap—a question that psychology today should attempt to answer.

Unfortunately, all we have to offer now—besides to cry "Problem! Problem!"—are a few distinctions suggested by other hypotheses to be discussed at a later date.

Source: A.H. Maslow essay (January 1950), reprinted with the permission of Ann R. Kaplan and the *Archives of the History of American Psychology.*

First, we must not think of *an* aesthetic need as if it were merely one particular impulse. Rather, there clearly seem to be discernible various kinds of aesthetic impulses, some or all of which also may serve as needs.

The aesthetic reaction is a subjective, introspective, and conscious response that most people consider ineffable; that is, it cannot be described in words but must be experienced to be known. However, some phrases are, in fact, used commonly to describe this type of experience. Thus, people frequently report such sensations as a faster heartbeat, a holding of the breath, feelings of fascination and mental absorption, sensations of sharp pleasure, and cold shivers moving up and down the back.

Indeed, I have often thought that the aesthetic experience may share a similarity with what physiologists call "sensory shock." For example, this encompasses a person's set of responses when suddenly immersed in ice-cold water. For now, I'm only guessing about this possible similarity, but at least it is easily testable.

The aesthetic experience may lead to various simple, habitual responses, such as collecting the particular objects (paintings, musical recordings, and so forth) that give so much pleasure or going to art museums or musical concerts. In general, we may speak here of appreciation, fun, pleasure, and connoisseurship but not yet of *actual aesthetic creation!*

In both theory and practice, aesthetic creativity is separable from aesthetic connoisseurship and should be treated differently by psychologists. We needn't point only to the legendary violin virtuoso who hated music but also to the well-known fact that connoisseurs notable for their good taste are often not creative at all. Even in principle, the battle between critics and creative artists is endless.

In the realm of analyzing artistic creativity, an infinite number of distinctions and classifications seems possible. Most of these are of little use to psychology, and we shall not concern ourselves with them. However, there is one differentiation that is almost surely necessary, namely, that between expressive versus imitative inventiveness.

Expressive inventiveness needn't be communicative or social and is of considerable importance in the theory of psychotherapy. For example, a purely expressive painting may or may not have meaning for anyone other than its creator. Regardless of the painting's actual beauty, it may give its creator great pleasure and emotional release.

Avowedly communicative art is another thing altogether, for it may have any or all of the motivations that involve other kinds of communications—such as an academic lecture—and it may produce as many diverse kinds of effects. If our primary interest is aesthetic enjoyment and creation, then we are far less interested in communicative or purposive art than in expressive art. Sometimes a poem or a painting is as didactic as an academic lecture, or, perhaps, its purpose, while communicative, is yet aesthetic—for example, to depict or remind us of a beautiful portion of the world (to induce an aesthetic experience) or to create a decoration.

Quite apart from aesthetics, our intrinsic fascination with research about aesthetic impulses also may harbor theoretical importance. It begins to appear as if the aesthetic realm may be an important bridge to join psychology's field-theorists with those theorists who are interested in human needs or instincts.

The most primitive example of the aesthetic impulse is our desire to set wrong things right, in the interest of symmetry or of pleasing order or of composition. Aspects like incorrect proportions, clashing contrasts, and displeasing arrangements all seem to call out in us the impulse to rearrange, to improve, and to correct.

Of great theoretical importance is the possibility of attributing this situation either to our inner need or to the external disarrangement—or, perhaps more accurately, to the total situation that comprehends both forces as a single unit.

Undoubtedly, empirical research will be necessary to shed light on all these questions.

PART FOUR

MOTIVATION AND BEHAVIOR

Thus man is a perpetually wanting animal. Any thwarting of these conditions upon which the basic human needs, or danger to the defenses which protect the rest, is considered a threat.

A. Maslow, *Toward a Psychology of Being, 3rd ed.*

INTRODUCTION

Leaders must have a basic understanding of human motivation and behavior if they are to be successful in their endeavors. Yet, very few leaders spend the time articulating and debating their own theories of human motivation and behavior. There are several major theories addressing these issues, ranging from B.F. Skinner's carrot-and-stick theories to Frederick Herzberg's famous hygiene-motivation theory. Yet, Abraham Maslow's theory of human motivation is probably best known.

Maslow's theory of human motivation was the cornerstone of Douglas McGregor's famous Theory X and Theory Y leadership theories. McGregor posed a question to leaders, asking them "How do you motivate employees?" He would surprise his audiences, after listening to their answers to the question, by stating: "You do not motivate employees." "Man is a living organism, not a machine." This belief in the relative "unmotivatability" of humans because they are living organisms led McGregor to Abraham Maslow's postulation that people are born motivated.

If we want a motivated workforce, we must build and continually modify an environment in which people can fulfill their needs while pursuing the goals of the organization. The obvious key to the successful implementation of this theory is alignment—of personal needs and organizational goals. Any discussion of motivation stemming from it must take this concept of alignment into primary consideration. This is particularly true if what we hope to achieve is more than mere compliance.

Once alignment is achieved, businesses can benefit from the natural tendency of employees to act to fulfill their needs and, as they go about doing so, their actions will be consonant with the best interests of the organization. The challenge then, for those who concur with Maslow's theories of human motivation and behavior, lies not in motivating people but in building an environment in which motivated people are willing to make a maximum contribution. In many cases, the problems with the workforce is not that they don't respond to motivation but with the methodology we have used to try to motivate them.

In beginning the journey towards building environments conducive to creativity, innovation, and maximum contributions, we need to begin to identify our beliefs about human motivation and behavior. The following essays, papers, and thoughts by Abraham Maslow will be helpful to those leaders who wish to embark upon this journey.

A Theory of
Human Motivation

*Capacities clamor to be used, and cease their clamor only
when they are well used . . . Not only is it fun to use our capacities, but it is necessary for growth. The unused skill or
capacity or organ can become a disease center or else atrophy
or disappear, thus diminishing the person.*

A.H. Maslow, *Toward a Psychology of Being, 3rd ed.*

In a previous paper[1] various propositions were presented which
would have to be included in any theory of human motivation that
could lay claim to being definitive. These conclusions may be
briefly summarized as follows:

1. The integrated wholeness of the organism must be one of the
foundation stones of motivation theory.

2. The hunger drive (or any other physiological drive) was rejected as a centering point or model for a definitive theory of motivation. Any drive that is somatically based and localizable was shown to
be atypical rather than typical in human motivation.

3. Such a theory should stress and center itself upon ultimate or
basic goals rather than partial or superficial ones, upon ends rather
than means to these ends. Such a stress would imply a more central
place for unconscious than for conscious motivations.

4. There are usually available various cultural paths to the same
goal. Therefore conscious, specific, local-cultural desires are not as fundamental in motivation theory as the more basic, unconscious goals.

Source: Psychological Review vol. 50 (July 1943), pp. 370–396. Footnotes and pertinent
references combined and renumbered; references not appearing in text have been omitted.

5. Any motivated behavior, either preparatory or consummatory, must be understood to be a channel through which many basic needs may be simultaneously expressed or satisfied. Typically an act has *more* than one motivation.

6. Practically all organismic states are to be understood as motivated and as motivating.

7. Human needs arrange themselves in hierarchies of prepotency. That is to say, the appearance of one need usually rests on the prior satisfaction of another, more pre-potent need. Man is a perpetually wanting animal. Also no need or drive can be treated as if it were isolated or discrete; every drive is related to the state of satisfaction or dissatisfaction of other drives.

8. Lists of drives will get us nowhere for various theoretical and practical reasons. Furthermore any classification of motivations must deal with the problem of levels of specificity or generalization of the motives to be classified.

9. Classifications of motivations must be based upon goals rather than upon instigating drives or motivated behavior.

10. Motivation theory should be human-centered rather than animal-centered.

11. The situation or the field in which the organism reacts must be taken into account but the field alone can rarely serve as an exclusive explanation for behavior. Furthermore the field itself must be interpreted in terms of the organism. Field theory cannot be a substitute for motivation theory.

12. Not only the integration of the organism must be taken into account, but also the possibility of isolated, specific, partial or segmental reactions.

It has since become necessary to add to these another affirmation.

13. Motivations theory is not synonymous with behavior theory. The motivations are only one class of determinants of behavior. While behavior is almost always motivated, it is also almost always biologically, culturally and situationally determined as well.

The present paper is an attempt to formulate a positive theory of motivation which will satisfy these theoretical demands and at the same time conform to the known facts, clinical and observational as well as experimental. It derives most directly, however, from clinical experience. This theory is, I think, in the functionalist tradition of

James and Dewey, and is fused with the holism of Wertheimer,[2] Goldstein,[3] and Gestalt Psychology, and with the dynamicism of Freud[4] and Adler.[5] This fusion or synthesis may arbitrarily be called a "general-dynamic" theory.

It is far easier to perceive and to criticize the aspects in motivation theory than to remedy them. Mostly this is because of the very serious lack of sound data in this area. I conceive this lack of sound facts to be due primarily to the absence of a valid theory of motivation. The present theory then must be considered to be a suggested program or framework for future research and must stand or fall, not so much on facts available or evidence presented, as upon researches yet to be done, researches suggested perhaps, by the questions raised in this paper.

THE BASIC NEEDS

The "physiological" needs.—The needs that are usually taken as the starting point for motivation theory are the so-called physiological drives. Two recent lines of research make it necessary to revise our customary notions about these needs, first, the development of the concept of homeostasis, and second, the finding that appetites (preferential choices among foods) are a fairly efficient indication of actual needs or lacks in the body.

Homeostasis refers to the body's automatic efforts to maintain a constant, normal state of the blood stream. Cannon[6] has described this process for (1) the water content of the blood, (2) salt content, (3) sugar content, (4) protein content, (5) fat content, (6) calcium content, (7) oxygen content, (8) constant hydrogen-ion level (acid-base balance) and (9) constant temperature of the blood. Obviously this list can be extended to include other minerals, the hormones, vitamins, and so forth.

Young in a recent article[7] has summarized the work on appetite in its relation to body needs. If the body lacks some chemical, the individual will tend to develop a specific appetite or partial hunger for that food element.

Thus it seems impossible as well as useless to make any list of fundamental physiological needs for they can come to almost any number one might wish, depending on the degree of specificity of description. We can not identify all physiological needs as homeostatic. That sexual desire, sleepiness, sheer activity and maternal behavior in animals, are homeostatic, has not yet been demonstrated. Furthermore, this list would not include the various sensory pleasures (tastes, smells, tickling, stroking) which are probably physiological and which may become the goals of motivated behavior.

In a previous paper[8] it has been pointed out that these physiological drives or needs are to be considered unusual rather than typical because they are isolable, and because they are localizable somatically. That is to say, they are relatively independent of each other, of other motivations and of the organism as a whole, and secondly, in many cases, it is possible to demonstrate a localized, underlying somatic base for the drive. This is true less generally than has been thought (exceptions are fatigue, sleepiness, maternal responses) but it is still true in the classic instances of hunger, sex, and thirst.

It should be pointed out again that any of the physiological needs and the consummatory behavior involved with them serve as channels for all sorts of other needs as well. That is to say, the person who thinks he is hungry may actually be seeking more for comfort, or dependence, than for vitamins or proteins. Conversely, it is possible to satisfy the hunger need in part by other activities such as drinking water or smoking cigarettes. In other words, relatively isolable as these physiological needs are, they are not completely so.

Undoubtedly these physiological needs are the most prepotent of all needs. What this means specifically is, that in the human being who is missing everything in life in an extreme fashion, it is most likely that the major motivation would be the physiological needs rather than any others. A person who is lacking food, safety, love, and esteem would most probably hunger for food more strongly than for anything else.

If all the needs are unsatisfied, and the organism is then dominated by the physiological needs, all other needs may become simply nonexistent or be pushed into the background. It is then fair to characterize the whole organism by saying simply that it is hungry, for consciousness is almost completely preempted by hunger. All capacities are put into the service of hunger-satisfaction, and the organization of these capacities is almost entirely determined by the one purpose of satisfying hunger. The receptors and effectors, the intelligence, memory, habits, all may now be defined simply as hunger-gratifying tools. Capacities that are not useful for this purpose lie dormant, or are pushed into the background. The urge to write poetry, the desire to acquire an automobile, the interest in American history, the desire for a new pair of shoes are, in the extreme case, forgotten or become of secondary importance. For the man who is extremely and dangerously hungry, no other interests exist but food. He dreams food, he remembers food, he thinks about food, he emotes only about food, he perceives only food and he wants only food. The more subtle determinants that ordinarily fuse with the physiological drives in organizing even feeding, drinking or sexual behavior, may now be so completely overwhelmed as to allow us to speak at this time (but *only* at this time) of pure hunger drive and behavior, with the one unqualified aim of relief.

Another peculiar characteristic of the human organism when it is dominated by a certain need is that the whole philosophy of the future tends also to change. For our chronically and extremely hungry man, Utopia can be defined very simply as a place where there is plenty of food. He tends to think that, if only he is guaranteed food for the rest of his life, he will be perfectly happy and will never want anything more. Life itself tends to be defined in terms of eating. Anything else will be defined as unimportant. Freedom, love, community feeling, respect, philosophy, may all be waved aside as fripperies which are useless since they fail to fill the stomach. Such a man may fairly be said to live by bread alone.

It cannot possibly be denied that such things are true but their *generality* can be denied. Emergency conditions are, almost by definition, rare in the normally functioning peaceful society. That this truism can be forgotten is due mainly to two reasons. First, rats have few motivations other than physiological ones, and since so much of the research upon motivation has been made with these animals, it is easy to carry the rat-picture over to the human being. Secondly, it is too often not realized that culture itself is an adaptive tool, one of whose main functions is to make the physiological emergencies come less and less often. In most of the known societies, chronic extreme hunger of the emergency type is rare, rather than common. In any case, this is still true in the United States. The average American citizen is experiencing appetite rather than hunger when he says "I am hungry." He is apt to experience sheer life-and-death hunger only by accident and then only a few times through his entire life.

Obviously a good way to obscure the "higher" motivations, and to get a lop-sided view of human capacities and human nature, is to make the organism extremely and chronically hungry or thirsty.

Anyone who attempts to make an emergency picture into a typical one, and who will measure all of man's goals and desires by his behavior during extreme physiological deprivation is certainly being blind to many things. It is quite true that man lives by bread alone—when there is no bread. But what happens to man's desires when there *is* plenty of bread and when his belly is chronically filled?

At once other (and "higher") needs emerge and these, rather than physiological hungers, dominate the organism. And when these in turn are satisfied, again new (and still "higher") needs emerge and so on. This is what we mean by saying that the basic human needs are organized into a hierarchy of relative prepotency.

One main implication of this phrasing is that gratification becomes as important a concept as deprivation in motivation theory, for it releases the organism from the domination of a relatively more physiological need, permitting thereby the emergence of other more social goals. The physiological needs, along with their partial goals, when chronically gratified cease to exist as active determinants or organizers of behavior. They now exist only in a potential fashion in the sense that they may emerge again to dominate the organism if they are thwarted. But a want that is satisfied is no longer a want. The organism is dominated and its behavior organized only by unsatisfied needs. If hunger is satisfied, it becomes unimportant in the current dynamics of the individual.

This statement is somewhat qualified by a hypothesis to be discussed more fully later, namely that it is precisely those individuals in whom a certain need has always been satisfied who are best equipped to tolerate deprivation of that need in the future, and that furthermore, those who have been deprived in the past will react differently to current satisfactions than the one who has never been deprived.

The safety needs.—If the physiological needs are relatively well gratified, there then emerges a new set of needs, which we may categorize roughly as the safety needs. All that has been said of the physiological needs is equally true, although in lesser degree, of these desires. The organism may equally well be wholly dominated by them. They may serve as the almost exclusive organizers of behavior, recruiting all the capacities of the organism in their service, and we may then fairly describe the whole organism as a safety-seeking mechanism. Again we may say of the receptors, the effectors, of the intellect and the other capacities that they are primarily safety-seeking tools.

Again, as in the hungry man, we find that the dominating goal is a strong determinant not only of his current world-outlook and philosophy but also of his philosophy of the future. Practically everything looks less important than safety, (even sometimes the physiological needs which being satisfied, are now underestimated). A man, in this state, if it is extreme enough and chronic enough, may be characterized as living almost for safety alone.

Although in this paper we are interested primarily in the needs of the adult, we can approach an understanding of his safety needs perhaps more efficiently by observation of infants and children, in whom these needs are much more simple and obvious. One reason for the clearer appearance of the threat or danger reaction in infants, is that they do not inhibit this reaction at all, whereas adults in our society have been taught to inhibit it at all costs. Thus even when adults do feel their safety to be threatened we may not be able to see this on the surface. Infants will react in a total fashion and as if they were endangered, if they are disturbed or dropped suddenly, startled by loud noises, flashing light, or other unusual sensory stimulation, by rough handling, by general loss of support in the mother's arms, or by inadequate support.[9]

In infants we can also see a much more direct reaction to bodily illnesses of various kinds. Sometimes these illnesses seem to be immediately and *per se* threatening and seem to make the child feel unsafe. For instance, vomiting, colic or other sharp pains seem to make the child look at the whole world in a different way. At such a moment of pain, it may be postulated that, for the child, the appearance of the whole world suddenly changes from sunniness to darkness, so to speak, and becomes a place in which anything at all might happen, in which previously stable things have suddenly become unstable. Thus a child who because of some bad food is taken ill may, for a day or two, develop fear, nightmares, and a need for protection and reassurance never seen in him before his illness.

Another indication of the child's need for safety is his preference for some kind of undisrupted routine or rhythm. He seems to want a predictable, orderly world. For instance, injustice, unfairness, or inconsistency in the parents seems to make a child feel anxious and unsafe. This attitude may be not so much because of the injustice *per se* or any particular pains involved, but rather because this treatment threatens to make the world look unreliable, or unsafe, or unpredictable. Young children seem to thrive better under a system which has at least a skeletal outline of rigidity, in which there is a schedule of a kind, some sort of routine, something that can be counted upon, not only for the present but also far into the future. Perhaps one could express this more accurately by saying that the child needs an organized world rather than an unorganized or unstructured one.

The central role of the parents and the normal family setup are indisputable. Quarreling, physical assault, separation, divorce or death within the family may be particularly terrifying. Also parental outbursts of rage or threats of punishment directed to the child, calling him names, speaking to him harshly, shaking him, handling him roughly, or actual physical punishment sometimes elicit such total panic and terror in the child that we must assume more is involved than the physical pain alone. While it is true that in some children this terror may represent also a fear of loss of parental love, it can also occur in completely rejected children, who seem to cling to the hating parents more for sheer safety and protection than because of hope of love.

Confronting the average child with new, unfamiliar, strange, unmanageable stimuli or situations will too frequently elicit the danger or terror reaction, as for example, getting lost or even being separated from the parents for a short time, being confronted with new faces, new situations or new tasks, the sight of strange, unfamiliar or uncontrollable objects, illness or death. Particularly at such times, the child's frantic clinging to his parents is eloquent testimony to their role as protectors (quite apart from their roles as food-givers and love-givers).

From these and similar observations, we may generalize and say that the average child in our society generally prefers a safe, orderly, predictable, organized world, which he can count on, and in which unexpected, unmanageable or other dangerous things do not happen, and in which, in any case, he has all-powerful parents who protect and shield him from harm.

That these reactions may so easily be observed in children is in a way a proof of the fact that children in our society, feel too unsafe (or, in a word, are badly brought up). Children who are reared in an unthreatening, loving family do *not* ordinarily react as we have described above.[10] In such children the danger reactions are apt to come mostly to objects or situations that adults too would consider dangerous.[11]

The healthy, normal, fortunate adult in our culture is largely satisfied in his safety needs. The peaceful, smoothly running, "good" society ordinarily makes its members feel safe enough from wild animals, extremes of temperature, criminals, assault and murder, tyranny, and so forth. Therefore, in a very real sense, he no longer has any safety needs as active motivators. Just as a sated man no longer feels hungry, a safe man no longer feels endangered. If we wish to see these needs directly and clearly we must turn to neurotic or near-neurotic individuals, and to the economic and social underdogs. In between these extremes, we can perceive the expressions of safety needs only in such phenomena as, for instance, the common preference for a job with tenure and protection, the desire for a savings account, and for insurance of various kinds (medical, dental, unemployment, disability, old age).

Other broader aspects of the attempt to seek safety and stability in the world are seen in the very common preference for familiar rather than unfamiliar things, or for the known rather than the unknown. The tendency to have some religion or world-philosophy that organizes the universe and the men in it into some sort of satisfactorily coherent, meaningful whole is also in part motivated by safety-seeking. Here too we may list science and philosophy in general as partially motivated by the safety needs (we shall see later that there are also other motivations to scientific, philosophical or religious endeavor).

Otherwise the need for safety is seen as an active and dominant mobilizer of the organism's resources only in emergencies, for example, war, disease, natural catastrophes, crime waves, societal disorganization, neurosis, brain injury, chronically bad situation.

Some neurotic adults in our society are, in many ways, like the unsafe child in their desire for safety, although in the former it takes on a somewhat special appearance. Their reaction is often to unknown, psychological dangers in a world that is perceived to be hostile, overwhelming and threatening. Such a person behaves as if a great catastrophe were almost always impending, that is, he is usually responding as if to an emergency. His safety needs often find specific expression in a search for a protector, or a stronger person on whom he may depend, or perhaps, a Fuehrer.

The neurotic individual may be described in a slightly different way with some usefulness as a grown-up person who retains his childish attitudes toward the world. That is to say, a neurotic adult may be said to behave "as if" he were actually afraid of a spanking, or of his mother's disapproval, or of being abandoned by his parents, or having his food taken away from him. It is as if his childish attitudes of fear and threat reaction to a dangerous world had gone underground, and untouched by the growing up and learning processes, were now ready to be called out by any stimulus that would make a child feel endangered and threatened.[12]

The neurosis in which the search for safety takes its clearest form is in the compulsive-obsessive neurosis. Compulsive-obsessives try frantically to order and stabilize the world so that no unmanageable, unexpected or unfamiliar dangers will ever appear.[13] They hedge themselves about with all sorts of ceremonials, rules and formulas so that every possible contingency may be provided for and so that no new contingencies may appear. They are much like the brain injured cases, described by Goldstein,[14] who manage to maintain their equilibrium by avoiding everything unfamiliar and strange and by ordering their restricted world in such a neat, disciplined, orderly fashion that everything in the world can be counted upon. They try to arrange the world so that anything unexpected (dangers) cannot possibly occur. If, through no fault of their own, something unexpected does occur, they go into a panic reaction as if this unexpected occurrence constituted a grave danger. What we can see only as a none-too-strong preference in the healthy person, for example, preference for the familiar, becomes a life-and-death necessity in abnormal cases.

The love needs.—If both the physiological and the safety needs are fairly well gratified, then there will emerge the love and affection and belongingness needs, and the whole cycle already described will repeat itself with this new center. Now the person will feel keenly, as never before, the absence of friends, or a sweetheart, or a wife, or children. He will hunger for affectionate relations with people in general, namely, for a place in his group, and he will strive with great intensity to achieve this goal. He will want to attain such a place more than anything else in the world and may even forget that once, when he was hungry, he sneered at love.

In our society the thwarting of these needs is the most commonly found core in cases of maladjustment and more severe psychopathology. Love and affection, as well as their possible expression in sexuality, are generally looked upon with ambivalence and are customarily hedged about with many restrictions and inhibitions. Practically all theorists of psychopathology have stressed thwarting of the love needs as basic in the picture of maladjustment. Many clinical studies have therefore been made of this need and we know more about it perhaps than any of the other needs except the physiological ones.[15]

One thing that must be stressed at this point is that love is not synonymous with sex. Sex may be studied as a purely physiological need. Ordinarily sexual behavior is multi-determined, that is to say, determined not only by sexual but also by other needs, chief among which are the love and affection needs. Also not to be overlooked is the fact that the love needs involve both giving *and* receiving love.[16]

The esteem needs.—All people in our society (with a few pathological exceptions) have a need or desire for a stable, firmly based, (usually) high evaluation of themselves, for self-respect, or self-esteem, and for the esteem of others. By firmly based self-esteem, we mean that which is soundly based upon real capacity, achievement and respect from others. These needs may be classified into two subsidiary sets. These are, first, the desire for strength, for achievement, for adequacy, for confidence in the face of the world, and for independence and freedom.[17] Secondly, we have what we may call the desire for reputation or prestige (defining it as respect or esteem from other people), recognition, attention, importance or appreciation.[18] These needs have been relatively stressed by Alfred Adler and his followers, and have been relatively neglected by Freud and the psychoanalysts. More and more today however there is appearing widespread appreciation of their central importance.

Satisfaction of the self-esteem need leads to feelings of self-confidence, worth, strength, capability and adequacy of being useful and necessary in the world. But thwarting of these needs produces feelings of inferiority, of weakness and of helplessness. These feelings in turn give rise to either basic discouragement or else compensatory or neurotic trends. An appreciation of the necessity of basic self-confidence and an understanding of how helpless people are without it, can be easily gained from a study of severe traumatic neurosis.[19]

The need for self-actualization.—Even if all these needs are satisfied, we may still often (if not always) expect that a new discontent and restlessness will soon develop, unless the individual is doing what he is fitted for. A musician must make music, an artist must paint, a poet must write, if he is to be ultimately happy. What a man *can* be, he *must* be. This need we may call self-actualization.

This term, first coined by Kurt Goldstein, is being used in this paper in a much more specific and limited fashion. It refers to the desire for self-fulfillment, namely, to the tendency for him to become actualized in what he is potentially. This tendency might be phrased as the desire to become more and more what one is, to become everything that one is capable of becoming.

The specific form that these needs will take will of course vary greatly from person to person. In one individual it may take the form of the desire to be an ideal mother, in another it may be expressed athletically, and in still another it may be expressed in painting pictures or in inventions. It is not necessarily a creative urge although in people who have any capacities for creation it will take this form.

The clear emergence of these needs rests upon prior satisfaction of the physiological, safety, love and esteem needs. We shall call people who are satisfied in these needs, basically satisfied people, and it is from these that we may expect the fullest (and healthiest) creativeness.[20] Since, in our society, basically satisfied people are the exception, we do not know much about self-actualization, either experimentally or clinically. It remains a challenging problem for research.

The preconditions for the basic need satisfactions.—There are certain conditions which are immediate prerequisites for the basic need satisfactions. Danger to these is reacted to almost as if it were a direct danger to the basic needs themselves. Such conditions as freedom to speak, freedom to do what one wishes so long as no harm is done to others, freedom to express one's self, freedom to investigate and seek for information, freedom to defend one's self, justice, fairness, honesty, orderliness in the group are examples of such preconditions for basic need satisfactions. Thwarting in these freedoms will be reacted to with a threat or emergency response. These conditions are not ends in themselves but they are *almost* so since they are so closely related to the basic needs, which are apparently the only ends in themselves. These conditions are defended because without them the basic satisfactions are quite impossible, or at least, very severely endangered.

If we remember that the cognitive capacities (perceptual, intellectual, learning) are a set of adjustive tools, which have, among other functions, that of satisfaction of our basic needs, then it is clear that any danger to them, any deprivation or blocking of their free use, must also be indirectly threatening to the basic needs themselves. Such a statement is a partial solution of the general problems of curiosity, the search for knowledge, truth and wisdom, and the ever-persistent urge to solve the cosmic mysteries.

We must therefore introduce another hypothesis and speak of degrees of closeness to the basic needs, for we have already pointed out that *any* conscious desires (partial goals) are more or less important as they are more or less close to the basic needs. The same statement may be made for various behavior acts. An act is psychologically important if it contributes directly to satisfaction of basic needs. The less directly it so contributes, or the weaker this contribution is, the less important this act must be conceived to be from the point of view of dynamic psychology. A similar statement may be made for the various defense or coping mechanisms. Some are very directly related to the protection or attainment of the basic needs, others are only weakly and distantly related. Indeed if we wished, we could speak of more basic and less basic defense mechanisms, and then affirm that danger to the more basic defenses is more threatening than danger to less basic defenses (always remembering that this is so only because of their relationship to the basic needs).

The desires to know and to understand.—So far, we have mentioned the cognitive needs only in passing. Acquiring knowledge and systematizing the universe have been considered as, in part, techniques for the achievement of basic safety in the world, or, for the intelligent man, expressions of self-actualization. Also freedom of inquiry and expression have been discussed as preconditions of satisfactions of the basic needs. True though these formulations may be, they do not constitute definitive answers to the question as to the motivation role of curiosity, learning, philosophizing, experimenting, and so forth. They are, at best, no more than partial answers.

This question is especially difficult because we know so little about the facts. Curiosity, exploration, desire for the facts, desire to know may certainly be observed easily enough. The fact that they often are pursued even at great cost to the individual's safety is an earnest of the partial character of our previous discussion. In addition, the writer must admit that, though he has sufficient clinical evidence to postulate the desire to know as a very strong drive in intelligent people, no data are available for unintelligent people. It may then be largely a function of relatively high intelligence. Rather tentatively, then, and largely in the hope of stimulating discussion and research, we shall postulate a basic desire to know, to be aware of reality, to get the facts, to satisfy curiosity, or as Wertheimer phrases it, to see rather than to be blind.

This postulation, however, is not enough. Even after we know, we are impelled to know more and more minutely and microscopically on the one hand, and on the other, more and more extensively in the direction of world philosophy, religion, and so forth. The facts that we acquire, if they are isolated or atomistic, inevitably get theorized about, and either analyzed or organized or both. This process has been phrased by some as the search for "meaning." We shall then postulate a desire to understand, to systematize, to organize, to analyze, to look for relations and meanings.

Once these desires are accepted for discussion, we see that they too form themselves into a small hierarchy in which the desire to know is prepotent over the desire to understand. All the characteristics of a hierarchy of prepotency that we have described above, seem to hold for this one as well.

We must guard ourselves against the too easy tendency to separate these desires from the basic needs we have discussed above, that is, to make a sharp dichotomy between "cognitive" and "conative" needs. The desire to know and to understand are themselves conative, that is, have a striving character, and are as much personality needs as the "basic needs" we have already discussed.[21]

FURTHER CHARACTERISTICS OF THE BASIC NEEDS

The degree of fixity of the hierarchy of basic needs.—We have spoken so far as if this hierarchy were a fixed order but actually it is not nearly as rigid as we may have implied. It is true that most of the people with whom we have worked have seemed to have these basic needs in about the order that has been indicated. However, there have been a number of exceptions.

(1) There are some people in whom, for instance, self-esteem seems to be more important than love. This most common reversal in the hierarchy is usually due to the development of the notion that the person who is most likely to be loved is a strong or powerful person, one who inspires respect or fear, and who is self confident or

aggressive. Therefore such people who lack love and seek it, may try hard to put on a front of aggressive, confident behavior. But essentially they seek high self-esteem and its behavior expressions more as a means-to-an-end than for its own sake; they seek self-assertion for the sake of love rather than for self-esteem itself.

(2) There are other, apparently innately creative people in whom the drive to creativeness seems to be more important than any other counter-determinant. Their creativeness might appear not as self-actualization released by basic satisfaction, but in spite of lack of basic satisfaction.

(3) In certain people the level of aspiration may be permanently deadened or lowered. That is to say, the less prepotent goals may simply be lost, and may disappear forever, so that the person who has experienced life at a very low level, that is, chronic unemployment, may continue to be satisfied for the rest of his life if only he can get enough food.

(4) The so-called "psychopathic personality" is another example of permanent loss of the love needs. These are people who, according to the best data available,[22] have been starved for love in the earliest months of their lives and have simply lost forever the desire and the ability to give and to receive affection (as animals lose sucking or pecking reflexes that are not exercised soon enough after birth).

(5) Another cause of reversal of the hierarchy is that when a need has been satisfied for a long time, this need may be underevaluated. People who have never experienced chronic hunger are apt to underestimate its effects and to look upon food as a rather unimportant thing. If they are dominated by a higher need, this higher need will seem to be the most important of all. It then becomes possible, and indeed does actually happen, that they may, for the sake of this higher need, put themselves into the position of being deprived in a more basic need. We may expect that after a long-time deprivation of the more basic need there will be a tendency to reevaluate both needs so that the more prepotent need will actually become consciously prepotent for the individual who may have given it up very lightly. Thus, a man who has given up his job rather than lose his self-respect, and who then starves for six months or so, may be willing to take his job back even at the price of losing his self-respect.

(6) Another partial explanation of *apparent* reversals is seen in the fact that we have been talking about the hierarchy of prepotency in

terms of consciously felt wants or desires rather than of behavior. Looking at behavior itself may give us the wrong impression. What we have claimed is that the person will *want* the more basic of two needs when deprived in both. There is no necessary implication here that he will act upon his desires. Let us say again that there are many determinants of behavior other than the needs and desires.

(7) Perhaps more important than all these exceptions are the ones that involve ideals, high social standards, high values and the like. With such values people become martyrs; they will give up everything for the sake of a particular ideal, or value. These people may be understood, at least in part, by reference to one basic concept (or hypothesis) which may be called "increased frustration-tolerance through early gratification." People who have been satisfied in their basic needs throughout their lives, particularly in their earlier years, seem to develop exceptional power to withstand present or future thwarting of these needs simply because they have strong, healthy character structure as a result of basic satisfaction. They are the "strong" people who can easily weather disagreement or opposition, who can swim against the stream of public opinion and who can stand up for the truth at great personal cost. It is just the ones who have loved and been well loved, and who have had many deep friendships who can hold out against hatred, rejection or persecution.

I say all this in spite of the fact that there is a certain amount of sheer habituation which is also involved in any full discussion of frustration tolerance. For instance, it is likely that those persons who have been accustomed to relative starvation for a long time, are partially enabled thereby to withstand food deprivation. What sort of balance must be made between these two tendencies, of habituation on the one hand, and of past satisfaction breeding present frustration tolerance on the other hand, remains to be worked out by further research. Meanwhile we may assume that they are both operative, side by side, since they do not contradict each other. In respect to this phenomenon of increased frustration tolerance, it seems probable that the most important gratifications come in the first two years of life. That is to say, people who have been made secure and strong in the earliest years, tend to remain secure and strong thereafter in the face of whatever threatens.

Degrees of relative satisfaction.—So far, our theoretical discussion may have given the impression that these five sets of needs are somehow in a step-wise, all-or-none relationships to each other. We have spoken in such terms as the following: "If one need is satisfied, then another emerges." This statement might give the false impression that a need must be satisfied 100 per cent before the next need emerges. In actual fact, most members of our society who are normal, are partially satisfied in all their basic needs and partially unsatisfied in all their basic needs at the same time. A more realistic description of the hierarchy would be in terms of decreasing percentages of satisfaction as we go up the hierarchy of prepotency. For instance, if I may assign arbitrary figures for the sake of illustration, it is as if the average citizen is satisfied perhaps 85 per cent in his physiological needs, 70 per cent in his safety needs, 50 per cent in his love needs, 40 per cent in his self-esteem needs, and 10 per cent in his self-actualization needs.

As for the concept of emergence of a new need after satisfaction of the prepotent need, this emergence is not a sudden, saltatory phenomenon but rather a gradual emergence by slow degrees from nothingness. For instance, if prepotent need A is satisfied only 10 per cent then need B may not be visible at all. However, as this need A becomes satisfied 25 per cent, need B may emerge 5 per cent, as need A becomes satisfied 75 per cent need B may emerge 90 per cent, and so on.

Unconscious character of needs.—These needs are neither necessarily conscious nor unconscious. On the whole, however, in the average person, they are more often unconscious rather than conscious. It is not necessary at this point to overhaul the tremendous mass of evidence which indicates the crucial importance of unconscious motivation. It would by now be expected, on a priori grounds alone, that unconscious motivations would on the whole be rather more important than the conscious motivations. What we have called the basic needs are very often largely unconscious although they may, with suitable techniques, and with sophisticated people become conscious.

Cultural specificity and generality of needs.—This classification of basic needs makes some attempt to take account of the relative unity behind the superficial differences in specific desires from one culture to another. Certainly in any particular culture an individual's conscious motivational content will usually be extremely different from the conscious motivational content of an individual in another society. However, it is the common experience of anthropologists that people, even in different societies, are much more alike than we would think from our first contact with them, and that as we know them better we seem to find more and more of this commonness. We then recognize the most startling differences to be superficial rather than basic, for example, differences in style of hairdress, clothes, tastes in food, and so forth. Out classification of basic needs is in part an attempt to account for this unity behind the apparent diversity from culture to culture. No claim is made that it is ultimate or universal for all cultures. The claim is made only that it is relatively *more* ultimate, more universal, more basic, than the superficial conscious desires from culture to culture, and makes a somewhat closer approach to common-human characteristics. Basic needs are *more* common-human than superficial desires or behaviors.

Multiple motivations of behavior.—These needs must be understood *not* to be *exclusive* or single determiners of certain kinds of behavior. An example may be found in any behavior that seems to be physiologically motivated, such as eating, or sexual play or the like. The clinical psychologists have long since found that any behavior may be a channel through which flow various determinants. Or to say it in another way, most behavior is multi-motivated. Within the sphere of motivational determinants any behavior tends to be determined by several or *all* of the basic needs simultaneously rather than by only one of them. The latter would be more an exception than the former. Eating may be partially for the sake of filling the stomach, and partially for the sake of comfort and amelioration of other needs. One may make love not only for pure sexual release, but also to convince one's self of one's masculinity, or to make a conquest, to feel powerful, or to win more basic affection. As an illustration, I may point out that it would be possible (theoretically if not practically) to analyze a single act of an individual and see in it the expression of his physiological needs, his safety needs, his love needs, his esteem needs and self-actualization. This contrasts sharply with the more naive brand of trait psychology in which one trait or one motive accounts for a certain kind of act, that is, an aggressive act is traced solely to a trait of aggressiveness.

Multiple determinants of behavior.—Not all behavior is determined by the basic needs. We might even say that not all behavior is motivated. There are many determinants of behavior other than motives.[23] For instance, one other important class of determinants is the so-called "field" determinants. Theoretically, at least, behavior may be determined completely by the field, or even by specific isolated external stimuli, as in association of ideas, or certain conditioned reflexes.

If in response to the stimulus word "table," I immediately perceive a memory image of a table, this response certainly has nothing to do with my basic needs.

Secondly, we may call attention again to the concept of "degree of closeness to the basic needs" or "degree of motivation." Some behavior is highly motivated, other behavior is only weakly motivated. Some is not motivated at all (but all behavior is determined).

Another important point[24] is that there is a basic difference between expressive behavior and coping behavior (functional striving, purposive goal seeking). An expressive behavior does not try to do anything; it is simply a reflection of the personality. A stupid man behaves stupidly, not because he wants to, or tries to, or is motivated to, but simply because he *is* what he is. The same is true when I speak in a bass voice rather than tenor or soprano. The random movements of a healthy child, the smile on the face of a happy man even when he is alone, the springiness of the healthy man's walk, and the erectness of his carriage are other examples of expressive, non-functional behavior. Also the *style* in which a man carries out almost all his behavior, motivated as well as unmotivated, is often expressive.

We may then ask, is *all* behavior expressive or reflective of the character structure? The answer is "No." Rote, habitual, automatized, or conventional behavior may or may not be expressive. The same is true for most "stimulus-bound" behaviors.

It is finally necessary to stress that expressiveness of behavior, and goal-directedness of behavior are not mutually exclusive categories. Average behavior is usually both.

Goals as centering principle in motivation theory.—It will be observed that the basic principle in our classification has been neither the instigation nor the motivated behavior but rather the functions, effects, purposes, or goals of the behavior. It has been proven sufficiently by various people that this is the most suitable point for centering in any motivation theory.[25]

Animal- and human-centering.—This theory starts with the human being rather than any lower and presumably "simpler" animal. Too many of the findings that have been made in animals have been proven to be true for animals but not for the human being. There is no reason whatsoever why we should start with animals in order to study human motivation. The logic or rather illogic behind this general fallacy of "pseudo-simplicity" has been exposed often enough by philosophers and logicians as well as by scientists in each of the various fields. It is no more necessary to study animals before one can study man than it is to study mathematics before one can study geology or psychology or biology.

We may also reject the old, naive, behaviorism which assumed that it was somehow necessary, or at least more "scientific" to judge human beings by animal standards. One consequence of this belief was that the whole notion of purpose and goal was excluded from motivational psychology simply because one could not ask a white rat about his purposes. Tolman[26] has long since proven in animal studies themselves that this exclusion was not necessary.

Motivation and the theory of psychopathogenesis.—The conscious motivational content of everyday life has, according to the foregoing, been conceived to be relatively important or unimportant accordingly as it is more or less closely related to the basic goals. A desire for an ice cream cone might actually be an indirect expression of a desire for love. If it is, then this desire for the ice cream cone becomes extremely important motivation. If however the ice cream is simply something to cool the mouth with, or a casual appetitive reaction, then the desire is relatively unimportant. Everyday conscious desires are to be regarded as symptoms, as *surface indicators of more basic needs.* If we were to take these superficial desires at their face value we would find ourselves in a state of complete confusion which could never be resolved, since we would be dealing seriously with symptoms rather than with what lay behind the symptoms.

Thwarting of unimportant desires produces no psychopathological results; thwarting of a basically important need does produce such results. Any theory of psychopathogenesis must then be based on a sound theory of motivation. A conflict or a frustration is not necessarily pathogenic. It becomes so only when it threatens or thwarts the basic needs, or partial needs that are closely related to the basic needs.[27]

The role of gratified needs.—It has been pointed out above several times that our needs usually emerge only when more prepotent needs have been gratified. Thus gratification has an important role in motivation theory. Apart from this, however, needs cease to play an active determining or organizing role as soon as they are gratified.

What this means is that, for example, a basically satisfied person no longer has the needs for esteem, love, safety, and so forth. The only sense in which he might be said to have them is in the almost metaphysical sense that a sated man has hunger, or a filled bottle has emptiness. If we are interested in what *actually* motivates us, and not in what has, will, or might motivate us, then a satisfied need is not a motivator. It must be considered for all practical purposes simply not to exist, to have disappeared. This point should be emphasized because it has been either overlooked or contradicted in every theory of motivation I know.[28] The perfectly healthy, normal, fortunate man has no sex needs or hunger needs, or needs for safety, or for love, or for prestige, or self-esteem, except in stray moments of quickly passing threat. If we were to say otherwise, we should also have to aver that every man had all the pathological reflexes, for example, Babinski, and so forth, because if his nervous system were damaged, these would appear.

It is such considerations as these that suggest the bold postulation that a man who is thwarted in any of his basic needs may fairly be envisaged simply as a sick man. This is a fair parallel to our designation as "sick" of the man who lacks vitamins or minerals. Who is to say that a lack of love is less important than a lack of vitamins? Since we know the pathogenic effects of love starvation, who is to say that we are invoking value-questions in an unscientific or illegitimate way, any more than the physician does who diagnoses and treats pellagra or scurvy? If I were permitted this usage, I should then say simply that a healthy man is primarily motivated by his needs to develop and actualize his fullest potentialities and capacities. If a man has any other basic needs in any active, chronic sense, then he is simply an unhealthy man. He is as surely sick as if he had suddenly developed a strong salt-hunger or calcium hunger.[29]

If this statement seems unusual or paradoxical the reader may be assured that this is only one among many such paradoxes that will appear as we revise our ways of looking at man's deeper motivations. When we ask what man wants of life, we deal with his very essence.

Summary

(1) *There are at least five sets of goals, which we may call basic needs.* These are briefly physiological, safety, love, esteem, and self-actualization. In addition, we are motivated by the desire to achieve or maintain the various conditions upon which these basic satisfactions rest and by certain more intellectual desires.

(2) *These basic goals are related to each other, being arranged in a hierarchy of prepotency.* This means that the most prepotent goal will monopolize consciousness and will tend of itself to organize the recruitment of the various capacities of the organism. The less prepotent needs are minimized, even forgotten or denied. But when a need is fairly well satisfied, the next prepotent ("higher") need emerges, in turn to dominate the conscious life and to serve as the center of organization of behavior, since gratified needs are not active motivators.

Thus man is a perpetually wanting animal. Ordinarily the satisfaction of these wants is not altogether mutually exclusive, but only tends to be. The average member of our society is most often partially satisfied and partially unsatisfied in all of his wants. The hierarchy principle is usually empirically observed in terms of increasing percentages of non-satisfaction as we go up the hierarchy. Reversals of the average order of the hierarchy are sometimes observed. Also it has been observed that an individual may permanently lose the higher wants in the hierarchy under special conditions. There are not only ordinarily multiple motivations for usual behavior, but in addition many determinants other than motives.

(3) *Any thwarting or possibility of thwarting of these basic human goals, or danger to the defenses which protect them, or to the conditions upon which they rest, is considered to be a psychological threat.* With a few exceptions, all psychopathology may be partially traced to such threats. A basically thwarted man may actually be defined as a "sick" man, if we wish.

(4) *It is such basic threats which bring about the general emergency reactions.*

(5) *Certain other basic problems have not been dealt with because of limitations of space.* Among these are (a) the problem of values in any definitive motivation theory, (b) the relation between appetites, desires, needs and what is "good" for the organism, (c) the etiology of the basic needs and their possible derivation in early childhood, (d) redefinition of motivational concepts, that is, drive, desire, wish, need, goal, (e) implication of our theory for hedonistic theory, (f) the nature of the uncompleted act, or success and failure, and of aspiration-level, (g) the role of association, habit and conditioning, (h) relation to the theory of inter-personal relations, (i) implications for psychotherapy, (j) implication for theory of society, (k) the theory of selfishness, (l) the relation between needs and cultural patterns,

(m) the relation between this theory and Allport's theory of functional autonomy. These as well as certain other less important questions must be considered as motivation theory attempts to become definitive.

NOTES

1. Maslow, A.H. A preface to motivation theory. *Psychosomatic Med.*, 1943, 5, 85–92.

2. Wertheimer, M. Unpublished lectures at the New School for Social Research.

3. Goldstein, K. *The organism.* New York: American Book Co., 1939.

4. Freud, S. *New introductory lectures on psychoanalysis.* New York: Norton, 1933.

5. Adler, A. *Social interest.* London: Faber & Faber, 1938.

6. Cannon, W.B. *Wisdom of the body.* New York: Norton, 1932.

7. Young, P.T. The experimental analysis of appetite. *Psychol. Bull.*, 1941, 38, 129–164.

8. Maslow, A.H. A preface to motivation theory, *op cit.*

9. As the child grows up, sheer knowledge and familiarity as well as better motor development make these "dangers" less and less dangerous and more and more manageable. Throughout life it may be said that one of the main conative functions of education is this neutralizing of apparent dangers through knowledge, for example, I am not afraid of thunder because I know something about it.

10. Shirley, M. Children's adjustments to a strange situation. *J. abnorm. (soc.) Psychol.,* 1942, 37, 201–217.

11. A "test battery" for safety might be confronting the child with a small exploding firecracker, or with a bewhiskered face, having the mother leave the room, putting him upon a high ladder, a hypodermic injection, having a mouse crawl up to him, and so forth. Of course I cannot seriously recommend the deliberate use of such "tests" for they might very well harm the child being tested. But these and similar situations come up by the score in the child's ordinary day-to-day living and may be observed. There is no reason why these stimuli should not be used with, for example, young chimpanzees.

12. Not all neurotic individuals feel unsafe. Neurosis may have at its core a thwarting of the affection and esteem needs in a person who is generally safe.

13. Maslow, A.H., & Mittelmann, B. *Principles of abnormal psychology.* New York: Harper & Bros., 1941.

14. Goldstein, *op cit.*

15. Maslow & Mittelmann, *op cit.*

16. For further details see Maslow, A.H. The dynamics of psychological security-insecurity. *Character & Pers.,* 1942, 10, 331–344 and Plant, J. *Personality and the cultural pattern.* New York: Commonwealth Fund, 1937, Chapter 5.

17. Whether or not this particular desire is universal we do not know. The crucial question, especially important today, is "Will men who are enslaved and dominated, inevitably feel dissatisfied and rebellious?" We may assume on the basis of commonly known clinical data that a man who has known true freedom (not paid for by giving up safety and security but rather built on the basis of adequate safety and security) will not willingly or easily allow his freedom to be taken away from him. But we do not know that this is true for the person born into slavery. The events of the next decade should give us our answer. See discussion of this problem in Fromm, E. *Escape from freedom.* New York: Farrar and Rinehart, 1941.

18. Perhaps the desire for prestige and respect from others is subsidiary to the desire for self-esteem or confidence in oneself. Observation of children seems to indicate that this is so, but clinical data give no clear support for such a conclusion.

19. Kardiner, A. *The traumatic neuroses of our time.* New York: Hoeber, 1941. For more extensive discussion of normal self-esteem, as well as for reports of various researchers, see Maslow, A.H., Dominance, personality and social behavior in women. *J. soc. Psychol.,* 1939, 10, 3–39.

20. Clearly creative behavior, like painting, is like any other behavior in having multiple determinants. It may be seen in "innately creative" people whether they are satisfied or not, happy or unhappy, hungry or sated. Also it is clear that creative activity may be compensatory, ameliorative or purely economic. It is my impression (as yet unconfirmed) that it is possible to distinguish the artistic and intellectual products of basically satisfied people from those of basically unsatisfied people by inspection alone. In any case, here too we must distinguish, in a dynamic fashion, the overt behavior itself from its various motivations or purposes.

21. Wertheimer, *op cit.*

22. Levy, D.M. Primary affect hunger. *Amer. J. Psychiat.,* 1937, 94, 643–652.

23. I am aware that many psychologists and psychoanalysts use the term "motivated" and "determined" synonymously, for example, Freud. But I consider this an obfuscating usage. Sharp distinctions are necessary for clarity of thought, and precision in experimentation.

24. To be discussed fully in a subsequent publication.

25. The interested reader is referred to the very excellent discussion of this point in Murray, H.A., *et al. Explorations in personality.* New York: Oxford University Press, 1938.

26. Tolman, E.C. *Purposive behavior in animals and men.* New York: Century, 1932.

27. Maslow, A.H. Conflict, frustration, and the theory of threat. *J. abnorm. (soc.) Psychol.,* 1943, 38, 81–86.

28. Note that acceptance of this theory necessitates basic revision of the Freudian theory.

29. If we were to use the word "sick" in this way, we should then also have to face squarely the relations of man to his society. One clear implication of our definition would be that (1) since a man is to be called sick who is basically thwarted, and (2) since such basic thwarting is made possible ultimately only by forces outside the individual, then (3) sickness in the individual must come ultimately from a sickness in the society. The "good" or healthy society would then be defined as one that permitted man's highest purposes to emerge by satisfying all his prepotent basic needs.

Is All
Behavior Motivated?

*Most of our theories of human motivation, whether applied
to the workplace or to human beings as a species, were developed in the 40s and 50s. Maslow's theories of human motivation still dominate the landscape. In this essay Maslow
answers the question he was often asked "Is All Behavior
Motivated?"*

We must recognize first that there are many other determinants of behavior besides motivation. Theoretically behavior may be determined completely by the field without
respect to motivation at all. Furthermore, in automatisms, in the
habits and conditionings it is very likely that often no motivation
need be involved.

Second we must definitely come to grips with the notion of the
degree of motivation. We have already spoken of the concept of degree of closeness to the basic need. It is quite clear that an implication
is that some behavior is highly motivated, other is not highly motivated, and some behavior may be so slightly involved in motivation so
as to be practically unmotivated behavior. This is all quite apart from
the known behavior that is unmotivated like reflexes and like various
expressive behaviors which have no purpose but simply are epiphenomena of the state of the organism. In a pathological extreme certain
tics would be such expressions as neither purposive nor motivation in
any other sense.

Source: A.H. Maslow papers (August 5, 1942; April 28, 1942; February 13, 1942),
reprinted with the permission of Ann R. Kaplan and the *Archives of the History of American Psychology.*

This general dichotomy between expressive behavior and coping behavior is an important one in this context (as well as in others). If I am a stupid man and I then behave stupidly, is this behavior motivated, or would it not be better to say that it was simply expressive? Anything that a horse does simply because he is a horse may be expressive rather than coping behavior. Also anything that a human being does simply because of the fact that he is a human being for instance like walking upright, shows that this need not be considered to be coping or motivated behavior, it may be simply expressive behavior. In the same way that if I speak in a base voice rather than in a soprano voice, this is simply an expression of the peculiar anatomical state of the organism and through any desire to do so.

THEORY OF MOTIVATION

Is all behavior motivated? There can be several answers to this question because it means different things. Is all behavior goal directed? The answer is no because there are random behaviors which are simply expressive, which are spontaneous overflowings or expressions of the nature of the character itself but which do not "try to do anything." The random movements of the healthy infant, the smile on a person's face when he is happy even when he is all alone, the springiness of the healthy man's walk, or the erectness of his carriage may be not goal directive but simply expressive.

But then we may ask, is all behavior indicative of character structure, or to rephrase the question, is all behavior expressive? The answer is no, even though most behavior is expressive in addition to being also goal directed. All the behaviors that are determined primarily by habit, by sheer conditioning, by external situational or cultural forces need not be expressive. Tipping the hat to a lady doesn't express politeness since this is a function of the culture, and has become quite automatized.

Another point about expressive behavior is that it seems to include what I have hitherto called discouragement expression. I suppose we could also include disorganization behavior as well.

It is important to point out that these are not mutually exclusive categories. Behavior may be both expressive and goal directed and, as a matter of fact, is usually both. The point here is simply not to make any 100 percent generalizations.

NOTES ON THEORY OF MOTIVATION

The question of unmotivated behavior. Sometimes the argument between the proponents of organismic theory and field theory is apt to assume the form of two extreme caricatures fighting against each other. Either everything is organism or everything is field; everything comes from within or everything comes from without. Neither extreme is correct. In order to avoid any suspicion of this tendency to extremeness it is well to lay a good deal of stress on the various types of unmotivated behavior, quite apart from the reflexes which are generally accepted as being in this category.

There are many examples of behavior which is determined so much by the field or by the immediate situation or by cultural forces that individual variation, individual motivation becomes completely unimportant. We have already given examples of this.

But an additional type of example may be brought up which throws open a wide new field for speculation. I refer to Bateson's paper on motivation in the Balinese. Bateson tried hard to show that here was a whole society in which average behavior seemed not to be goal oriented as we understand this phrase. At most we could say of it that in contrast with our own typical behavior Balinese behavior is certainly only mildly goal oriented if at all. These people seem to proceed along at a very even pace without any heights or depressions, with no beginning and no end, but seem to find rather the justification for anything in the activity itself. It is characteristic of them that they will practically never complete a task as we do—start at the beginning and carry it through right on to the end. More characteristic for them is the tendency to do 15 tasks at the same time alternating between them, doing a little of one, then doing a little of another so that life seems to have for them no natural climaxes, no points of definite achievement, no moment that they can say, "I am finished." It is hard to find words to describe their attitude. The best I can do with it is to call it a pure acting out of cultural patterns in almost pure automatic response to the immediate environment. Life for them runs on smoothly with few ups or downs. It is Bateson's conclusion from these considerations that being goal oriented is not a universal human characteristic.

Perhaps in our own society we can find some instances which might give us a feeling for the Balinese attitude in life. Sheer placid enjoyment of the spectator type seems not to be goal organized or perhaps this itself is the goal, not coming in a peak but spread out in a long plateau. There are many other situations in life in which we are simply placid and contented over a period of time, perhaps like the mother who calmly and contentedly watches her baby disporting itself. She does nothing about it, she has no goal, she is not striving, she does not go in any particular direction, she is not fulfilling anything. Still this is behavior.

Deficiency Motivation
and Growth Motivation

This excerpt is a condensed version of a lecture presented at the University of Nebraska Symposium on Motivation, January 13, 1955. The conceptual groundwork for the motivational ideas presented in this and subsequent chapters had been laid in two of Maslow's earlier papers: "A Preface to Motivation Theory," Psychosomatic Medicine, 1943, 5, 85–92; and "A Theory of Human Motivation," Psychological Review, 1943, 50, 370–396. Both of these germinal papers appeared in his Motivation and Personality (New York: Harper & Bros., 1954; second edition, 1970; third edition [posthumous], 1987).

The concept "basic need" can be defined in terms of the questions which it answers and the operations which uncovered it. My original question was about psychopathogenesis. "What makes people neurotic?" My answer (a modification of and, I think, an improvement upon the analytic one) was, in brief, that neurosis seemed at its core, and in its beginning, to be a deficiency disease; that it was born out of being deprived of certain satisfactions which I called needs in the same sense that water and amino acids and calcium are needs, namely that their absence produces illness. Most neuroses involved, along with other complex determinants, ungratified wishes for safety, for belongingness and identification, for close love relationships and for respect and prestige. My "data" were gathered

Source: A.H. Maslow, *Toward a Psychology of Being, 3rd ed.* (New York: John Wiley & Sons, 1968, 1999). Copyright © 1968, 1999 by Ann R. Kaplan, used with permission.

through twelve years of psychotherapeutic work and research and twenty years of personality study. One obvious control research (done at the same time and in the same operation) was on the effect of replacement therapy which showed, with many complexities, that when these deficiencies were eliminated, sicknesses tended to disappear.

These conclusions, which are now in effect shared by most clinicians, therapists, and child psychologists (many of them would not phrase it as I have) make it more possible year by year to define need, in a natural, easy, spontaneous way, as a generalization of actual experiential data (rather than by fiat, arbitrarily and prematurely, *prior* to the accumulation of knowledge rather than subsequent to it simply for the sake of greater objectivity).

The long-run deficiency characteristics are then the following. It is a basic or instinctoid need if:

1. Its absence breeds illness.
2. Its presence prevents illness.
3. Its restoration cures illness.
4. Under certain (very complex) free choice situations, it is preferred by the deprived person over other satisfactions.
5. It is found to be inactive, at a low ebb, or functionally absent in the healthy person.

Two additional characteristics are subjective ones, namely, conscious or unconscious yearning and desire, and feeling of lack or deficiency, as of something missing on the one hand, and, on the other, palatability. ("It tastes good.")

One last word on definition. Many of the problems that have plagued writers in this area, as they attempted to define and delimit motivation, are a consequence of the exclusive demand for behavioral, externally observable criteria. The original criterion of motivation and the one that is still used by all human beings except behavioral psychologists is the subjective one. I am motivated when I feel desire or want or yearning or wish or lack. No objectively observable state has yet been found that correlates decently with these subjective reports, that is, no good behavioral definition of motivation has yet been found.

Now of course we ought to keep on seeking for objective correlates or indicators of subjective states. On the day when we discover such a public and external indicator of pleasure or of anxiety or of desire, psychology will have jumped forward by a century. But *until* we find it we ought not make believe that we have. Nor ought we neglect the subjective data that we do have. It is unfortunate that we cannot ask a rat to give subjective reports. Fortunately, however, we *can* ask the human being, and there is no reason in the world why we should refrain from doing so until we have a better source of data.

It is these needs which are essentially deficits in the organism, empty holes, so to speak, which must be filled up for health's sake, and furthermore must be filled from without by human beings *other* than the subject, that I shall call deficits or deficiency needs for purposes of this exposition and to set them in contrast to another and very different kind of motivation.

It would not occur to anyone to question the statement that we "need" iodine or vitamin C. I remind you that the evidence that we "need" love is of exactly the same type.

In recent years more and more psychologists have found themselves compelled to postulate some tendency to growth or self-perfection to supplement the concepts of equilibrium, homeostasis, tension-reduction, defense and other conserving motivations. This was so for various reasons.

1. *Psychotherapy.* The pressure toward health makes therapy possible. It is an absolute *sine qua non*. If there were no such trend, therapy would be inexplicable to the extent that it goes beyond the building of defenses against pain and anxiety.

2. *Brain-injured soldiers.* Goldstein's[1] work is well known to all. He found it necessary to invent the concept of self-actualization to explain the reorganization of the person's capacities after injury.

---

[1] Kurt Goldstein (1878–1965) was a neuropsychiatrist whose work with brain-injured patients was very influential in the development of Maslow's concept of self-actualization. Goldstein had offered many acute observations of how the brain-injured organism spontaneously reorganizes its capacities and strives to actualize its potential through whatever avenues remain open to it. As Maslow acknowledged, it was Goldstein who first used the term "self-actualization" in a psychological context. See Kurt Goldstein, *The Organism,* New York: American Book Co., 1939; first published as *Der Aufbau des Organismus,* 1934.

3. *Psychoanalysis*. Some analysts, notably Fromm and Horney,[2] have found it impossible to understand even neuroses unless one postulates that they are a distorted version of an impulse toward growth, toward perfection of development, toward the fulfillment of the person's possibilities.

4. *Creativeness*. Much light is being thrown on the general subject of creativeness by the study of healthy growing and grown people, especially when contrasted with sick people. Especially does the theory of art and art education call for a concept of growth and spontaneity.

5. *Child Psychology*. Observation of children shows more and more clearly that healthy children *enjoy* growing and moving forward, gaining new skills, capacities and powers. This is in flat contradiction to that version of Freudian theory which conceives of every child as hanging on desperately to each adjustment that it achieves and to each state of rest or equilibrium. According to this theory, the reluctant and conservative child has continually to be kicked upstairs, out of its comfortable, preferred state of rest *into* a new frightening situation.

While this Freudian conception is continually confirmed by clinicians as largely true for insecure and frightened children, and while it is partially true for all human beings, in the main it is *untrue* for healthy, happy, secure children. In these children we see clearly an eagerness to grow up, to mature, to drop the old adjustment as outworn, like an old pair of shoes. We see in them with special clarity not only the eagerness for the new skill but also the most obvious delight in repeatedly enjoying it, the so-called *Funktions-lust* of Karl Buhler.

---

[2] Erich Fromm (1900–1980) and Karen Horney (1885–1952) were classically trained psychoanalysts who eventually came into conflict with Freudian orthodoxy. Among their deviations from the Freudian path was their insistence that human personality could only be understood within the context of particular societies, cultures, and historical periods, and their respective views—not precisely the same as Maslow's, but certainly congenial—that the satisfaction of basic needs can open the way to the expression of "a higher human nature." The works of Fromm that Maslow found most *simpático* were: *Man For Himself*, New York: Rinehart, 1947 (also New York: Fawcett Premier, 1965); and *The Sane Society*, New York: Holt, Rinehart, and Winston, 1955 (also New York: H. Holt, 1990). For an introduction to the psychological views of Karen Horney see: *The Neurotic Personality of Our Time*, New York: Norton, 1937; and *Neurosis and Human Growth*, New York: Norton, 1950.

For the writers in these various groups, notably Fromm, Horney, Jung , C. Buhler, Angyal, Rogers, and G. Allport, Schachtel, and Lynd , and recently some Catholic psychologists, growth, individuation, autonomy, self-actualization, self-development, productiveness, self-realization, are all crudely synonymous, designating a vaguely perceived area rather than a sharply defined concept. In my opinion, it is *not* possible to define this area sharply at the present time. Nor is this desirable either, since a definition which does not emerge easily and naturally from well-known facts is apt to be inhibiting and distorting rather than helpful, since it is quite likely to be wrong or mistaken if made by an act of the will, on a priori grounds. We just don't know enough about growth yet to be able to define it well.

Its meaning can be *indicated* rather than defined, partly by positive pointing, partly by negative contrast, that is, what is *not*. For example, it is not the same as equilibrium, homeostasis, tension-reduction, and so forth.

Its necessity has presented itself to its proponents partly because of dissatisfaction (certain newly noticed phenomena simply were not covered by extant theories); partly by positive needs for theories and concepts which would better serve the new humanistic value systems emerging from the breakdown of the older value systems.

This present treatment, however, derives mostly from a direct study of psychologically healthy individuals. This was undertaken not only for reasons of intrinsic and personal interest but also to supply a firmer foundation for the theory of therapy, of pathology and therefore of values. The true goals of education, of family training, of psychotherapy, of self-development, it seems to me, can be discovered only by such a direct attack. The end product of growth teaches us much about the processes of growth. In a recent book, I have described what was learned from this study and in addition theorized very freely about various possible consequences for general psychology of this kind of direct study of good rather than bad human beings, of healthy rather than sick people, of the positive as well as the negative. (I must warn you that the data cannot be considered reliable until someone else repeats the study. The possibilities of projection are very real in such a study and of course are unlikely to be detected by the investigator himself.) I want now to discuss some of the differences that I have observed to exist between the motivational lives of healthy people and of others, that is, people motivated by growth needs contrasted with those motivated by the basic needs.

So far as motivational status is concerned, healthy people have sufficiently gratified their basic needs for safety, belongingness, love, respect and self-esteem so that they are motivated primarily by trends to self-actualization (defined as ongoing actualization of potentials, capacities and talents, as fulfillment of mission [or call, fate, destiny, or vocation], as a fuller knowledge of, and acceptance of, the person's own intrinsic nature, as an unceasing trend toward unity, integration or synergy within the person).

Much to be preferred to this generalized definition would be a descriptive and operational one which I have already published. These healthy people are there defined by describing their clinically observed characteristics. These are:

1. Superior perception of reality.
2. Increased acceptance of self, of others and of nature.
3. Increased spontaneity.
4. Increase in problem-centering.
5. Increased detachment and desire for privacy.
6. Increased autonomy, and resistance to enculturation.
7. Greater freshness of appreciation, and richness of emotional reaction.
8. Higher frequency of peak experiences.
9. Increased identification with the human species.
10. Changed (the clinician would say, improved) interpersonal relations.
11. More democratic character structure.
12. Greatly increased creativeness.
13. Certain changes in the value system.

Furthermore, in this book are described also the limitations imposed upon the definition by unavoidable shortcomings in sampling and in availability of data.

One major difficulty with this conception as so far presented is its somewhat static character. Self-actualization, since I have studied it mostly in older people, tends to be seen as an ultimate or final state of affairs, a far goal, rather than a dynamic process, active throughout life, Being, rather than Becoming.

If we define growth as the various processes which bring the person toward ultimate self-actualization, then this conforms better with the observed fact that it is going on *all* the time in the life history. It discourages also the stepwise, *all* or none, saltatory conception of motivational progression toward self-actualization in which the basic needs are completely gratified, one by one, before the next higher one emerges into consciousness. Growth is seen then not only as progressive gratification of basic needs to the point where they "disappear," but also in the form of specific growth motivations over and above these basic needs, for example, talents, capacities, creative tendencies, constitutional potentialities. We are thereby helped also to realize that basic needs and self-actualization do not contradict each other any more than do childhood and maturity. One passes into the other and is a necessary prerequisite for it.

The differentiation between these growth-needs and basic needs which we shall explore here is a consequence of the clinical perception of qualitative differences between the motivational lives of self-actualizers and of other people. These differences, listed below, are fairly well though not perfectly described by the names deficiency-needs and growth-needs. For instance, not all physiological needs are deficits, for example, sex, elimination, sleep and rest.

In any case, the psychological life of the person, in many of its aspects, is lived out differently when he is deficiency-need-gratification-bent and when he is growth-dominated or "metamotivated" or growth-motivated or self-actualizing. The following differences make this clear.

ATTITUDE TOWARD IMPULSE: IMPULSE-REJECTION AND IMPULSE-ACCEPTANCE

Practically all historical and contemporary theories of motivation unite in regarding needs, drives and motivating states in general as annoying, irritating, unpleasant, undesirable, as something to get rid of.

Motivated behavior, goal seeking, consummatory responses are all techniques for reducing these discomforts. This attitude is very explicitly assumed in such widely used descriptions of motivation as need reduction, tension reduction, drive reduction, and anxiety reduction.

This approach is understandable in animal psychology and in the behaviorism which is so heavily based upon work with animals. It may be that animals have *only* deficiency needs. Whether or not this turns out to be so, in any case we have treated animals *as if* this were so for the sake of objectivity. A goal object has to be something outside the animal organism so that we can measure the effort put out by the animal in achieving this goal.

It is also understandable that the Freudian psychology should be built upon the same attitude toward motivation that impulses are dangerous and to be fought. After all, this whole psychology is based upon experience with sick people, people who in fact suffer from bad experiences with their needs, and with their gratifications and frustrations. It is no wonder that such people should fear or even loathe their impulses which have made so much trouble for them and which they handle so badly, and that a usual way of handling them is repression.

This derogation of desire and need has, of course, been a constant theme throughout the history of philosophy, theology and psychology. The Stoics, most hedonists, practically all theologians, many political philosophers and most economic theorists have united in affirming the fact that good or happiness or pleasure is essentially the consequence of amelioration of this unpleasant state-of-affairs of wanting, of desiring, of needing.

To put it as succinctly as possible, these people all find desire or impulse to be a nuisance or even a threat and therefore will try generally to get rid of it, to deny it or to avoid it.

This contention is sometimes an accurate report of what is the case. The physiological needs, the needs for safety, for love, for respect, for information are in fact often nuisances for many people, psychic troublemakers, and problem-creators, especially for those who have had unsuccessful experiences at gratifying them and for those who cannot now count on gratification.

Even with these deficiencies, however, the case is very badly overdrawn: one can accept and enjoy one's needs and welcome them to consciousness if (a) past experience with them has been rewarding, and (b) if present and future gratification can be counted on. For example, if one has in general enjoyed food and if good food is now available, the emergence of appetite into consciousness is welcomed instead of dreaded. ("The trouble with eating is that it kills my appetite.") Something like this is true for thirst, for sleepiness, for sex, for dependency needs and for love needs. However, a far more powerful refutation of the "need-is-a-nuisance" theory is found in the recently merging awareness of, and concern with, growth (self-actualization) motivation.

The multitude of idiosyncratic motives which come under the head of "self-actualization" can hardly be listed since each person has different talents, capacities, potentialities. But some characteristics are general to all of them. And one is that these impulses are desired and welcomed, are enjoyable and pleasant, that the person wants more of them rather than less, and that if they constitute tensions, they are *pleasurable* tensions. The creator ordinarily welcomes his creative impulses, the talented person enjoys using and expanding his talents.

It is simply inaccurate to speak in such instances of tension-reduction, implying thereby the getting rid of an annoying state. For these states are not annoying.

DIFFERENTIAL EFFECTS OF GRATIFICATION

Almost always associated with negative attitudes toward the need is the conception that the primary aim of the organism is to get rid of the annoying need and thereby to achieve a cessation of tension, an equilibrium, a homeostasis, a quiescence, a state of rest, a lack of pain.

The drive or need presses toward its own elimination. Its only striving is toward cessation, toward getting rid of itself, toward a state of not wanting. Pushed to its logical extreme, we wind up with Freud's death-instinct.

Angyal, Goldstein, G. Allport, C. Buhler, Schachtel and others have effectively criticized this essentially circular position. If the motivational life consists essentially of a defensive removal of irritating tensions, and if the only end product of tension-reduction is a state of passive waiting for more unwelcome irritations to arise and in their turn, to be dispelled, then how does change, or development or movement or direction come about? Why do people improve? Get wiser? What does zest in living mean?

Charlotte Buhler has pointed out that the theory of homeostasis is different from the theory of rest. The latter theory speaks simply of removing tension which implies that zero tension is best.

Homeostasis means coming not to a zero but to an optimum level. This means sometimes reducing tension, sometimes increasing it, for example, blood pressure may be too low as well as too high.

In either case the lack of constant direction through a lifespan is obvious. In both cases, growth of the personality, increases in wisdom, self-actualization, strengthening of the character, and the planning of one's life are not and cannot be accounted for. Some long-time vector, or directional tendency, must be invoked to make any sense of development through the lifetime.

This theory must be put down as an inadequate description even of deficiency motivation. What is lacking here is awareness of the dynamic principle which ties together and interrelates all these separate motivational episodes. The different basic needs are related to each other in a hierarchical order such that gratification of one need and its consequent removal from the center of the stage brings about not a state of rest or Stoic apathy, but rather the emergence into consciousness of another "higher" need; wanting and desiring continues but at a "higher" level. Thus the coming-to-rest theory isn't adequate even for deficiency motivation.

However, when we examine people who are predominantly growth-motivated, the coming-to-rest conception of motivation becomes completely useless. In such people gratification breeds increased rather than decreased motivation, heightened rather than lessened excitement. The appetites become intensified and heightened. They grow upon themselves and instead of wanting less and less, such a person wants more and more of, for instance, education. The person rather than coming to rest becomes more active. The appetite for growth is whetted rather than allayed by gratification. Growth is, *in itself*, a rewarding and exciting process, for example, the fulfilling of yearnings and ambitions, like that of being a good doctor; the acquisition of admired skills, like playing the violin or being a good carpenter; the steady increase of understanding about people or about the universe, or about oneself; the development of creativeness in whatever field, or, most important, simply the ambition to be a good human being.

Wertheimer long ago stressed another aspect of this same differentiation by claiming, in a seeming paradox, that true goal-seeking activity took up less than 10 percent of his time. Activity can be enjoyed either intrinsically, for its own sake, or else have worth and value only because it is instrumental in bringing about a desired gratification. In the latter case it loses its value and is no longer pleasurable when it is no longer successful or efficient. More frequently, it is simply *not enjoyed at all,* but only the goal is enjoyed. This is similar to that attitude toward life which values it less for its own sake than because one goes to Heaven at the end of it. The observation upon which this generalization is based is that self-actualizing people enjoy life in general and in practically all its aspects, while most other people enjoy only stray moments of triumph, of achievement or of climax or peak experience.

Partly this intrinsic validity of living comes from the pleasurableness inherent in growing and in being grown. But it also comes from the ability of healthy people to transform means-activity into end-experience, so that even instrumental activity is enjoyed as if it were end activity. Growth motivation may be long-term in character. Most of a lifetime may be involved in becoming a good psychologist or a good artist. All equilibrium or homeostasis or rest theories deal only with short-term episodes, each of which has nothing to do with each other. Allport particularly has stressed this point. Planfulness and looking into the future, he points out, are of the central stuff or healthy human nature. He agrees that "Deficit motives do, in fact, call for the reduction of tension and restoration of equilibrium. Growth motives, on the other hand, maintain tension in the interest of distant and often unattainable goals. As such they distinguish human from animal becoming, and adult from infant becoming."

CLINICAL AND PERSONOLOGICAL EFFECTS OF GRATIFICATION

Deficit-need gratifications and growth-need gratifications have differential subjective and objective effects upon the personality. If I may phrase what I am groping for here in a generalized way, it is this: satisfying deficiencies avoids illness; growth satisfactions produce positive health. I must grant that this will be difficult to pin down for research purposes at this time. And yet there is a real *clinical* difference between fending off threat or attack and positive triumph and achievement, between protecting, defending and preserving oneself and reaching out for fulfillment, for excitement and for enlargement. I have tried to express this as a contrast between living fully and *preparing* to

292 MOTIVATION AND BEHAVIOR

live fully, between growing up and being grown. Another contrast that I have used is between defense mechanisms (to cut pain) and coping mechanisms (to be successful and to win out over difficulties).

DIFFERENT KINDS OF PLEASURE

Erich Fromm has made an interesting and important effort to distinguish higher from lower pleasures, as have so many others before him. This is a crucial necessity for breaking through subjective ethical relativity and is a prerequisite for a scientific value theory.

He distinguishes scarcity-pleasure from abundance-pleasure, the "lower" pleasure of satiation of a need from the "higher" pleasure of production, creation and growth of insight. The glut, the relaxation, and the loss of tension that follows deficiency-satiation can at best be called "relief" by contrast with the *Funktions-lust,* the ecstasy, the serenity that one experiences when functioning easily, perfectly and at the peak of one's powers—in overdrive, so to speak (see Chapter 6).

"Relief," depending so strongly on something that disappears, is itself more likely to disappear. It must be less stable, less enduring, less constant than the pleasure accompanying growth, which can go on forever.

ATTAINABLE (EPISODIC) AND UNATTAINABLE GOAL STATES

Deficiency-need gratification tends to be episodic and climactic. The most frequent schema here begins with an instigating, motivating state which sets off motivated behavior designed to achieve a goal-state, which, mounting gradually and steadily in desire and excitement, finally reaches a peak in a moment of success and consummation. From this peak curve of desire, excitement and pleasure fall rapidly to a plateau of quiet tension-release, and lack of motivation.

This schema, though not universally applicable, in any case contrasts very sharply with the situation in growth-motivation, for here, characteristically, there is no climax or consummation, no orgasmic moment, no end-state, even no goal if this be defined climactically. Growth is instead a continued, more or less steady upward or forward development. The more one gets, the more one wants, so that this kind of wanting is endless and can never be attained or satisfied.

It is for this reason that the usual separation between instigation, goal-seeking behavior, the goal object and the accompanying effect breaks down completely. The behaving is itself the goal, and to differentiate the goal of growth from the instigation to growth is impossible. They too are the same.

SPECIES-WIDE GOALS AND IDIOSYNCRATIC GOALS

The deficit-needs are shared by all members of the human species and to some extent by other species as well. Self-actualization is idiosyncratic since every person is different. The deficits, that is., the species requirements, must ordinarily be fairly well satisfied before real individuality can develop fully.

Just as all trees need sun, water, and foods from the environment, so do all people need safety, love and status from *their* environment. However, in both cases this is just where real development of individuality can begin, for once satiated with these elementary, species-wide necessities, each tree and each person proceeds to develop in his own style, uniquely, using these necessities for his own private purposes. In a very meaningful sense, development then becomes more determined from within rather than from without.

DEPENDENCE ON, AND INDEPENDENCE OF, THE ENVIRONMENT

The needs for safety, belongingness, love relations and for respect can be satisfied only by other people, that is, only from outside the person. This means considerable dependence on the environment. A person in this dependent position cannot really be said to be governing himself, or in control of his own fate. He *must* be beholden to the sources of supply of needed gratifications. Their wishes, their whims, their rules and laws govern him and must be appeased lest he jeopardize his sources of supply. He *must* be, to an extent, "other-directed," and *must* be sensitive to other people's approval, affection and good will. This is the same as saying that he must adapt and adjust by being flexible and responsive and by changing himself to fit the external situation. *He* is the dependent variable; the environment is the fixed, independent variable.

Because of this, the deficiency-motivated man must be more afraid of the environment, since there is always the possibility that it may fail or disappoint him. We now know that this kind of anxious dependence breeds hostility as well. All of which adds up to a lack of freedom, more or less, depending on the good fortune or bad fortune of the individual.

In contrast, the self-actualizing individual, by definition gratified in his basic needs, is far less dependent, far less beholden, far more autonomous and self-directed. Far from needing other people, growth-motivated people may actually be hampered by them. I have already reported their special liking for privacy, for detachment and for meditativeness (see also Chapter 13).

Such people become far more self-sufficient and self-contained. The determinants which govern them are now primarily inner ones, rather than social or environmental. They are the laws of their own inner nature, their potentialities and capacities, their talents, their latent resources, their creative impulses, their needs to know themselves and to become more and more integrated and unified, more and more aware of what they really are, of what they really want, of what their call or vocation or fate is to be.

Since they depend less on other people, they are less ambivalent about them, less anxious and also less hostile, less needful of their praise and their affection. They are less anxious for honors, prestige and rewards.

Autonomy or relative independence of environment means also relative independence of adverse external circumstances, such as ill fortune, hard knocks, tragedy, stress, deprivation. As Allport has stressed, the notion of the human being as essentially reactive, the S-R man, we might call him, who is set into motion by external stimuli, becomes completely ridiculous and untenable for self-actualizing people. The sources of *their* actions are more internal than reactive. This *relative* independence of the outside world and its wishes and pressures, does not mean of course, lack of intercourse with it or respect for its "demand-character." It means only that in these contacts, the self-actualizer's wishes and plans are the primary determiners, rather than stresses from the environment. This I have called psychological freedom, contrasting it with geographical freedom.

Allport's expressive contrast between "opportunistic" and "propriate"[3] determination of behavior parallels closely our outer-determined, inner-determined opposition. It reminds us also of the uniform agreement among biological theorists in considering increasing autonomy and independence of environmental stimuli as *the* defining characteristics of full individuality, of true freedom, of the whole evolutionary process.

Interested and Disinterested Interpersonal Relations

In essence, the deficit-motivated man is far more dependent upon other people than is the man who is predominantly growth-motivated. He is more "interested," more needful, more attached, more desirous.

This dependency colors and limits interpersonal relations. To see people primarily as need-gratifiers or as sources of supply is an abstractive act. They are seen not as wholes, as complicated, unique individuals, but rather from the point of view of usefulness. What in them is not related to the perceiver's needs is either overlooked altogether, or else bores, irritates, or threatens. This parallels our relations with cows, horses, and sheep, as well as with waiters, taxicab drivers, porters, policemen or others whom we *use*.

Fully disinterested, desireless, objective and holistic perception of another human being becomes possible only when nothing is needed from him, only when *he* is not needed. Idiographic, aesthetic perception of the whole person is far more possible for self-actualizing people (or in moments of self-actualization), and furthermore approval, admiration, and love are based less upon gratitude for usefulness and more upon the objective, intrinsic qualities of the perceived person. He is admired for objectively admirable qualities rather than because he flatters or praises. He is loved because he is love-worthy rather than because he

---

[3] Gordon Allport (1897–1967) coined the terms "proprium" and "propriate" (from the Latin *proprius,* one's own) to denote all aspects of a person that are deeply rooted in the core of personality. "Opportunistic" was the term he used to describe the less deeply rooted aspects of personality. See: *The Nature of Personality,* Cambridge, MA: Addison-Wesley, 1950; and *Becoming,* New Haven: Yale University Press, 1955.

gives out love. This is what will be discussed below as unneeding love, for example, for Abraham Lincoln.

One characteristic of "interested" and need-gratifying relations to other people is that to a very large extent these need-gratifying persons are interchangeable. Since, for instance, the adolescent girl needs admiration per se, it therefore makes little difference who supplies this admiration; one admiration-supplier is about as good as another. So also for the love-supplier or the safety-supplier.

Disinterested, unrewarded, useless, desireless perception of the other as unique, as independent, as end-in-himself—in other words, as a person rather than as a tool—is the more difficult, the more hungry the perceiver is for deficit satisfaction. A "high-ceiling" interpersonal psychology, that is, an understanding of the highest possible development of human relationships, cannot base itself on deficit theory of motivation.

EGO-CENTERING AND EGO-TRANSCENDENCE

We are confronted with a difficult paradox when we attempt to describe the complex attitude toward the self or ego of the growth-oriented, self-actualized person. It is just this person, in whom ego-strength is at its height, who most easily forgets or transcends the ego, who can be most problem-centered, most self-forgetful, most spontaneous in his activities, most homonomous, to use Angyal's term. In such people, absorption in perceiving, in doing, in enjoying, in creating can be very complete, very integrated and very pure.

This ability to center upon the world rather than to be self-conscious, egocentric and gratification-oriented becomes the more difficult the more need-deficits the person has. The more growth-motivated the person is the more problem-centered he can be, and the more he can leave self-consciousness behind him as he deals with the objective world.

INTERPERSONAL PSYCHOTHERAPY
AND INTRAPERSONAL PSYCHOLOGY

A major characteristic of people who seek psychotherapy is a former and/or present deficiency of basic-need gratification. Neurosis can be seen as a deficiency-disease. Because this is so, a basic necessity for cure is supplying what has been lacking or making it possible for the patient to do this himself. Since these supplies come from other people, ordinary therapy *must* be interpersonal.

But this fact has been badly over-generalized. It is true that people whose deficiency needs have been gratified and who are primarily growth-motivated are by no means exempt from conflict, unhappiness, anxiety, and confusion. In such moments they too are apt to seek help and may very well turn to interpersonal therapy. And yet it is unwise to forget that frequently the problems and the conflicts of the growth-motivated person are solved by himself by turning inward in a meditative way, that is, self-searching, rather than seeking for help from someone. Even in principle, many of the tasks of self-actualization are largely intrapersonal, such as the making of plans, the discovery of self, the selection of potentialities to develop, the construction of a life-outlook.

In the theory of personality improvement, a place must be reserved for self-improvement and self-searching, contemplation and meditation. In the later stages of growth the person is essentially alone and can rely only upon himself. This improvement of an already well person, Oswald Schwarz has called "psychogogy." If psychotherapy makes sick people not-sick and removes symptoms, then psychogogy takes up where therapy leaves off and tries to make not-sick people healthy. I was interested to notice in Rogers that successful therapy raised the patients' average score in The Willoughby Maturity Scale from he twenty-fifth to the fiftieth percentile. Who shall then lift him to the seventy-fifth percentile? Or the one hundredth? And are we not likely to need new principles and techniques to do this with?

INSTRUMENTAL LEARNING AND PERSONALITY CHANGE

So-called learning theory in this country has based itself almost entirely on deficit-motivation with goal objects usually external to the organism, that is, learning the best way to satisfy a need. For this reason, among others, our psychology of learning is a limited body of knowledge, useful only in small areas of life and of real interest only to other "learning theorists."

This is of little help in solving the problem of growth and self-actualization. Here the techniques of repeatedly acquiring from the outside world satisfactions of motivational deficiencies are much less needed. Associative learning and canalizations give way more to perceptual learning, to the increase of insight and understanding, to knowledge of self and to the steady growth of personality, that is, increased synergy, integration and inner consistency. Change becomes much less an acquisition of habits or associations one by one, and much more a total change of the total person, that is, a new person rather than the same person with some habits added like new external possessions.

This kind of character-change-learning means changing a very complex, highly integrated, holistic organism, which in turn means that many impacts will make no change at all because more and more such impacts will be rejected as the person becomes more stable and more autonomous.

The most important learning experiences reported to me by my subjects were very frequently single life experiences such as tragedies, deaths, traumata, conversations, and sudden in-sights, which forced change in the life-outlook of the person and consequently in everything that he did. (Of course the so-called "working through" of the tragedy or of the insight took place over a longer period of time but this, too, was not primarily a matter of associative learning.)

To the extent that growth consists in peeling away inhibitions and constraints and then permitting the person to "be himself," to emit behavior—"radiantly," as it were—rather than to repeat it, to allow his inner nature to express itself, to this extent the behavior of self-actualizers is unlearned, created and released rather than acquired, expressive rather than coping.

DEFICIENCY-MOTIVATED AND GROWTH-MOTIVATED PERCEPTION

What may turn out to be the most important difference of all is the greater closeness of deficit-satisfied people to the realm of Being . Psychologists have never yet been able to claim this vague jurisdiction of the philosophers, this area dimly seen but nevertheless having undoubted basis in reality. But it may now become feasible through the study of self-fulfilling individuals to have our eyes opened to all sorts of basic insights, old to the philosophers but new to us.

For instance, I think that our understanding of perception and therefore of the perceived world will be much changed and enlarged if we study carefully the distinction between need-interested and need-disinterested or desireless perception. Because the latter is so much more concrete and less abstracted and selective, it is possible for such a person to see more easily the intrinsic nature of the percept. Also, he can perceive simultaneously the opposites, the dichotomies, the polarities, the contradictions and the incompatibles. It is as if less developed people lived in an Aristotelian world in which classes and concepts have sharp boundaries and are mutually exclusive and incompatible, for example, male-female, selfish-unselfish, adult-child, kind-cruel, good-bad. A is A and everything else is not-A in the Aristotelian logic, and never the twain shall meet. But seen by self-actualizing people is the fact that A and not-A interpenetrate and are one, that any person is simultaneously good and bad, male *and* female, adult *and* child. One cannot place a whole person on a continuum, only an abstracted aspect of a person. Wholenesses are non-comparable.

We may not be aware when *we* perceive in a need-determined way. But we certainly are aware of it when *we* ourselves are perceived in this way, for example, simply as a money-giver, a food-supplier, a safety-giver, someone to depend on, or as a waiter or other anonymous servant or means-object. When this happens we don't like it at all. We want to be taken for ourselves, as complete and whole individuals. We dislike being perceived as useful objects or as tools. We dislike being "used."

Because self-actualizing people ordinarily do not have to abstract need-gratifying qualities nor see the person as a tool, it is much more possible for them to take a non-valuing, non-judging, non-interfering, non-condemning attitude toward others, a desirelessness, a "choiceless awareness." This permits much clearer and more insightful perception and understanding of what is there. This is the kind of untangled and uninvolved, detached perception that surgeons and therapists are supposed to try for and which self-actualizing people attain *without* trying for.

Especially when the structure of the person or object seen is difficult, subtle, and not obvious is this difference in style of perception most important. Especially then must the perceiver have respect for the nature of the object. Perception must then be gentle, delicate, un-intruding, undemanding, able to fit itself passively to the nature of things as water gently soaks into crevices. It must *not* be the need-motivated kind of perception which *shapes* things in a blustering, over-riding, exploiting, purposeful fashion, in the manner of a butcher chopping apart a carcass.

The most efficient way to perceive the intrinsic nature of the world is to be more receptive than active, determined as much as pos-sible by the intrinsic organization of that which is perceived and as little as possible by the nature of the perceiver. This kind of detached, Taoist, passive, non-interfering awareness of all the simultaneously ex-isting aspects of the concrete, has much in common with some de-scriptions of the aesthetic experience and of the mystic experience. The stress is the same. Do we see the real, concrete world or do we see our own system of rubrics, motives, expectations and abstractions which we have projected onto the real world? Or, to put it very bluntly, do we see or are we blind?

NEEDING LOVE AND UNNEEDING LOVE

The love need as ordinarily studied, for instance by Bowlby, Spitz, and Levy, is a deficit need. It is a hole which has to be filled, an emptiness into which love is poured. If this healing necessity is not available, severe pathology results; if it *is* available at the right time, in the right quantities and with proper style, then pathology is averted. Intermediate states of pathology and health follow upon in-termediate states of thwarting or satiation. If the pathology is not too severe and if it is caught early enough, replacement therapy can cure. That is to say the sickness, "love-hunger," can be cured in certain cases by making up the pathological deficiency. Love hunger is a de-ficiency disease, like salt hunger or the avitaminoses.

The healthy person, not having this deficiency, does not need to receive love except in steady, small, maintenance doses and he may even do without these for periods of time. But if motivation is entirely a matter of satisfying deficits and thus getting rid of needs, then a con-tradiction appears. Satisfaction of the need should cause it to disappear, which is to say that people who have stood in satisfying love relation-ships are precisely the people who should be *less* likely to give and to receive love! But clinical study of healthier people, who have been love-need-satiated, show that although they need less to *receive* love, they are more able to *give* love. In this sense, they are *more* loving people.

This finding in itself exposes the limitation of ordinary (deficiency-need-centered) motivation theory and indicates the necessity for "meta-motivation theory" (or growth-motivation or self-actualization theory).

I have already described in a preliminary fashion the contrasting dynamics of B-love (love for the Being of another person, unneed-ing love, unselfish love) and D-love (deficiency-love, love need, selfish love). At this point, I wish only to use these two contrasting groups of people to exemplify and illustrate some of the generalizations made above.

1. B-love is welcomed into consciousness, and is completely enjoyed. Since it is non-possessive, and is admiring rather than needing, it makes no trouble and is practically always pleasure-giving.

2. It can never be sated; it may be enjoyed without end. It usually grows greater rather than disappearing. It is intrinsically enjoyable. It is end rather than means.

3. The B-love experience is often described as being the same as, and having the same effects as the aesthetic experience or the mystic experience. (See Chapters 6 and 7 on "Peak-Experiences.")

4. The therapeutic and psychogogic effects of experiencing B-love are very profound and widespread. Similar are the characterological effects of the relatively pure love of a healthy mother for her baby, or the perfect love of their God that some mystics have described.

5. B-love is, beyond the shadow of a doubt, a richer, "higher," more valuable subjective experience than D-love (which all B-lovers have also previously experienced). This preference is also reported by my other older, more average subjects, many of whom experience both kinds of love simultaneously in varying combinations.

6. D-love *can* be gratified. The concept "gratification" hardly applies at all to admiration-love for another person's admiration-worthiness and love-worthiness.

7. In B-love there is a minimum of anxiety-hostility. For all practical human purposes, it may even be considered to be absent. There *can*, of course, be anxiety-for-the-other. In D-love one must always expect some degree of anxiety-hostility.

8. B-lovers are more independent of each other, more autonomous, less jealous or threatened, less needful, more individual, more disinterested, but also simultaneously more eager to help the other toward self-actualization, more proud of his triumphs, more altruistic, generous and fostering.

9. The truest, most penetrating perception of the other is made possible by B-love. It is as much a cognitive as an emotional-conative reaction, as I have already emphasized. So impressive is this, and so often validated by other people's later experience, that, far from accepting the common platitude that love makes people blind, I become more and more inclined to think of the *opposite* as true, namely that non-love makes us blind.

10. Finally, I may say that B-love, in a profound but testable sense, creates the partner. It gives him a self-image, it gives him self-acceptance, a feeling of love-worthiness, all of which permit him to grow. It is a real question whether the full development of the human being is possible without it.

Letter to B.F. Skinner

Dr. B.F. Skinner
Department of Psychology
Harvard University
Cambridge, MA 02138

Dear Fred:

Thank you for your letter *and* for its bluntness, which is helpful.

If values and the life of values are your professional concern, poetry, art, and so on, you must make a better theoretical place in your structure for experiential knowledge. At least, it must be accepted as a beginning of knowledge and this must be done in a *systematic* way (as part of the theory of science). I think this is quite compatible with my methodological or epistemological behaviorism that thinks of objective, public, respectable knowledge as most reliable, most certain, most solid, an ideal toward which to press. But there is no need to exclude experience as datum for science and then to hope to objectify it eventually.

Beyond that, what you choose to specialize in is a matter of (characterological) taste. I like playing around with the beginnings of knowledge, raising new questions, and so on. Other people like to work on more solid ground. Both approaches are okay. I think I know both pleasures. It was John B. Watson's writings that brought me into psychology. At the University of Wisconsin, Clark Hull, Norman Cameron, Bill Sheldon, and everyone else was a behaviorist—and so was I. All my research was in this line. The feeling of building something solid, firm, and reliable is a very good one. But it need not exclude the speculating, groping, trying things out in some preliminary, heuristic way.

For instance, my analysis of *Being-values* is very meaningful to me, and it keeps on groping to express matters in ways that are thus far poetic and figurative. Well, I am very confident that I am pointing in the direction of a dimly cognizable reality, which one day we will know well enough to put to the test, objectify, confirm, or disconfirm. Let's check on this in 10 years.

I am so interested in what you say of your *peak-experiences* and of your interest in the impulsive, emotional, and so on. May I suggest that

(continued)

(Continued)

you expand on this in your autobiography? It will correct the erroneous picture people have. I accept the correction and am glad to hear about it. Also, about translating your stuff [into behavioral language] as you were reading it. It is good that it is translatable.

Yes, please send me your writings on these matters when you finish them.

Cordially,

A.H. Maslow

Source: A.H. Maslow letter to B.F. Skinner, reprinted with the permission of Ann R. Kaplan and the *Archives of the History of American Psychology.*

Management as a
Psychological Experiment

. . . Accountants must try to figure out some way of turning into balance sheet terms the intangible personnel values that come from improving the people of the organization . . . .

A.H. Maslow, *Maslow on Management*

There are enough data available, and enough industrial experiences, and also enough clinical-psychological data on human motivations, to warrant taking a chance on the experiment of Theory Y type of management. And yet it is well to keep in mind always that this will be a kind of a pilot experiment for the simple reason that the data which justify this experiment are definitely not final data, not clearly convincing beyond a shadow of a doubt. There is still plenty of room for doubt, as is evidenced by the fact that many academic people and many managers still do, in fact, doubt the validity of the whole line of thinking involved, and this is not entirely arbitrary. They do bring up evidence, experience, data against the new kind of management. We must certainly agree that there is plenty of doubt, and that the whole business is an experiment, and we must also be very aware of the fact that we need lots of data, lots of answers to a lot of questions yet to come.

For instance, the whole philosophy of this new kind of management may be taken as an expression of faith in the goodness of human beings, in trustworthiness, in enjoyment of efficiency, of knowledge, of respect, and so forth. But the truth is that we don't really have exact and quantitative information on the proportion of the human population which does in fact have some kind of feeling for workmanship, some kind of desire for all the facts and all the truth, some sort of desire for efficiency over inefficiency, and so forth. We know certainly that some individual human beings have these needs, and we know a little about the conditions under which these needs will appear, but we don't have any mass surveys of large populations that would give us some quantitative indication of just how many people prefer to have somebody else do their thinking for them, for instance. We don't know the answers to the question: What proportion of the population is irreversibly authoritarian?

These are all crucial kinds of information that we would need in order to be absolutely certain about enlightened management policy. We don't know how many people or what proportion of the working population would actually prefer to participate in management decisions, and how many would prefer not to have anything to do with them. What proportion of the population take a job as simply any old kind of a job which they must do in order to earn a living, while their interests are very definitely centered outside of the job.

An example is the woman who works only because she has to support her children. It's perfectly true that she'll prefer a nice and pleasant job to a rotten job, but just how does she define rotten job? How much involvement does she really want in the enterprise if the center of her life is definitely in her children rather than in her job? What proportion of the population prefer authoritarian bosses, prefer to be told what to do, don't want to bother thinking, and so forth.? What proportion of the population is reduced to the concrete and so finds planning for the future totally incomprehensible and boring? How many people prefer honesty and how strongly do they prefer it to dishonesty, how strong a tendency is there in people against being thieves? We know very little about physical inertia or psychic inertia. How lazy are people and under what circumstances and what makes them not lazy? We just don't know.

All of this then is an experiment (because of inadequate final data) in just about the same way that political democracy is an experiment which is based upon a scientifically unproven assumption: namely that human beings like to participate in their own fate, that given sufficient information they will make wise decisions about their own lives, and that they prefer freedom to being bossed, that they prefer to have a say in everything which affects their future, and so forth. None of these assumptions have been adequately enough proven so that we would call it scientific fact in about the same way that we would label biological fact scientific. We have to know more about these psychological factors than we do. Because this is so, we ought to again be very aware, very conscious, of the fact that these are articles of faith rather than articles of final knowledge, or perhaps better said that they are articles of faith with some grounding in fact though not yet enough to convince people who are characterologically against these articles of faith.

I suppose that the ultimate test of scientific fact is that those people who are by temperament and character unsympathetic to the conclusion must accept it as a fact anyway. We will know that our knowledge of the authoritarian character structure is truly scientific final fact when an average authoritarian character will be able to read the information on the subject and then regard his own authoritarian character as undesirable or sick or pathological and will go about trying to get rid of it. Just so long as an authoritarian character can wave aside all the evidence which indicates that he is sick, just so long are those facts not sufficient, not final enough.

After all, if we take the whole thing from Douglas McGregor's point of view of a contrast between a Theory X view of human nature, a good deal of the evidence upon which he bases his conclusions comes from my researches and my papers on motivations, self-actualization, and so forth. But I of all people should know just how shaky this is as a final foundation. My work on motivations came from the clinic, from a study of neurotic people. The carry-over of this theory to the industrial situation has some support from industrial studies, but certainly I would like to see a lot more studies of this kind before feeling finally convinced that this carry-over from the study of neurosis to the study of labor in factories is legitimate.

The same thing is true of my studies of self-actualizing people—there is only this one study of mine available. There were many things wrong with the sampling, so many in fact that it must be considered to be, in the classical sense anyway, a bad or poor or inadequate experiment. I am quite willing to concede this—as a matter of fact, I am eager to concede it—because I'm a little worried about this stuff which I consider to be tentative being swallowed whole by all sorts of enthusiastic people, who really should be a little more tentative, in the way that I am. The experiment needs repeating and checking—it needs working over in other societies—it needs a lot of things which it doesn't yet have. The main support of this theory—and, of course, there's plenty of this support—has come mostly from psychotherapists like Rogers and Fromm.

This, of course, leaves the problem of carry-over from the therapeutic situation to the industrial situation still open to testing. It needs to be validated as a legitimate carry-over. I may say also that my paper on the need for knowledge, on curiosity in the human being, is also practically the only thing of its kind, and while I trust it and believe my own conclusions, I am still willing to admit like a cautious scientist that it ought to be checked by other people before being taken as final. As we become aware of the probable errors of the data, we must underscore the necessity for more research and more research and more research. Smugness and certainty tend to stop research rather than to stimulate it.

On the other hand, of course, I should make clear that the evidence upon which Theory X management is based is practically nil; that there is even less evidence for Theory X than there is for Theory Y. It rests entirely on habit and tradition. It's no use saying that it rests on long experience, as most of its proponents would say, because this experience is a kind of self, or at least *can* be a kind of self-fulfilling prophecy. That is to say that the people who support Theory X on nonscientific grounds then proceed to use it as a management philosophy, which brings about just that behavior in the workers which Theory X would predict. But with this kind of Theory X treatment of workers, no other kind of behavior would be possible as a result.

To sum this up I would say that there is insufficient grounding for a firm and final trust in Theory Y management philosophy; but then I would hastily add that there is even less firm evidence for Theory X. If one adds up all the researches that have actually been done under scientific auspices and in the industrial situation itself, practically all of them come out on the side of one or another version of Theory Y; practically none of them come out in favor of Theory X philosophy except in small and detailed and specific special circumstances.

The same is true for the studies of the authoritarian personality. These also come out generally in favor of the democratic personality. And yet there are a few specific special instances in which it is better to have an authoritarian personality, in which the authoritarian will get

better results. For instance, an authoritarian personality will get better results for a transitional period as a teacher with authoritarian
students than will a democratic and permissive Theory Y kind of
teacher. This is the same order of evidence which indicates that practically *any* human being, however sick, can be used some place in a
complex industrial civilization. I think, for instance, of Bob Holt's
demonstration of the adaptive value even of the paranoid character; he
showed that such people tend to make better detectives than do normal people—or at least that they do as well.

Another point here comes from my reading of the chapter by Scoutten in the book edited by Mason Haire called *Organization Theory in
Industrial Practice.* Scoutten brings to mind that as soon as we take
into account such factors as the long-range health of the business (instead of merely short-range health), the duties to a democratic society,
the need in an individualized situation for pretty highly developed
human beings as workers and managers, and so forth, and so on, *then*
the necessity for Theory Y management becomes greater and greater.
He speaks of production and sales as the only functions, the only goals,
of the company with which he is connected, the Maytag Company.
Everything else he considers unnecessary or subsidiary to these two
functions. But it should be pointed out that this is a kind of isolated or
encapsulated view of the situation, that is, as if this company had no relationship with the community, the environment, or the society, nor
any debt to it. He takes an awful lot for granted in a situation like this,
including a democratic society with high levels of education, with great
respect for law and property, and so forth, and so on. He leaves these
things out entirely. If you include them, then it becomes obvious also
that the company or the enterprise has to give certain things to the society as well as receive certain things from the society, and this makes
a different picture altogether. The picture that Scoutten gives of an enterprise might work perfectly well in a fascist economy, but it would not
work at all if it were taken seriously in our democratic society, where
any enterprise—as a matter of fact, any individual—has also its obligations to the whole society.

(At this point there should be a reference to my memorandum on
the patriot, and on the enlightened industrialist as a patriot.)

More should be said on the relations between the enterprise and
the society, especially if we take into account the ways to keep the organization healthy over a period of a hundred years. It then becomes

most obvious about the mutual ties between the enterprise and the society—for one thing the healthy organization will need a steady supply of fairly well-matured and well-educated personalities (it cannot use delinquents, criminals, cynical kids, spoiled and indulged kids, hostile people, warmongers, destroyers, vandals, and so forth., but exactly these people are the products of a poor society). This is very much like saying that a poor society cannot support healthy enterprises, in the long run at least. (Although it probably is true that some kinds of products can be well made in the authoritarian society or the authoritarian enterprise, or under conditions of fear and starvation. I really should find out what kinds of exports for instance, can come from Spain today, or how good are Negro workers in South Africa? What kind of production do they have?)

It is also true that the healthy enterprise cannot function at all well under conditions of riots and civil war, of epidemics, of sabotage and murder, of class warfare, or caste warfare. The culture itself has to be healthy for this reason as well. Also there cannot be conditions of corruption, political corruption, nor can there be religious corruption or religious domination. The enterprise must be free to develop itself in all ways which do not interfere with the goodness and the health of the society. This means also that there ought not to be too much political domination either.

In effect any company that restricts its goals purely to its own profits, its own production, and its own sales is getting a kind of a free ride from me and other taxpayers. I help pay for the schools and the police departments and the fire departments and the health departments and everything else in order to keep the society healthy, which in turn supplies high-level workers and managers to such companies at little expense to them. I feel that they should, in order to be fair, make more returns to the society than they are making—that is, in terms of producing good citizens, people who because of their good work situation can themselves be benevolent, charitable, kind, altruistic, and so forth, and so on, in the community.

I am impressed again with the necessity, however difficult the job may be, of working out some kind of moral or ethical accounting scheme. Under such a scheme tax credits would be given to the company that helps to improve the whole society, that helps to improve the local population, and helps to improve the democracy by helping to create more democratic individuals. Some sort of tax penalty should be assessed against enterprises that undo the effects of a political democracy, of good schools, and so forth, and so on, and that make their people more paranoid, more hostile, more nasty, more malevolent, more destructive, and so forth. This is like sabotage against the whole society. And they should be made to pay for it.

Partly it must be put up to the accountants to try to figure out some way of turning into balance sheet terms the intangible personnel values that come from improving the personality level of the workers, making them more cooperative, better workers, less destructive, and so forth. It does cost money to hire this kind of personnel; it costs money to train and teach them and to build them into a good team, and there are all sorts of other costs involved in making the enterprise attractive to this kind of worker and this kind of engineer, and so forth. All these real expenditures of money and effort ought somehow to be translated into accounting terms so that the greater value of the enterprise that contributes to the improvement of the whole society can somehow be put on the balance sheets. We all know that such a company for instance, is a better credit risk and lending banks will take this into account. So will investors. The only ones who don't take these things into account are the accountants.

The Jonah Complex:
Understanding Our Fear of Growth

Why don't more people achieve their full potential in life? What inwardly stands in their way? In the following article written in November 1966, Maslow offered a tentative, intriguing answer as to why people don't reach self-actualization.

Most humanistic and existential psychologists today believe that a universal aspect of human nature is the impulse to grow, to enhance and actualize oneself, and to be all that one is capable of becoming. If we regard this viewpoint as accurate, then it is obviously necessary to explain why most people don't grow to their full inner height—why they *don't* actualize themselves.

The model that I have found most useful in grappling with this problem is the old Freudian notion involving psychodynamics, that is, the dialectic between an impulse's existence and the defense against its actual expression. Thus, once we have accepted the postulate that there is a basic human impulse to grow toward health, full humanness, self-actualization, or perfection, then we face the necessity of analyzing all the blocks, defenses, evasions, and inhibitions that get in the way of the growth tendency.

For instance, it is useful to apply the Freudian terms of *fixation* and *regression.* We can certainly use the psychoanalytic findings of the past half-century to help us understand the fear of growth, its cessation, or even renunciation in favor of regression. However, I find that the Freudian concepts are insufficient in this domain. Therefore, several new concepts must be formulated.

Source: A.H. Maslow article (November 1966), reprinted with the permission of Ann R. Kaplan and the *Archives of the History of American Psychology.*

As we take our stand on psychoanalytic knowledge and transcend Freud, we inevitably make the discovery of what I've called the "healthy unconscious." To state it very simply, not only do we repress our dangerous, distasteful, or threatening impulses, we often repress our best and noblest impulses.

For instance, in our society, there is a widespread taboo on tenderness. People often are ashamed of being altruistic, compassionate, kind, and loving and certainly of being noble or saintlike. Most obviously, this fleeing from one's own best nature is manifested among adolescent males. They tend to renounce ferociously all attributes that might conceivably be called feminine, sissy, weak, or soft in order to appear completely tough, fearless, and cool.

But this phenomenon is hardly limited to teenage males. Unfortunately, it is pervasive in our society. Often the highly intelligent person is ambivalent about her intelligence. Sometimes, she may even deny it altogether in an effort to be like the common or "average" person—in an effort, so to speak, to flee her fate as did the biblical Jonah. It frequently takes half a lifetime for the creatively talented individual to come to terms with one's own talent, to accept it fully, and to unleash oneself, that is, to be postambivalent about one's talent.

I have found something of the sort to be true for strong people: those who are natural leaders, bosses, or generals. They too get into a tangle about how to handle and regard themselves. The defenses against paranoia—or perhaps better said, against hubris or sinful pride—are all involved in such internal conflicts. On the one hand, the person has his normal tendency for open and joyful self-expression, for actualizing his best tendencies. Yet, he finds himself frequently in situations in which he must camouflage these very same capacities.

In our society, the superior individual generally learns to put on a chameleon-like cloak of false modesty or humility. Or at the very least, she has learned not to say openly what she thinks of herself and her high capacities. It is just not permitted in our society for a very intelligent individual to say, "I am an extremely intelligent person." In our society, such an attitude offends. It is called boasting and generally arouses counterreactions, hostility, and even attack.

Thus, a statement of one's superiority—even though it is justified, realistic, and proven—is frequently experienced by others as an assertion of the speaker's dominance and a concomitant demand for the listener's subordination. It is hardly surprising, then, that the listener will reject such a statement and become aggressive. Such a phenomenon seems common to many cultures around the globe. Accordingly, the superior individual derogates herself in order to avoid counterattack from others.

Yet, the problem confronts us all. We all must feel strong enough or self-loving enough to be creative, to achieve our goals, or to fulfill our potentialities. As a result, the superior athlete, dancer, musician, or scientist is forced into a conflict between his normal, intrapsychic tendency to grow to his fullest height and the socially acquired recognition that other people are apt to regard his true stature as a threat to their own self-esteem.

The individual whom we call neurotic may be said to be one so impressed with the possibility of punishment—so afraid of counter-hostility—that, in effect, she gives up her highest capacities, her right to grow to her fullest height. In order to avoid punishment, she becomes humble, ingratiating, appeasing, or even masochistic. In short, due to fear of punishment for being superior, she becomes inferior and throws away some of her capacity; that is, she voluntarily diminishes her possibilities of humanness. For the sake of safety and security, she cripples and stunts herself.

Yet, one's deepest nature cannot be altogether denied. If it does not show itself in a direct, spontaneous, uninhibited, and unleashed form, it must inevitably express itself in a concealed, covert, ambiguous, and even sneaky form. At the very least, one's lost capacities will express themselves in troubling dreams, unsettling free associations, strange slips of the tongue, or inexplicable emotions. For such a person, life becomes a continuous struggle, a conflict of the kind with which psychoanalysis has familiarized us.

If the neurotic person has strongly renounced his growth potentialities and self-actualization, then he typically seems "good," humble, modest, obedient, shy, timid, and even self-effacing. In its most dramatic form, this renunciation and its harmful consequences can be seen in the dissociated personality—the "multiple personality"—in which the denied, repressed, and suppressed possibilities finally break out in a dissociated form of another personality.

In all such cases of which I know, the presenting personality before split was of a totally conventional, obedient, passive, modest individual who asked nothing for herself, that is, who couldn't really enjoy herself and be selfish in a biological way. In such instances, the new personality that dramatically emerges is generally more selfish, fun-loving, immaturely impulsive, and less able to delay gratification.

What most superior people do, therefore, is to make a compromise with the wider society. They reach out toward their goals and advance toward self-actualization. They seek to express and enjoy their special talents and abilities. But they also mask such tendencies with a thin veneer of apparent modesty and humility or, at the very least, silence.

This model will help us to understand the neurotic person in another way, mainly as one who is simultaneously reaching out for his birthright of full humanness, wanting to grow toward self-actualization and full being, yet who, constrained by fear, will disguise or hide his normal impulses and contaminate them with a mixture of guilt with which he soothes his fear and appeases others.

To say it even more simply, neurosis can be seen as containing the same impulse of growth and expression that all animals and plants share but with a mixture of fear. Therefore, growth will take place in a crooked, tortuous, or joyless way. One may thus be said to be "evading one's growth," as the psychologist Angyal (1965) aptly observed.

If we concede that the core self is at least partially biological in the sense of anatomy, constitution, physiology, temperament, and preferred, biologically driven behaviors, then it also may be said that one is evading one's biological fate or destiny. Or, I could even say that such a person is evading her vocation, mission, and calling.

That is, she is evading the task for which her peculiarly idiosyncratic constitution fits her, the task for which she was born, so to speak. She is evading her destiny.

That is why the historian Frank Manuel has called this phenomenon the *Jonah complex*. As we remember, the biblical tale of Jonah was that he was called by God to prophesy, but he was afraid of the task. He tried to run away from it. But no matter where Jonah ran, he could find no hiding place. Finally, he understood that he had to accept his fate. He had to do what he was called to do.

In this sense, we each are called to a particular task for which our nature fits us. To run away from it, fear it, become half-hearted, or ambivalent about it are all "neurotic" reactions in the classic sense. They can be considered illnesses, in the sense of breeding anxiety and inhibitions, producing classic neurotic and even psychosomatic symptoms of all kinds, and generating costly and crippling defenses.

Yet, from another perspective, it is possible to see these very same mechanisms as instances of our drive toward health, self-actualization, and full humanness. The difference between the diminished individual, wistfully yearning toward full humanness but never quite daring to make it, versus the unleashed individual, growing well toward her destiny, is simply the difference between fear and courage.

Neurosis may be said to be the process of actualizing oneself under the aegis of fear and anxiety. It thus may be considered the same healthy and universal process but hindered, blocked, and shackled. Such a neurotic person can certainly be seen as moving toward self-actualization, even though he limps rather than runs and zigzags rather than moves directly forward.

Epilogue

The world that Abraham Maslow spoke of is here today. It is a world where we are fond of saying that the Internet has changed everything. A world where brainpower fuels the economic engine and where technology has forced us to rely more on the human connection than every before. Thus, Maslow's work in the areas of human motivation, creativity, innovation, and the human experience do indeed speak to us in a voice that is timely, critical, and relevant.

Businesses and organizations that are able to tap human potential, to organize effectively around human effort, and satisfy the inherent need for human beings to do meaningful work, will endure. Maslow seemed to realize that as a world and its people became more complex, the importance of building environments where people could reach their potential would become imperative. His writings, his essays, and his many books give us a roadmap into the next century of work.

Index